Orientalism

Orientalism

History, theory and the arts

John M. MacKenzie

Manchester University Press

Manchester and New York

distributed exclusively in the USA and Canada by St Martin's Press

Published by Manchester University Press
Oxford Road, Manchester M13 9NR, UK
and Room 400, 175 Fifth Avenue, New York, NY 10010, USA

Distributed exclusively in the USA and Canada
by St Martin's Press, Inc., 175 Fifth Avenue, New York,
NY 10010, USA

British Library Cataloguing-in-Publication Data
A catalogue record is available from the British Library

Library of Congress Cataloging-in-Publication Data
MacKenzie, John M.
    Orientalism : history, theory, and the arts / John MacKenzie.
        p.   cm.
    Includes bibliographical references and index.
    ISBN 0–7190–1861–7 (hardback). — ISBN 0–7190–4578–9 (paperback)
    1. Exoticism in art. 2. Arts, Modern. I. Title.
    NX650.E85M33 1995
    700—dc20
                                                            94–43434
                                                            CIP

ISBN 0 7190 1861 7 *hardback*
ISBN 0 7190 4578 9 *paperback*

Typeset in Galliard by Graphicraft Typesetters Ltd., Hong Kong
Printed in Great Britain
by Redwood Books, Trowbridge

FOR ALISTAIR, TRIXIE, LORNA,
AMANDA, NICOLA, NEIL AND MELANIE
who all love the arts
and live in the 1990 European City of Culture

Contents

The plates

ILLUSTRATING a work of this sort is not easy. In order to develop complex arguments, it has been necessary to refer to a great deal of visual material only a tiny proportion of which can be included here. Moreover, despite the heroic efforts of picture researcher and editor, it was not always possible to secure the illustrations which, in an ideal world, would have focused the arguments most effectively. Generally, an effort has been made to illustrate less familiar works, even when they are sometimes aesthetically less appealing than better known pieces. Much of the other visual material can be found in standard works cited in text and footnotes. Musical and theatrical examples would, of course, have presented an even greater problem. To have included them would have made the text unwieldy and, possibly, less accessible. They have, therefore, been omitted. The arguments are sufficiently underpinned by descriptive exegesis to be able to stand by themselves.

Colour plates

Sources/credits

Preface

THIS IS an essay in cultural history. Some may think, perhaps, that this is no more than a euphemism for the impossibly ambitious, since what is attempted is an overview of a major debate and a reassessment of the manifestations and influence of the Orient in the pictorial and plastic arts, architecture, design, music and the theatre between the late eighteenth and twentieth centuries. Since entire books can clearly be written about each of these, this may seem like a reversal of the usual scholarly sin, an attempt to write less and less about more and more. It is written, however, in the conviction that historians must not only compress and synthesise, but also have the courage to plunder other disciplines in order to make the widest connections.

The relationship between the cultures of different continents, as mediated by imperialism, is a crucial aspect of modern history. So far it has tended to be treated through the lens of individual disciplines and primarily in the context of high art. The most extensive debate has been about the western literature of Orientalism and the literary critics who have conducted it, working well in arrears of their historian colleagues, have concentrated on studying representations of the Orient and imperial relations through elite, metropolitan and centrifugal formations. But imperial culture also needs to be understood through the heterogeneity of its forms and in popular, intra-imperial and centripetal terms. History is a synoptic discipline. The historian is perhaps best equipped to bring the arts together and consider them in their relationship with the events and intellectual movements of specific periods, as well as in terms of audience reactions based upon social class.

Such a project is, however, greatly complicated by the fact that the word 'Orientalism' has changed its import over the past twenty years. It has always had a multiplicity of meanings, but the significant new shift is one of normative tone. The word originally had a wholly sympathetic ring: the study of the languages, literature, religions, thought, arts and social life of the East in order to make them available to the West, even in order to protect them from occidental cultural arrogance in the age of imperialism. For Edward Said, in his highly influential book *Orientalism* of 1978, far from protecting oriental cultures from overwhelming imperial power, far from permitting eastern cultural forms to survive, Orientalist studies became themselves an expression of intellectual and technical dominance and a means to the extension of political, military and economic supremacy. Orientalism came to represent a construct, not a reality, an emblem of domination and a weapon of power. It lost its status as a sympathetic concept, a product of scholarly admiration for diverse and exotic cultures, and became the literary means of creating a stereotypical and mythic East through which European rule could be more readily asserted. It is this new and negative meaning which has come to predominate in the 1980s and 1990s.

Refigured in this radical and dissenting form, Orientalism has stimulated an extraordinarily extensive debate, mainly among literary critics, which has drawn on all the principal intellectual movements of the late twentieth century – poststructuralism, discourse theory and postmodernism. With a few exceptions, historians who feel more comfortable with analysis firmly grounded in an empirical base have tended to avoid these highly theoretical disputes. However, it is difficult to embark upon a study of Orientalism without some consideration of the direction these discussions have taken and the reasons for the indifference, even hostility of historians. This is perhaps particularly timely, since in the last three to four years a number of books have been published, from a variety of different disciplinary standpoints, which purport to offer insights into the culture of imperialism, particularly in relation to British rule in South Asia.

The older concept of Orientalism means something very specific in terms of British *policy* in India, representing a conservative and romantic approach not only utilising the languages and laws of both Muslim and Hindu India, but also desiring the preservation of allegedly traditional social relations. From the turn of the nineteenth century this was assaulted by the combined forces of evangelicalism and utilitarianism and in many respects was overwhelmed by the new 'Anglicist' approach from the 1830s. In the past, the historical discussion of these shifts in the intellectual and political climate which had such significant effects on British imperial rule was conducted on cleanly delineated analytical grounds. The new approach to Orientalism has injected considerable confusion, not only in the meaning and use of terms but also involving a repeated realignment of sympathies, which needs to be set into its wider theoretical contexts. This debate and its implications for cultural history and for the study of British rule in India will be discussed in Chapters 1 and 2.

The word 'Orientalism' has also been used since the early nineteenth century to describe a genre of painting, pioneered by the French, but developed by artists from Britain and several other European countries, with predominantly Middle Eastern and North African subjects. Historians of architecture and design have occasionally adopted the word to embrace work which has an oriental inspiration, in this case often Islamic, sometimes Indian, occasionally Chinese or Japanese. In this sense it has been used to identify the cross-cultural influences upon patterns, textiles, ceramics, furniture and certain building styles. In recent years some of these artistic manifestations of Orientalism have been reinterpreted in the light of Said's radical theory. Visual representations of the East, no less than literary ones, apparently offer further evidence that Orientalism represents the epitome of occidental power, paralleling the monolithic discourse identified by Said in literary renderings of the East and expressing a set of binary oppositions, turning the represented Orient into the moral negative of the West. In arguing in this way, art historians (as will be suggested in Chapter 3) have narrowed and restricted the possible readings of paintings and other visual forms in extraordinarily limiting ways. Moreover, by a curious irony, they have critically reinterpreted Orientalist art at the very time when these paintings have come back into vogue, not least among Middle Eastern buyers.

In short, the word 'Orientalism' has come to have a complex life of its own. In this book, its compass is going to be stretched further, though in ways that seem entirely logical. Art, architecture and design will be discussed in Chapters 3, 4 and 5, and the concept will then be used to represent, first, the attempts by western classical composers to extend and develop the language and mood of music and its associated drama, opera, by adopting oriental influences (Chapter 6) and second, depictions of the Orient in popular and topical plays, panoramas, pageantry and spectacular displays, as well as the 'intercultural' theatre of the twentieth century (Chapter 7). As with all other 'Orientalisms', the concern is not with genuine oriental artefacts transmitted to the West, but with their reflection and reworking in western art.

The intention in adopting such a range of arts is twofold: to examine the extent to which the Orientalist thesis can be revised in more positive and constructive ways by escaping the literary obsession and to consider the relationships among different cultural forms, both elite and popular in character. (Said, by his own admission, is generally uncomfortable with popular culture.) For the historian interested in the arts, the Orientalist debate raises a number of profoundly interesting problems. To what extent do the various arts march in a sort of rough parallel, deeply sensitive to their intellectual environment and therefore to their political and social context? How far are they on different paths that occasionally cross or coincide, but generally go their own way? Why do they seem at times consensual, at other times oppositional? What is the relationship between innovation in the arts and fresh intellectual directions in related disciplines? Is it possible to establish time-lags in responses as between the 'high arts' and popular culture? Thus, can one move on while others remain in old grooves? These are eternal questions which a short work like this can only touch upon, but they are pertinent to, and can perhaps be illuminated by Orientalism because it had expressions in so many different arts. Many practitioners of Orientalism were interested in more than one art: painting, craft and design; painting and architecture; writing and painting; music, theatre and design; and so on.

But Victorian and Edwardian artists (in the widest sense) were not only eclectic in their approach to the arts, they were also massively eclectic in their response to cultures. Theirs was the first age in which almost all the cultures of the world had been made available through writings, illustrations, museums, photography (later film) and increased opportunities for safe travel itself. Given the immense quantity of information pouring in upon them, it is perhaps not surprising that they were obsessed with classification, attempting through codification to control and understand this welter of material. Their concern with taxonomies ran from zoology to botany, geology to human cultures, and it was perhaps the last period when amateurs could have an informed interest in all of these. The celebrated disorder of many of the 'cabinets of curiosities' of the seventeenth and early eighteenth centuries, the ordering of which had begun in the Age of Reason, gave way to systematisation following Linnaean precedent. Artists were of course influenced by and involved in these efforts to control the flow of information through organisation.

It may be that in order to understand the cultural eclecticism of the arts in the late nineteenth and early twentieth centuries, we have to attempt to be thoroughly eclectic in our approach to these arts and their related ideas, an ambition which does not come easily to the late twentieth-century scholar. In an age of strict specialisms, the scholar hesitates to betray *naïveté* at best, ignorance at worst, by entering the preserves of others. But a full understanding of Orientalism can only come from artistic promiscuity, however dangerously audacious the approach may be. This is, perhaps, the prime rationale for this book.

Even audacity requires some limits. A chronological concentration on the nineteenth and early twentieth centuries supplies one limit, although there will of course be references to other periods. The prime focus, moreover, will be on the British. This does not, however, create rigid national parameters, for the British were consumers as well as producers. In painting, music and design, the products of other Europeans will be considered, particularly those which secured a ready market in Britain. The focus of certain arts, notably architecture, and to a certain extent the theatre (and some passing references to the cinema) will be more restricted, for the obvious reason that in these the relationship between production and consumption is somewhat more circumscribed.

Concentrating on Britain can be justified not only because Orientalism was a notable preoccupation of the British, but also because the Orientalist debate has been so closely related to imperialism. Since the British were the major imperial power of the period, perhaps the artistic connections with the possession of empire can be most clearly established by examining their reactions and tastes. Here indeed is one of the principal problems of the strongly ideological approach to Orientalism. Said and his followers purport to write about certain arts within the matrix of imperialism. But they are not imperial historians, and their 'imperialism' has a disturbing vagueness about it. It becomes a generalised concept inadequately rooted in the imperial facts, lacking historical dynamic, innocent of imperial theory or the complexities of different forms of imperialism and varieties of economic and political relationship. When Orientalist ideas are fitted into the grand progression of the historian's periodisation, a curious counterpoint establishes itself. Orientalism and imperialism, as the subsequent chapters will demonstrate, did not march in parallel.

Music seems to illustrate this well. Composers certainly dealt in oriental stereotypes in order to create programmatic music about the East, but at the high point of imperialism in the later nineteenth century, composers began to discover in eastern music the opportunity to extend the language of their art. In an age when so many old conventions were breaking up, in music as in all the arts, composers found new tone rows, fresh harmonic and rhythmic potential, a different sound world, particularly of percussion and wind, which they could adapt to their own purposes. Their exposure to oriental music was at first limited, and they were in no sense accurately reproducing it, but they were securing stimulation from it, revitalising their craft in the process. In some cases, the oriental effect was merely a musical arabesque, a derived ornament of little structural significance, but in others there was a genuine extension of language, form and mood. The influence of the Orient had a profound effect on both French musical Impressionism and the late Romanticism of the Viennese school. Even Italian opera made expressive nods in its direction. This influence has extended through twentieth-century Modernism and into minimalism. At times the cross-fertilisation has seemed close to producing genuine syncretic forms.

Curiously, despite his great interest in music, Said has made little attempt to apply his model to western classical forms, perhaps because he seems to be highly ambivalent about their degree of aesthetic autonomy. His one essay in this direction, recently republished as a significant section in his *Culture and Imperialism* of 1993, analyses Verdi's opera *Aida* in terms of its allegedly imperial context. This was originally delivered as a keynote address to the conference of the British Association of Art Historians in Brighton in 1988. I was wholly unconvinced by it then, and expressed some of my reservations. This view is powerfully confirmed by encountering Said's analysis in cold print. He reverses the true import of the opera, misunderstands its conclusion and fails to contextualise it adequately in terms of intra-European conflict (particularly that between Germany and France) and Verdi's views on nationalism and imperialism. The opera illustrates the power of love to transcend not only national differences, but also the gulf between the dominant and subordinate in a conquest situation as explored in Verdi's reworking of the personal story of an Egyptian general and an Ethiopian princess.

Although Verdi achieved an intriguing sense of exoticism in his music for *Aida*, it was done by wholly western means. He toyed with 'Orientalist' approaches, including the use of Egyptian instruments, but he rejected these. Other composers, however, did embrace oriental forms, and although they were 'Orientalist' in the sense of being impure adaptations, they had a revivifying effect. Such a positive revitalisation can also be found in other arts. This is not to suggest that the Orient and oriental peoples were not frequently presented as a set of stereotypes: they unquestionably were, particularly in popular cultural forms, but this was but one half of a striking duality. In the 'high arts', at least, the effects of the depiction and adaptation of the Orient were powerful and positive.

Indeed it may be that the contrast lies precisely in this distinction between different levels of representation. While all forms of representation are of course filtered through the lens of the beholder, some purport to offer a realistic facsimile; others thrive on stereotypical depiction, in which both clothes (literally and figuratively) and mannerisms heighten alleged characteristics to the point of caricature; while yet others seek to absorb and adapt in a conscious effort to find a syncretic art. The realistic approach may offer positive or negative sentiment, sometimes in almost equal measure. Caricatural depiction is direct, crude and filled with certainties. Adaptation and the search for hybridisation are perhaps more the business of the arts of design, architecture and music, where representation is indirect. Yet we should surely be wary of distinguishing too rigidly between these different arts, just as we should be cautious about creating too great a gulf between the popular and the intellectual, what used to be called 'lowbrow' and 'highbrow'. The strivings to extend language, form and mood were common to all, and the effects could be superficial or profound in all of them, depending on creator, performer or consumer.

But if creator, performer, consumer are involved in efforts to extend artistic experience through such innovation, they are also implicated in the transmission and assimilation of message. Message does not of course have a life of its own. It is embedded in and contributes to contemporary discourse, but it is also inseparable from the language, forms and moods which are, in a sense, its essential constituent elements. The deciphering of message is, of course, immensely difficult, but of one thing we can be sure: it can only be done in terms of the meanings of its own age and not those of others. The message conveyed to us may well be different from the one the creator intended or his/her audience received. Allowance must be made for almost infinite variation in the latter, but still we can recognise that arts which secure a degree of contemporary acceptability and popularity must be using elements of a common language and meanings shared by producer and consumer.

If the 'Orientalist' interpretation misses the complexities and dualities of the western representations of the East and adaptations of eastern forms, it also takes disturbingly ahistorical forms. As developed by the art historian Linda Nochlin or the poet and literary critic Rana Kabbani, we find the susceptibilities of the late twentieth century applied to nineteenth-century art; we find moral condemnation befogging intellectual clarity and at times negating the essential characteristics of the critical faculty; and we find an entire epoch condemned out of hand as though historical ages themselves can be divided into 'goodies' and 'baddies'. At its worst, this type of activity, surprisingly favourably hailed in some quarters, is reduced to the level of grotesquerie.

Much of this work is a response to 'the burden of the present'. It is focused upon the Middle East and purports to demonstrate that the Palestinian problem is influenced by the unfavourable attitudes towards Arabs encapsulated in Orientalism. Feminist ideas provide an important sub-plot since so many aspects of western attitudes to the East were bound up with notions of gender, the role of women in western society and perceptions of the position of women in that of the East. Rana Kabbani, who devotes a great deal of time to the exploration of the depiction of women in Orientalism, is quite explicit about the contemporary political objectives of her work. In her book *Europe's Myths of Orient: Devise and Rule*, she writes of Europe's 'projection of evil onto a faraway culture', of a 'bulwark of bigotry', 'a polemic highly charged with hostility', originating in the Middle Ages, but continuing into the nineteenth century, a heightened demonisation which has led her to 'feel very strongly indeed that in order to arrive at a West–East discourse liberated from the obstinacy of the colonial legacy, a serious effort has to be made to review and reject a great many inherited representations' (pp. 5, 13). Thus, sympathies can only be built upon the exposure of areas of alleged misunderstanding of the past. But the identification of negative stereotyping, slights and insults on the basis of late twentieth-century perceptions has the opposite effect. It poisons the deep wells of sympathy and respect which artists of all sorts felt for the East in the nineteenth century, which they expressed in distinctively nineteenth-century ways, not necessarily amenable to the critical values of the twentieth century. The work of Said, Nochlin, Kabbani and others is riddled with such misconceptions. This is a pity, for the effect of their work is to further the very misunderstandings they seek to allay.

In some respects, I have been surprised by the development of my own views. I originally found Said's book so provocative and stimulating that I felt its range could be widened to include the popular arts, that its analytical techniques could be extended to the theatre, cinema, exhibitions, and so on. But further consideration of some of Said's sources and the theoretical critique developed by many of his critics, and above all a re-examination of other art forms made me more aware of the complexity of western approaches to the East, and of the need to understand the dualities and polarities that are inherent in the artistic cross-cultural grapplings of the nineteenth and early twentieth centuries. I also came to realise that, in this field perhaps more than any other, a particular selection of paintings, or a specific set of quotations can be used to prove anything. In the hands of Nochlin and Kabbani, the Said model seemed to go haywire, and it became abundantly apparent that a revision was necessary, although, perhaps because, my own contemporary sympathies lie very close to theirs.

While my doubts about Said's methods and conclusions, and the incompatibility rather than applicability of his approach to conventional historical studies, particularly as expressed in *Culture and Imperialism*, have developed to the point of rejection, my admiration for the man remains undimmed. His cultural interests, his scholarly good manners, and his striving for international understanding, if sometimes bordering on a naïve cosmopolitanism, are admirable. His castigation of conservative politicians in the West, particularly the populist nationalism of the New Right and their intrusion of state power into scholarship and learning, is particularly timely in Britain, where schools and universities have been placed under such threat. Academics everywhere should join with Said in identifying and resisting the highly slanted approach to literary and historical education which insists upon a surface canonical correctness, infused by a misplaced 'patriotism', rather than the critically exciting plumbing of the interpretative depths. The ascription of 'political motivation' to opponents and the concomitant claims of objectivity – always a reflection of the arrogance of power and a tool in its preservation – reflect the fact that the main threat of 'political correctness' comes not from the libertarian Left, to which it is shackled, but from the New Right. Moreover, to take two other points of sympathy, like many British academics, I am profoundly disturbed by the hatreds and oppressions of some elements of modern Zionism, and I find some, though by no means all feminist reinterpretations necessary and satisfying. But causes are not advanced by bile, and appropriate forms of historical understanding remain more important to contemporary sympathies than the wilful misreading of the historical record.

As the above paragraph amply illustrates, Said's books are profoundly polemical, both because scholarship and ideology are seen to be so inseparably intertwined and because he insists upon the necessity of the scholar being involved in the hurly-burly of politics. In the distinction between the 'organic' and 'abstracted' intellectual, he naturally places himself in the former category (although it must be said that his political objectives and ideological standpoint are unclear). In my view, the historian must indeed be organically involved and ideologically committed and all my work has reflected this position. In consequence, this book will also be polemical. Indeed, it would surely be impossible to grapple with Said in any other way.

Another word of personal and professional explanation is perhaps necessary. This may seem like an idiosyncratic choice of subject, at the very least a slightly unusual new direction, for a historian of British imperialism who has previously written about imperial propaganda, the relationship of ideology to popular culture, the social history of railway stations, and the dissemination of hunting practices and environmental ideas from Britain to its Empire. But in fact a number of tracks seem to have led inexorably to these Orientalist thickets. No Glaswegian interested in the arts can be unaware of the nineteenth-century preoccupation

with the Orient. The distinguished Glasgow architect, Alexander 'Greek'
Thomson, mixed and elaborated his classicism with extraordinary Egyptian, Assyrian and other oriental elements. The 1888 Glasgow Exhibition, which was mounted in Joseph Paxton's great Kelvingrove Park
opposite the tenement in which I was brought up, was known as 'Baghdad by the Kelvin' because of its strikingly Orientalist architecture. Eld-
erly inhabitants of the locality remembered it, and told me of it when I
was a boy. Sir John Lavery recorded its ephemeral, almost ethereal
buildings in some highly atmospheric paintings. More recently, a much-
visited local cinema, the Kelvin in Finnieston, boasted an oriental tab-
leau, mosque, palace, palm trees and a curiously grounded onion dome,
on a platform beside the screen. Further up the artistic scale, members
of the school of artists known as the 'Glasgow boys' – Melville, Lavery,
Hornel, Henry – secured inspiration from various parts of the East. And
elements of oriental patterning, screens, and approaches to colour, responding to oriental sensibilities, even if ill-defined, passed into the art
nouveau of the Glasgow style, epitomised by the work of Charles Rennie
Mackintosh. And nearby there was Paisley and its mills as a constant
reminder of the power of oriental design in British textile production.
Thus my interest in the visual, plastic and musical arts was stimulated by
a typically improving education in a city which I never tired of exploring
and which finally received its due recognition as European City of Culture in 1990. It will now be readily apparent why this book has more
than its fair share of examples drawn from Glasgow.

     In recent years, Orientalism has been a constant thread running
through various, and seemingly disparate research interests. Imperial
propaganda abounded in Orientalism, the Orientalism of the imperial
exhibitions, of theatrical and cinematic representations of empire, of
juvenile literature and magazines, and some at least of the iconography
of war reporting, of the engravings of battles and heroic legends.
Orientalism was also a frequent feature of the popular culture of leisure. Oriental motifs made their appearance in the architecture of railway stations, just as they did, more prominently, in seaside piers,
bandstands, kiosks and garden pavilions. And oriental images were a
central aspect of the hunt. Both the Persian 'paradise' and the Chinese
'Xanadu' contained animals ripe for hunting. Falconry was introduced to
Europe by the Normans who had learnt it from the Arabs in Sicily.
Images of the hunt and of the East were inseparably intertwined in
Orientalist painting. The British adopted and adapted the Mughal traditions of the hunt such that it became both a spectacular act of imperial
state and a rich source of painting, photography and publishing.

     Even this list from one city and one individual's research experi-
ence reflect diversity and variety of positive and negative imports. It may

be that books which concentrate attacks upon straw theories are undermined by the weakness of their targets. But the Orientalist thesis is a
highly influential one, which has not yet received the full critical scrutiny
(at least from outside the literary field) it deserves. This relatively brief
work is offered only as a start. By extending into other areas of the
Orient and into other arts, it will range beyond the specific preoccupations of the Said school. But at all times it will seek understanding
through an appropriate historical and cultural contextualisation. For it
will argue that when techniques of cultural cross-referencing are used,
twentieth-century slights and insults often become nineteenth-century
compliments and sympathies.

I have only compliments for those who have helped in the formulation
of the material and ideas that have gone into this book. The Leverhulme
Foundation generously provided a grant to cover some of the costs of its
research. I am particularly grateful to them as they have had to wait a
long time for the fruits. Among the many helpful librarians at Lancaster
University library, I should like to single out Thelma Goodman and her
efficient inter-library loan service and Winnie Clark, who allowed me to
take out more than my fair share of books. Before his retirement, Donald
Simpson of the Royal Commonwealth Society library (now sadly removed from its atmospheric premises in Northumberland Avenue) expressed great interest in this project and, as always, tracked down useful
starting-points. At the same library, Terry Barringer and Pauline Foster
continued to be cheerfully co-operative even as their bibliophilic world
seemed to collapse around them. Librarians and archivists at the national
art library at the Victoria and Albert Museum and the Theatre Museum
in Covent Garden have been unfailingly helpful, as have been the members of staff at various galleries who have supplied slides and illustrations.
    References, books, offprints, ideas and various other forms of help
were provided by David Arnold, Terry Barringer, Phillip Dalziel, Felix
Driver, Alain Frogley, Paul Greenhalgh, Mike Heffernan, Kevin Hamel,
Enid Hobba, Adrian Kiernander, Andrew Lyle, Denis McCaldin, Peter
Marshall, David Mayer, Tom Metcalf, Hugh Tinker, Patrick Williams,
Mike Pickering and Nigel Whiteley. The editors of *Nineteenth-Century
Contexts*, Greg Kucic and Keith Hanley, invited me to contribute an
article to the 'Colonialism' issue of that journal (18, 1994, pp. 9–25).
This was based on sections of Chapters 1 and 2 and I am grateful to
them for persuading me to crystallise my thoughts at a crucial stage in
the development of this book.
    The contributors to the Manchester University Press series
'Studies in Imperialism' have been an endless source of stimulation and
inspiration. They have collectively pushed forward the study of cultural
imperialism and of the imperial effects upon Britain in strikingly innovative and extensive ways. Before his retirement from the Press, I was

prevented by a house rule from acknowledging Ray Offord. It is now possible for me to place my debt to this model publisher's editor on record. He showed boundless interest and enthusiasm in my research from his first encounter with my *Propaganda and Empire* and, together with the late Martin Spencer, encouraged me in the founding of the 'Studies in Imperialism' series. He advised me as to content and style with a quiet restraint which belied his unfailing sureness of judgement and taste. He eagerly commissioned this work and persuaded me to persevere with a difficult and unusual project even when I was diverted into other things. It is now being seen through the press by his equally attentive successor.

As I indicated above, something of my own past is in this book since it has been influenced both by a Glasgow upbringing and by personal connections. Miss Kate Thomson, a photographer born in the 1870s, regaled me as a boy with stories of the Glasgow exhibitions which had so excited her in late Victorian and Edwardian times. During my twenty-five years at Lancaster, two colleagues have had an enduring influence upon me and have contributed greatly to its reputation for imperial and cultural history. Stephen Constantine, who shares so many of my convictions, has donated books to this project, as well as providing a superb example of meticulous care, enduring patience and hard-headed, sceptical scholarship. I owe an equal debt to Jeffrey Richards, who, after twenty-five years as colleague, collaborator and friend, continues to offer books from his extensive library as well as facts from his amazingly capacious memory, together with copious bibliographical help and stimulating interpretation, not just about the theatre and the cinema, but about other arts as well. These two, among other colleagues and students at Lancaster, have contributed immeasurably to my scholarly life. This book will probably do no more than reveal how far short of their expectations and ideals I have fallen. My prime debt is to Rob, who was present when I first had the idea for the book in 1983, and with whom I have explored aspects of the Orient and Orientalism from the Alhambra to *Aida*, from the Taj to *Turandot*.

                                                              J. M.

1

The 'Orientalism' debate

BETWEEN 1941 and 1945 the British Council published a series of pamphlets on British contributions to the study of oriental cultures. Some of these had been wartime radio talks on the BBC and were obviously intended to illustrate to the British public the long-standing and admiring connections between Britain and those eastern territories which it was trying to hold steady (in either neutral status or open support of the Allies) against the Axis powers. To further this end, their publication by the British Council was clearly designed to give them wider currency, including circulation among the elites of the countries concerned. The first pamphlet, by Bernard Lewis, dealt with Arabic studies, while subsequent ones examined the British scholarly connection with Persia (Arthur J. Arberry), India (Sir Attul Chatterjee and Sir Richard Burn) and Turkey (Harold Bowen).[1]

'Orientalism' operates at a number of different levels in this wartime project. Here the study of the Orient is obviously presented in a largely positive light. British scholarship is used as a propaganda weapon, an emblem of respect and support. The relatively new technology of broadcasting, recognised since at least the early 1930s as a potent means of disseminating information and propaganda for national and international ends, is used as the vehicle for this projection of a beneficent Orientalism,[2] while the British Council, founded in 1934 to spread the influence of British culture, politics and ideas, gave the material additional

currency through the widely distributed printed page.[3] The inclusion of
Sir Attul Chatterjee, who had entered the Indian Civil Service in 1896
and was Indian High Commissioner in London from 1925 to 1931, was
clearly intended to convey the emollient power of scholarship in bringing
together members of both the British and Indian elites.

The authors duly complied with the propagandist purpose. Lewis
emphasised the friendship between British and Arabic peoples, which it
was the 'solemn responsibility' of contemporaries 'to preserve and enrich'.[4] Each sought to highlight the particular achievements of the culture in question: mathematics, science, medicine and philosophy for the
Arabs, art and literature for the Persians, astronomy, astrology, religious scholarship, architecture and arts for India, poetry, stained glass,
architecture for Turkey. Only Bowen reflected on the rise and fall in the
reputation of his chosen culture, Turkey, in the West. Indeed, given the
growing antagonism between Britain and the Ottomans in the late nineteenth century and the role of the latter in the First World War, he
could scarcely have done otherwise. He categorised descriptions of Turkey and Turkish culture according to whether they tended to be hostile
or sympathetic and he delicately described those who had attacked the
Turks, among whom he included Cardinal Newman, as being 'infected
with Gladstonian prejudice'.[5] Bowen, however, was able to climax his
story with a supposedly new and more sympathetic relationship with
Atatürk's secular state of the 1920s and 1930s. By the time his pamphlet was published, Turkey had abandoned its neutrality and joined
the Allies against Germany.

While Bowen acknowledged that the study of the Orient was a
complex and sometimes ambivalent process, the pamphlets generally
saw oriental scholarship as leading to understanding rather than misunderstanding, as capable even of contributing to wartime solidarity. It
is not surprising in such a project that the emphasis was on personalities,
publications, cultural scope and representational form rather than content. Propaganda works through ideological simplicity and certainty.
When the content is put back and subjected to rigorous analysis, ideological complexity becomes the order of the day. Something of that
complexity is conveyed by the changing meaning of the word
'Orientalism'.

In the past twenty years, the resonance of this much-used term
has been transformed. Until the publication of Edward Said's *Orientalism*
in 1978, it was generally used to describe either the corpus of scholarship and ideas, together with related administrative policy, associated
with the East India Company judge Sir William Jones and other members of the Asiatick Society of Bengal, in the later eighteenth century,
or an artistic movement, developed principally by the French, in the

nineteenth century. In both cases the word had a positive or at the very least neutral ring to it. British Orientalism suggested the notion that East India Company officials should govern India according to Indian laws and customs (or at least their perception of them), immersing themselves in the languages and culture of the subjects of the Company's Indian territories.[6] The first Governor-General, Warren Hastings, was one of its prime proponents and justified it on both practical and scholarly grounds. He wrote that 'every accumulation of knowledge, and especially such as is obtained by social communication with people over whom we exercise a dominion founded on the right of conquest, is useful to the state'.[7] This effort at mutual understanding through 'social communication' would be 'the gain of humanity' and 'cannot fail to open our minds, and to inspire us with that benevolence which our religion inculcates, for the whole race of mankind'.[8] This policy held sway until it was overwhelmed by the combined assault of Anglicising evangelicalism and utilitarianism in the first decades of the nineteenth century.[9]

Since then the relative status of the Orientalist and Anglicist policies has tended to be the litmus test of both British approaches to India and scholarly appraisals of them. Until Indian independence, the Anglicist policy, as the source of educated and westernised Indians, both elite collaborators and nationalist resisters, was the more highly valued, although the British indulged in a fresh burst of a different sort of Orientalism both in the post-Mutiny preservation of the Indian princely states and in their renewed interest in Islamic culture and rulers as a counterpoise to a Hindu-led nationalism. In more modern times, historians have tended to find eighteenth-century Orientalism more sympathetic than the cultural arrogance of the utilitarians.[10] Yet 'Orientalist' survived as a generally positive description of the scholar with interests in the East throughout this period, while among the extensive school of painters who considered themselves Orientalists it also remained a relatively value-free term, although their work experienced, from an aesthetic rather than an ideological standpoint, extremes of critical acclaim and abuse.

The valuation of the words 'Orientalism' and 'Orientalist' and the activities which they described came, of course, from within the cultures that had spawned them. The transformation in their meaning and use came from outside, from the world of comparative literature in a post-colonial and post-nationalist context. Edward Said combined and adapted two influential theoretical constructs of the twentieth century to produce his major revaluation of Orientalism.[11] He took Michel Foucault's concept of the discourse, the linguistic apparatus through which the articulation of knowledge becomes an expression of power, and linked it to Antonio Gramsci's notion of cultural hegemony through which elite control is maintained over the masses. But whereas Foucault was often more interested in the internal topography of his apparatus, Said was concerned to apply it to a large body of heterogeneous texts. And where Gramsci dealt with class in a European context, Said transferred his hegemonic principles to racial representation and control in an imperial frame. Said's work is thus strikingly eclectic, both in philosophical and theoretical terms as well as in his use of a mixture of literary and non-canonical sources. It transformed 'Orientalism', in which the Orient is appropriated by the Occident by being turned into a structure of myth prefabricated for western use, into one of the most ideologically charged words in modern scholarship. Moreover, its seemingly wide-ranging character and the power and freshness of its message prompted responses from a number of disciplines in both the humanities and the social sciences.

Indeed, few books have at the same time stimulated so much controversy or influenced so many studies. Colonial literary theory, anthropology, women's studies, art history, theatre history, media and communications studies, the history of philology, historical geography, even the modish study of 'heritage' and tourism have all come under its sway. Not only has it become almost impossible to consider the relationship between West and East without grappling with its insights, but its method has also been applied to Europe's relationship with other parts of the globe.[12] Yet, with a few rare exceptions, the conventional study of history, even that concerned with the highly relevant examination of travel in the Mediterranean, North Africa and the Levant has been notably absent from this list.[13] Moreover, historians of imperialism, for whom Said seems to have the clearest messages, have paid it relatively little attention. It is one of the purposes of this chapter and the next to consider why this should be so.

Like most books that acquire 'epochal' status, *Orientalism* has been seen both as merely enshrining a great truth and as constituting a major polemic. While Said has castigated the literary–cultural establishment in both *Orientalism* and his more recent *Culture and Imperialism* (1993) for having 'declared the serious study of imperialism and culture' as being 'off limits',[14] imperial historians have been concerned with the culture of imperialism for more than twenty years.[15] Indeed, since the early 1980s it has become a major historical preoccupation.[16] Most historians have little difficulty in seeing texts as 'worldly', as 'to some degree events' in their own right, as 'a part of the social world, human life, and of course the historical moments in which they are located and interpreted'.[17] For them 'rubbing culture's nose in the mud of politics'[18] is a perfectly conventional rather than iconoclastic activity.

Yet, as we shall see, historians continue to have problems both with *Orientalism* and, more particularly, with some of the work inspired by it, for, like Marx and Freud, Said has spawned followers (Saidians or Saidists), producing work both subtle and crude, some of which the master might wish to disown. However, if *Orientalism* at times conveyed the seductive ring of the codification of the obvious, *Culture and Imperialism* – as I shall demonstrate in Chapter 2 – presents far greater problems for historians as well as literary critics.[19]

But if Said's intellectual influence on a number of related disciplines in the humanities and the social sciences has been considerable, his work has also been seen as both highly polemical and distinctly schizophrenic. A large proportion of Said's examples are drawn from the Middle East and he is concerned, as he has insisted in a later commentary on *Orientalism*, not to defend Arabs or Islam, but to show that these terms exist as

> 'communities of interpretation' which gave them existence, and that, like the Orient itself, each designation represented interests, claims, projects, ambitions and rhetorics that were not only in violent disagreement, but were in a situation of open warfare. So saturated with meanings, so overdetermined by history, religion and politics are labels like 'Arab' or 'Muslim' as subdivisions of 'the Orient' that no one today can use them without some attention to the formidable polemical mediations that screen the objects, if they exist at all, that the labels designate.[20]

Given that this is indeed his starting-point, it is not surprising that his work has been seen as a product of rage, the anti-western and by extension anti-Zionist tract of a dispossessed Palestinian. It might reasonably be objected that other religious and ethnic designations are equally overdetermined and saturated with meanings, not only in the Orient, but also in other continents and the West itself. Indeed, it may be that Said himself contributes to this saturation by occidentalising the West, by 'essentialising' (describing by means of essences or stereotypes) the characteristics of European powers no less than they 'essentialised' the East. Moreover, 'Jew' and 'Zionist' are clearly overburdened terms, and it is, perhaps, inevitable that some of the most powerful critiques of Said have come from scholars of Jewish heritage. One proclaimed himself as 'tired of the Said phenomenon'.[21] Another became embroiled in a bitter correspondence in the *Times Literary Supplement* after a particularly hostile review of *Culture and Imperialism*.[22] Yet another, writing within Israel, has used the viewpoint of women's studies to deliver a powerful, if largely implicit critique of *Orientalism*.[23] For conventional literary critics, Said has had the audacity to attempt to implicate the literature of sensibility, the Leavisite great tradition, in the squalor and brutality of imperialism,[24] while scholars imbued in western liberal humanism have seen the Enlightenment tradition, the scholarly explorations celebrated by the writers of the British Council pamphlets, arraigned as the accomplices of colonialism.

Yet herein lies the schizophrenia. Said has declared himself to react to the word 'humanist' with 'contradictory feelings of affection and revulsion'.[25] He seeks to expose the humanistic tradition, while essentially writing within it himself. His works are a collective plea for a new kind of liberal humanity, which Ernest Gellner, in a magisterial review, found an unexceptionable truism.[26] He is steeped in the western musical tradition, but finds it compromised by its political context.[27] He admires the art of Kipling, valuing it above that of the more ambivalent Forster, for example, while loathing its imperialist assumptions.[28] Thus, though he has toyed with the language of base and superstructure, while he has been a member of the Palestine National Council, he writes outside Marxist or revolutionary traditions. Indeed, it is a characteristic of his work that neither economics nor class plays a particularly central role if indeed any role at all. He has said that he finds Marxism 'more limiting than enabling'[29] and that he is more interested in an ethic of individualism than class-consciousness.[30] He is atheistic in religion, agnostic in politics and has no general intellectual attachment beyond a respect for anarcho-syndicalism. Thus, influenced though he is by Gramsci and Foucault, he stands beyond any scholarly collective, his political objectives (except perhaps Palestinian freedom – though not through partition, which he decries – and wider global understanding) largely undefined.[31]

Further, Said is situated at the watershed of the modernist–postmodernist debate. In *Orientalism* he identifies an imperial totalising project, a 'master narrative' of western power. But his is of course a Whiggism in reverse. He exposes these constant leitmotifs of intercultural relations to condemn rather than to celebrate. Instead of 'progress' or an ineluctable historical dialectic, his master narrative is regressive, a tool of dominance which survives the end of formal imperialism to continue its destructive role in the world of today. As he has put it, decolonisation is an unfinished project.[32] Thus he totalises for the purpose of demolition. But his trade mark is continuity: his Orientalist programme has had continuous showings from at least the eighteenth century to the present day. It prepared the way for full-blown imperial rule and survives as the cultural and ideological superstructure of neo-colonialism, particularly America's self-satisfied and culturally blinkered role (as he sees it) as imperial world policeman in the late twentieth century.[33]

Yet he profoundly distrusts all other 'metanarratives' as interpretative tools. Instead of the 'theorization of the whole', he prefers a 'more unbuttoned, unfixed, and mobile mode' which he has dubbed (in a direct allusion to his own exiled status) nomadic and unhoused.[34] He is also disturbed by the cultural guerrillas which beset the fringes of the master narrative. These he has identified as 'nativism' (which extols the virtues of and seeks to resurrect individual indigenous cultures), 'nationalism' (which asserts the political creed of contesting nations) and 'fundamentalism' (which seeks to restore religious purity as a rallying cry of resistance).[35] Each is concerned to subdivide and separate, by cultural, political or religious means, in order to escape the western coils, and in doing so contributes to a reorientalisation by appearing to confirm the irrational, the divisive, the aberrant character of the West's Orient.

Thus we have an extraordinary, and some might think disabling paradox, that the author of a work purporting to identify a master discourse of the Orient operating over at least two centuries himself distrusts all global theorisation. It is as though his critical totalising head is at war with his nomadic, polymorphous heart. In *Orientalism* he seems to be a monolithic modernist; in all his ideological statements since, a committed postmodernist. And indeed the responses to Said have often been profoundly postmodernist, refusing to accept the juggernaut of a global cultural history trapped in a specific misrepresentational groove. They have substituted pluralism and ambivalence (or more likely multivalence), the polyglot and the contingent for Said's generalising discourse. They have sought to replace Said's Orientalist system-building with eclectic and fragmented structures of knowledge. To use the kind of musical metaphor so beloved of Said himself, they have composed a reedy polyphony (or perhaps cacophony) in place of the magisterial diapasons of Orientalism's great fugal project. And in doing so (and this is its considerable strength) they have extended the multidisciplinary character of the Orientalist debate, implicating it in the central intellectual developments of the late twentieth century.

On the face of it, Said's work should be of great interest to historians. He has said that he is particularly fascinated by history, that he regards his work as supremely historicist and that he has become totally unconcerned with literary theory.[36] He rejects both the concept of a literary canon and criticism that is purely textual. He sees deconstruction as exhausted and positions himself in the anti-Derrida camp.[37] He himself has taken up the 'Subaltern Studies' group of Indian historians, but although the initial publication of their work followed hard on the heels of *Orientalism* in the early 1980s, it is only more recently that they have become directly influenced by him, if at all.[38] In any case, they adhere to a much tougher ideological standpoint than he does. For the rest, historians have largely ignored him. Yet it would be wrong for historians to be wholly absent from this controversy, even if only to define their negative reactions. The debate conveys some messages for their discipline and offers explanations for cross-disciplinary misunderstandings as well as arguments for securing multidisciplinary insights.

For the imperial historian, there is a more practical necessity for involvement. Said has claimed that 'we would not have had empire itself without important philosophical and imaginative processes at work in the production as well as the acquisition, subordination and settlement of space'.[39] Indeed, that is one of the powerful underlying themes of Orientalism. The western discourse of the Orient paved the way for power and smoothed the route to its continuation in the neo-colonialist context. Patrick Brantlinger has similarly argued for the continuity of the imperial literary canon,[40] and other works have noted the imperial contexts and characteristics of cultural media and scientific endeavour in the nineteenth century.[41] The cultural continuity interpretation should come as no particular surprise to historians since they have themselves been stressing the importance of eighteenth-century imperialism,[42] identifying an imperial meridian in the early nineteenth century,[43] and have long rejected the notion of a mid-Victorian era of anti-imperialism.[44]

The rest of this chapter will be concerned with Said's arguments in *Orientalism* and subsequent commentaries, together with the variety of responses and criticisms that have been produced in recent years, while Chapter 2 will consider Said's new statement in *Culture and Imperialism*, and the continuing difficulties for historians inherent in these approaches.

Said's Orientalism revisited

For Disraeli, himself often viewed as a mysterious oriental presence in British politics, the West turned the East into a career.[45] For Said, the West transformed the East into a discourse.[46] From the late eighteenth to the twentieth centuries a vast corpus of scholarly, travel and imaginative writings consumed the Orient and disgorged it as a prefabricated construct. This 'Orientalism' duly 'overrode the Orient' (p. 96). Not only is it impossible for knowledge to be 'pure', but, following and developing Foucault, knowledge both represents and extends power, in this case the power to recreate the cultures of an entire continent solely in the light of sets of self-referents, thus implying if not inferiority, at the very least the need for correction. In the pursuit of this programme, Orientalism necessarily stressed contrast and difference. As a 'cultural contestant', the East was always one of the West's 'deepest and most recurring images of the Other' (p. 1), an Other which was 'mysterious, duplicitous and dark'.[47] This process of comparative characterisation tended to lead to the polarisation of distinctions between the two cultures, to the creation of what linguists call binary opposition (p. 46). The West became more western, the East more eastern, the West rational, mature and normal, the East irrational, backward, depraved. Orientalism as a political doctrine could be 'willed over the Orient because the Orient was weaker than the West, which elided the Orient's difference with its weakness' (p. 204) and therefore presumably with its alleged inferiority.

But Orientalism was much more than a self-regarding debate among scholars and writers. It was 'a scientific movement whose analogue in the world of empirical politics was the Orient's colonial accumulation and acquisition by Europe'. Thus the Orient was prevented from being Europe's interlocutor, but was its wholly silent Other.[48] Yet analogue does not seem to be the right word (these problems of language frequently recur in Said), for the whole point about Orientalism was that it was instrumental. Through the images formed by the Orientalists, 'European culture was able to manage – and even produce – the Orient politically, sociologically, militarily, ideologically, scientifically and imaginatively during the post-Enlightenment period.' Thus Orientalism was a 'Western style for dominating, restructuring, and having authority over the Orient' (p. 3), which was able to emerge from an uneven exchange of different sorts of power: political, intellectual, cultural and moral. Its relationship with such expressions of power was circular: it arose from them and in turn encouraged and re-emphasised them. Orientalism, as with culture generally, had a 'persistence and durability' that creates 'saturating hegemonic systems' (p. 14). Since it was Britain and France which primarily exercised such power from the late eighteenth century to 1914, Orientalism was essentially the product of these two western cultures. For reasons not wholly explained by Said, German and other Orientalisms seem to have been more disinterested (p. 18).

Such a theory, as Said recognises, needs to be predicated on the notion of 'unchallenged western dominance' (p. 73). Orientalists 'plotted Oriental history, character and destiny for hundreds of years' until Orientalism 'accomplished its self-metamorphosis from a scholarly discourse to an imperial institution' (p. 95). Orientalists, often viewed as heroic figures, set up 'a dynamic exchange between individual authors and large political concerns', but in doing so they established the essential 'interconnectedness of texts', frequently quoting each other (pp. 15, 23). This 'systematic accumulation' achieved its vindication through its later 'effectiveness, its usefulness, its authority' (p. 123). And from 'these complex rewritings the actualities of the modern Orient were systematically excluded' (p. 177). Indeed a central point of Said's argument is that Orientalism is not just a historical phenomenon. It has a 'continuing political actuality' which no less conditions the West's approach to the East (by which he means, of course, primarily the Middle East) in the late twentieth century as in the nineteenth century. The only difference is that the prime actor has become the United States rather than Britain or France.

However, in one of the more enigmatic and least developed passages in *Orientalism*, Said recognises that the traffic cannot all be one way, that Orientalism was forming the West as well as the Orient. The East 'has helped to define Europe' (p. 1), has been an 'integral part of European *material* civilisation and culture', a 'sort of surrogate and even underground self', at times (as for the Romantics) even a means of regenerating the West. Thus the discourse of Orientalism seems to go further than merely highlighting the alleged superiorities of Europe. It can modify and therefore surely even challenge the West. Said never follows through the logic of this, that the example of the Orient can become the means for a counter-western discourse, that it can offer opportunities for literary extension, spiritual renewal and artistic development. Thus the Orient, or at least its discourse, has the capacity to become the tool of cultural revolution, a legitimising source of resistance to those who challenge western conventions, introspection and complacency. This will constitute an important theme of this book.

Postmodernist revisions

Partha Chatterjee has written that for him, a child of a successful anticolonial struggle, '*Orientalism* was a book which talked of things I felt I had known all along but had never found the language to formulate with clarity. Like many great books, it seemed to say for the first time what one had always wanted to say.'[49] There is no doubt that Said's work had that kind of revelatory, almost self-revelatory effect on scholars in the Third World and the United States. As Benita Parry has suggested, critical engagement with *Orientalism* has been less sustained in Britain than elsewhere, although it is perhaps from Britain that the most dismissive attacks have come.[50] While Ernest Gellner has recently described the book as 'quite entertaining, but intellectually insignificant',[51] the majority of criticisms and revisions of Said have been delivered from the vantage-point of admiration. This is, perhaps, particularly true of those emanating from the field of literary criticism. The rest of this chapter will deal with some of these, particularly those which have operated on an essentially theoretical level. In Chapter 2, revisions more firmly rooted in an empirical base will be examined in terms of the norms and conventions of historians.

There have been at least four areas of challenge to Said: his binary approach to the 'Other' or 'alterity' as colonial discourse jargon has it; his notion of unchallenged western dominance and his handling of the character of imperial hegemony; his vacillations between truth and ideology and his lack of theoretical consistency (which he has himself acknowledged);[52] and his identification of a monolithic and predominantly male-originated discourse, which equally subjects the West to 'Occidentalism'. To these we can add (and these will be mainly discussed in Chapter 2) a historicism which is in itself essentially ahistorical, an unwillingness to grapple with political economy, with class, and the contrasting economic and social circumstances of different territories; and difficulties in connecting representation to agency, establishing the precise relationship between scholarly Orientalism and imperial instrumentality.

Said himself says very little about specific colonial moments and touches on particular territories only in passing. Homi K. Bhabha and Gayatri Chakravorty Spivak make even fewer, if any, attempts to anchor their work in the empirical depths of the imperial experience, tending to generalise in strikingly airy ways. Spivak has even been accused of collapsing ethnic categories and 'essentialising' colonial subjects no less than the Orientalists did.[53] But both Bhabha and Spivak seek to emphasise that the colonial cultural experience had mutually modifying effects and that it is an oversimplification to divide the dominant and the subordinate too rigidly into active and passive, imperial mugger and unresisting victim.[54] Spivak in particular has allied herself (if somewhat ambivalently) to the 'Subaltern Studies' group of scholars whose prime concern has been to give voice to the unvoiced, to highlight 'subaltern' resistance and illustrate the extent to which subordinate peoples retain control over their own destiny and subtly – and sometimes more directly – modify the designs of their rulers.[55] For the Subaltern School attempting to recover the consciousness of the non-elite subordinates of empire, the notion of helpless victim is anathema and indeed, even outside their deeply committed stance, few historians can today accept the concept of the irresistibility of imperial rule, the idea, expressed long ago by an Indian scholar, that from the days of Vasco da Gama Asia somehow lay at Europe's feet.[56] Recent imperial historiography has tended to emphasise the ephemerality of imperial rule ('The Colonial Moment in Africa'), its relative insecurity and its helplessness to effect real change.[57] Not even its limited economic objectives were pursued as comprehensively or successfully as used to be thought. Moreover, this historiography has tended to re-emphasise the influence of imperialism upon the mother country, in modifying its social and political systems, in serving the objectives of national integration – and in the post-imperial world potential disintegration.[58] None of this rests easily with Said's all-embracing commanding discourse serving the interests of an invincible western power.

Using the distinction between the centrifugal and centripetal in imperial influences,[59] critics have seen Said's lines of scholarly force and power as far too unidirectional. The discourse of Orientalism must also implicate the dominant imperial subject; the white man's subjectivity is equally worthy of study.[60] Indeed, this is the area where the work of historians has been most strong in recent years.[61] But literary critics have attempted to theorise this in psychological ways. The coloniser's strength is always prefigured by vulnerability.[62] Empire was traumatic as well as triumphal, as productive of apprehension as much as comprehension, fear as well as fantasy. Using ideas derived from Fanon and Freud, Homi Bhabha has seen the colonial stereotype as essentially ambivalent, part of the 'grotesque psychodrama' in which the discourse, far from being simply possessed by the coloniser, also possesses him.[63] His relationship with the colonised operates like a fetish, vacillating between fear and desire, doubt and confidence. The indigenous of empire are portrayed as degenerate in order to justify conquest, but as redeemable in order to justify their continuing rule. Thus: 'The black is both savage (cannibal) and yet the most obedient and dignified of servants (the bearer of food); he is the embodiment of rampant sexuality and yet innocent as a child; he is mystical, primitive, simple-minded and yet the most worldly and accomplished liar, and manipulator of social forces.'[64] Hence the violence of empire moves from the punitive to the disciplinary, initial conquest to reforming suppression of resistance.

If colonial stereotyping is essentially interactive, hegemony is never uncontested. A major theoretical inconsistency arises from the problems of attempting to reconcile Foucault with Gramsci.[65] Foucault is less concerned with historical process; yet hegemonic activity must always imply chronological dynamic. Just as scholarly paradigms like that of Said pass through the cycle of imitation, revision, subversion and rejection, so too is power asserted, modified, challenged, reasserted and transformed. Counter-hegemonic thought and activity are to be found both among the dominant and subordinate elements of the imperial relationship. Moreover, the hegemonic stereotypes can be taken over by the colonised and then used against the imperial masters, where characteristics (like the concept of the 'martial race' or the notion of a spiritual, pre-industrial India) attributed by the imperial power come to be wielded as sources of resistance. The anthropologist Richard Fox has shown the ways in which this was done both by the Sikhs in the Punjab and by Gandhi in his formulation of an Indian Utopian vision.[66] More-over, imperial texts can display considerable heterogeneity, revealing doubts and contradictions, both hegemonic and counter-hegemonic thought.[67]

Thus, culture is something more than simply a 'vital, enabling counterpoint to institutional practices'.[68] As Said has himself noted in another of his books, but apparently forgot in both *Orientalism* and *Culture and Imperialism*, culture is unstable, heterogeneous and inter-nally resistant.[69] In *Orientalism* he suggests not only that 'all cultures impose corrections upon raw reality, changing it from free-floating ob-jects into units of knowledge' (p. 67), but also that some form of truth is attainable.[70] When he ascribes virtue and vice to scholars, he seems to be searching for those who have arrived at some form of 'real' Orient, a representation that can be identified as truthful.[71] Thus he moves from a discursive determinism to a humanistic positivism in a short and breathtaking stride.

Yet in searching for the ideologically positive – or politically correct – he cannot avoid 'Occidentalism'. The culture that engenders such a self-perpetuating and interconnected discourse itself becomes reduced to a set of essences of power and dominance. This propensity is particularly pronounced in Said's *Culture and Imperialism*. Thus the imperative of misrepresentation becomes mutual: cultures seem con-demned to irredeemable misunderstanding. The optimistic purpose of the British Council pamphleteers is stood on its head. The removal of the solidarity inspired by opposition to totalitarian regimes produces an intellectual cold war of interpretations. While Said has himself called for a 'libertarian or a nonrepressive and nonmanipulative perspective' to be brought to bear on the study of other cultures, his implication is that so far this has seldom, if ever, been achieved.[72] While he has denied that his argument suggests that understanding can only come from inside, his examples of a more 'nonrepressive' approach have been few and sometimes bizarre.[73]

Said has singled out women's studies as offering one libertarian route. Yet he has made very little use of the insights of scholars in this field and, indeed, his Orientalist discourse is solely male-generated. Now an 'alternative female discourse' of the East has been identified, a dis-course which is highly fractured, multivocal and polyglot.[74] Billie Melman has analysed women's accounts of travel and residence in the Middle East, Said's intellectual heartland and ethnic homeland, as re-flecting the ambivalence and complexity of both eighteenth-century and Victorian attitudes. In this account (which will be discussed more extensively in Chapter 2), women's representations of the East are more clearly attributed to chronological periods and set into their historical contexts. They display major shifts in concepts of sexual liberty, ideas about race and social Darwinism and deep fissures between secular and evangelical standpoints. She concludes that social and gender differences were more important in conditioning writings about the Middle East than political attitudes or objectives.

With the exception of Melman's work, which is presented from a historical rather than a literary viewpoint, most of this critique has been expressed in unsubversive ways. Yet the cumulative effect is highly disruptive, if not destructive. Said's theoretical inconsistency and tend-ency to slip into precisely those sins he castigates undermines much of his Orientalist structure. Moreover, he fails to recognise that the arts and dominant political ideologies tend to operate in counterpoint rather than conformity. It is from the arts that a counter-hegemonic discourse invariably emerges. It is often tentative and cannot be expected to leap totally out of its period. (Thus Said's disappointment that neither Conrad nor Forster is capable of a full premonition of decolonisation seems hopelessly anachronistic.)[75] In some accounts, as we shall see in Chapter 3, an oppositional stance has actually been misrepresented by art historians as conformity.[76]

Further, Said has failed to make any distinction between 'high art' and popular culture. This may be because, by his own admission, he has little interest in popular culture.[77] Apart from acknowledging some of the work of the Frankfurt school of sociologists in debating the relationship between the two, he has said little or nothing about the intended audience of different areas of 'Orientalism' or the possibility of contrasting receptions based on historical phase, class and economic context.[78] Moreover, it is possible that there are periods of convergence and divergence in elite and popular culture. So far as the culture of the new imperialism is concerned, it is at least possible that there was a period of convergence in late Victorian and Edwardian times followed by an era of divergence in the inter-war years.[79] It may be that Orientalism follows a similar pattern.

Perhaps the greatest limitation on Said's analysis of Orientalism is the fact that he concentrates almost exclusively on elite texts. He claims heterogeneity for his choice, but although he ventures outside the purely literary, his sources consistently inhabit the realms of high culture. In fact, historians have already ranged out beyond this highly restricted field and have examined imperial materials extending from juvenile literature to ephemera, from stage presentations to advertising, from national ceremonial to popular music and the cinema.[80] Similarly, a full understanding of Orientalism requires some comprehension of the extensive range of artistic vehicles through which representations of the Orient were projected. Ideally (and this book can only make a tentative start to this process) these need to be analysed in terms of production, intention, content, audience and specific historical moment.

It is perhaps because the work of historians has been so much more adventurous and has attempted an analysis of the culture of imperialism within its specific national, class and historic contexts that Said's *Culture and Imperialism* seems such an unsatisfactory book. From the standpoint of the discipline of history, the literary critics give the impression of chasing their theoretical tails in ever-diminishing circles while never actually converting their historicism into any meaningful historical study. The next chapter turns a critical eye upon *Culture and Imperialism* and considers a new wave of contributions to the Orientalism debate.

Notes

1   Bernard Lewis, 'British Contributions to Arabic Studies' (London, 1941); Arthur J. Arberry, 'British Contributions to Persian Studies' (London, 1942); Sir Attul Chatterjee and Sir Richard Burn, 'British Contributions to Indian Studies' (London, 1943); Harold Bowen, 'British Contributions to Turkish Studies' (London, 1945).

2   John M. MacKenzie, 'Propaganda and the BBC Empire Service' in Jeremy Hawthorn (ed.), *Propaganda, Persuasion and Polemic* (London, 1987), pp. 37–53.

3   Philip M. Taylor, *The Projection of Britain: British Overseas Publicity and Propaganda, 1919–1939* (Cambridge, 1981).

4   Lewis, 'Arabic Studies', p. 6.

5   Bowen, 'Turkish Studies', pp. 43, 54.

6   S. N. Mukherjee, *Sir William Jones: a Study in Eighteenth-Century British Attitudes to India* (Cambridge, 1968); Garland Cannon, *Oriental Jones: a Biography* (London, 1964) and *The Life and Mind of Oriental Jones* (Cambridge 1990), in which he specifically takes issue with Said's *Orientalism*, pp. xv, xvi, 360–1, 385.

7   Quoted in Gauri Viswanathan, *Masks of Conquest* (London, 1989), p. 28.

8   Quoted in P. J. Marshall, 'Warren Hastings as scholar and patron' in Anne Whiteman, J. S. Bromley and P. G. M. Dickson (eds), *Statesmen, Scholars and Merchants: Essays in Eighteenth-Century History Presented to Dame Lucy Sutherland* (Oxford, 1973), pp. 253, 258.

9   Eric Stokes, *The English Utilitarians and India* (Oxford, 1959) and George D. Bearce, *British Attitudes towards India, 1784–1858* (Oxford, 1961).

10 For example, J. L. Brockington, 'Warren Hastings and Orientalism' in Geoffrey Carnall and Colin Nicholson (eds), *The Impeachment of Warren Hastings* (Edinburgh, 1989), pp. 91–108.

11 Edward W. Said, *Orientalism* (London, 1978) and 'Orientalism reconsidered' in Francis Barker *et al.* (eds), *Literature, Politics and Theory* (London, 1986), pp. 210–29.

12 Christopher L. Miller, *Blank Darkness: Africanist Discourse in French* (Chicago, 1985) and Malek Alloula, *The Colonial Harem* (Manchester, 1986) are two examples.

13 John Pemble, *The Mediterranean Passion: Victorians and Edwardians in the South*

(Oxford, 1987). For one of many popular accounts of travel in the Middle East that take no account of Said, see Naomi Shepherd, *The Zealous Intruders: the Western Rediscovery of Palestine* (London, 1987).

14 Said, *Orientalism*, p. 13; Edward W. Said, *Culture and Imperialism* (London, 1993).

15 A. P. Thornton was one of the first to consider the culture of imperialism: see his *Doctrines of Imperialism* (New York, 1963) and *For the File on Empire* (London, 1968).

16 William H. Schneider, *An Empire for the Masses: the French Popular Image of Africa, 1870–1900* (London, 1982); Thomas G. August, *The Selling of the Empire: British and French Imperialist Propaganda, 1890–1914* (London, 1985); John M. MacKenzie, *Propaganda and Empire* (Manchester, 1984) and the Manchester University Press 'Studies in Imperialism' series which was founded in 1986.

17 Edward W. Said, *The World, the Text and the Critic* (Cambridge, Mass., 1983), p. 4.

18 Said, *Orientalism*, p. 13.

19 See my review of *Culture and Imperialism*, 'Occidentalism, counterpoint and counter-polemic' in *Journal of Historical Geography*, 19 (1993), pp. 339–44.

20 Said, 'Orientalism reconsidered', p. 214.

21 Quoted in Michael Sprinker (ed.), *Edward Said: a Critical Reader* (Oxford, 1992), p. 1.

22 Ernest Gellner, 'The mightier pen', *Times Literary Supplement*, 19 February 1993, pp. 3–4; and the correspondence in *The Times Literary Supplement*, 19 March, p. 15; 2 April, p. 17 and 9 April, p. 15.

23 Billie Melman, *Women's Orients: English Women in the Middle East, 1718–1918* (London, 1992).

24 Peter Conrad, 'Empires of the senseless', *Observer*, 7 February 1993, p. 55. This abusive and largely unreasoning piece (neatly conveyed through the title) was carried in one of the very few left-of-centre newspapers remaining in Britain. Just about the only review in the British press which was sympathetic to Said, that by Terry Eagleton in the *Guardian*, 9 February 1993, p. 10, largely misunderstood Said's true purposes.

25 Edward W. Said, 'Opponents, audiences, constituencies and community' in H. Foster (ed.), *Postmodern Culture* (London, 1985), pp. 135–59.

26 Gellner, 'The mightier pen', p. 4.

27 Interview with Said in Sprinker, *Critical Reader*, pp. 245–6. The answer is curiously ambiguous, but he does talk of 'the complicity between music, ideology and social space'. See also Edward W. Said, *Musical Elaborations* (London, 1991). In another interview in Imre Salusinszky, *Criticism in Society* (New York, 1987, p. 141), he has said that 'Music is the great passion of my life.'

28 Said, *Culture and Imperialism*, pp. 159–96, 241–9.

29 Sprinker, *Critical Reader*, p. 260. See also Salusinszky, *Criticism*, pp. 137–9.

30 Salusinszky, *Criticism*, p. 146.

31 Salusinszky, *Criticism*, pp. 128–9.

32 Sprinker, *Critical Reader*, p. 236.

33 Said, *Culture and Imperialism*, pp. 341–408.

34 Sprinker, *Critical Reader*, p. 241. Here he is following the ideas of Gilles Deleuze.

35 Said, 'Orientalism reconsidered', p. 216.

36 Sprinker, *Critical Reader*, pp. 248–9.

37 Salusinszky, *Criticism*, p. 138.

38 Said wrote a foreword to the selection of their essays in Ranajit Guha and Gayatri Chakravorty Spivak (eds), *Selected Subaltern Studies* (Oxford, 1988), pp. v–x.

The first volume of *Subaltern Studies* was published in 1982. The use of the word 'subaltern' in this meaning (the largely unvoiced and disempowered masses) is of course derived from Gramsci. For some readers it has been highly confusing since the most common usage in English relates to 'junior officers', that is, those who mediate between the senior officer elite and the rank and file.

39 Edward W. Said, 'Representing the colonized: anthropology's interlocutors'. *Critical Inquiry* 15 (1989), p. 216. This theme is developed throughout *Culture and Imperialism*.

40 Patrick Brantlinger, *Rule of Darkness: British Literature and Imperialism, 1830–1914* (London, 1988).

41 See, for example, J. S. Bratton *et al.* (eds), *Acts of Supremacy: the British Empire and the Stage, 1790–1930* (Manchester, 1991) and Robert Stafford, *Scientist of Empire: Sir Roderick Murchison, Scientific Exploration and Victorian Imperialism* (Cambridge, 1989).

42 P. J. Marshall, 'An agenda for the history of imperial Britain', unpublished paper delivered at a conference, 'Issues in Imperial and Commonwealth History', King's College, London, 14 March 1992 and P. J. Marshall, 'No fatal impact? The elusive history of imperial Britain', *Times Literary Supplement*, 12 March 1993, pp. 8–10.

43 C. A. Bayly, *Imperial Meridian: the British Empire and the World, 1780–1830* (London, 1989).

44 J. A. Gallagher and R. E. Robinson, 'The imperialism of free trade', *Economic History Review*, vi (1953).

45 The quotation comes from Disraeli's novel *Tancred* of 1847. Sir William Harcourt described the purchase of the Suez Canal shares in 1875 in this way: 'There was something Asiatic in this mysterious melodrama. It was like something from the "Thousand and One Nights" when in the midst of the fumes of incense a shadowy Genius astonishes the bewildered spectators. The public mind was dazzled, fascinated, mystified.' Quoted in P. W. Clayden, *England under Lord Beaconsfield* (London, 1880), p. 155. A. J. P. Taylor once described Gladstone as the Victorian conscience, with Disraeli as the release from it: here is an analogue with the Orient itself.

46 In the summary that follows, all the page numbers in parentheses refer to *Orientalism*.

47 Salusinszky in *Criticism*, p. 125.

48 Said, 'Orientalism reconsidered', p. 215.

49 Partha Chatterjee, 'Their own words? An essay for Edward Said' in Sprinker, *Critical Reader*, p. 194.

50 Benita Parry, 'Overlapping territories and intertwined histories: Edward Said's postcolonial cosmopolitanism' in Sprinker, *Critical Reader*, p. 23. See also her 'Problems in current theories of colonial discourse', *Oxford Literary Review*, 9 (1987), pp. 1–2.

51 Gellner, letter, *TLS*, 9 April 1993, p. 15.

52 Salusinszky, *Criticism*, p. 137.

53 Laura Chrisman, 'The imperial unconscious? Representations of imperial discourse', *Critical Quarterly*, 32, 3 (1990), pp. 39–40.

54 See, for example, Homi K. Bhabha, 'The other question; difference, discrimination and the discourse of colonialism' in Francis Barker *et al.* (eds), *The Politics of Theory* (Colchester, 1983) and reprinted in Barker *et al.* (eds), *Literature, Politics and Theory*, pp. 148–72; 'Of mimicry and man: the ambivalence of colonial discourse', *October*, 28 (spring 1984); 'Signs taken for wonders; questions of ambivalence and authority under a tree outside Delhi, May 1817', *Critical Enquiry*, 12, 1 (1985), pp. 144–65; 'DissemiNation: time, narrative, and the

margins of the modern nation' in Homi K. Bhabha (ed.), *Nation and Narration* (London, 1990), pp. 291–321, together with his introduction to the same volume; and *The Location of Culture* (London, 1994). For Gayatri Chakravorty Spivak, see her collection *In Other Worlds: Essays in Cultural Politics* (London, 1987) and 'Poststructuralism, marginality, postcoloniality and value' in Peter Collier and Helga Geyer-Ryan (eds), *Literary Theory Today* (Cambridge, 1990).

55   Gayatri Chakravorty Spivak, 'Subaltern studies: deconstructing historiography' in *In Other Worlds*, pp. 196–221, reprinted as her introduction to *Selected Subaltern Studies*. In her 'Can the subaltern speak?' in Cary Nelson and Lawrence Gossberg (eds), *Marxism and the Interpretation of Culture* (London, 1988), she seems to argue against the possibility of a voicing of subaltern autonomy, a position somewhat different from that of the Subaltern Studies historians.

56   K. M. Panikkar, *Asia and Western Dominance* (London, 1953), a work which Said extols as a turning-point in *Culture and Imperialism*, p. 270, although for historians it is now out of date in providing far too much unresisted instrumentality to Europeans.

57   Andrew Roberts, *The Colonial Moment in Africa: Essays on the Movement of Minds and Materials, 1900–1940* (Cambridge, 1990), reprinted essays from the *Cambridge History of Africa*, Vol. 7 (Cambridge, 1987).

58   Tom Nairn, *The Break-up of Britain* (London, 1977); Linda Colley, *Britons: Forging the Nation, 1707–1837* (New Haven, 1992); and John M. MacKenzie, 'Scotland and the Empire', an inaugural lecture privately printed by the University of Lancaster (1992).

59   MacKenzie, *Propaganda and Empire*, p. 2.

60   David Trotter, 'Colonial subjects', *Critical Quarterly*, 32, 3 (1990), pp. 3–20.

61   See the contributions to John M. MacKenzie (ed.), *Imperialism and Popular Culture* (Manchester, 1986); *Imperialism and the Natural World* (Manchester, 1990); and *Popular Imperialism and the Military* (Manchester, 1992); and Jeffrey Richards, *Imperialism and Juvenile Literature* (Manchester, 1989), together with works in the Manchester University Press 'Studies in Imperialism' series by W. J. Reader, Paul Greenhalgh, J. W. M. Hichberger and collections edited by J. S. Bratton and J. A. Mangan; also Kathryn Tidrick, *Empire and the English Character* (London, 1990).

62   Trotter, 'Colonial subjects', p. 5.

63   Bhabha, 'The other question', p. 149 ff.

64   'The other question', p. 170.

65   Dennis Porter, 'Orientalism and its problems' in Barker *et al.* (eds), *The Politics of Theory*, pp. 179–93.

66   Richard G. Fox, 'East of Said' in Sprinker, *Critical Reader*, pp. 144–56.

67   Parry, 'Overlapping territories and intertwined histories', *passim*. See also Rosalind O'Hanlon, 'Recovering the subject: subaltern studies and histories of resistance in colonial South Asia', *Modern Asian Studies*, 22 (1988), pp. 189–224.

68   Parry, 'Overlapping territories', p. 24.

69   'In human history there is always something beyond the reach of dominating systems no matter how deeply they saturate society': *The World, the Text and the Critic*, pp. 246–7.

70   Said, *Orientalism*, pp. 67, 21. 'Indeed, I would go so far as saying that it is the critic's job to provide resistance to theory, to open it up towards historical reality': *The World, The Text and the Critic*, p. 242.

71   In *Culture and Imperialism*, he indulges in a similar ascription of virtue and vice and an assumption that European writers in the past – like Goldwyn Smith or J. A. Hobson – and the present – like Terence Ranger or Basil Davidson – can get nearer to truth, mainly because they are privileged by their dissenting political

position. Yet he acknowledges that 'reading and writing texts are never neutral activities', *Culture and Imperialism*, p. 385. How the impossibility of neutrality and a scale of acceptability can be reconciled is never made clear. The same problems beggar the correspondence in the *Times Literary Supplement* in March and April 1993.

72   Said calls for a 'non-coercive knowledge' in the closing pages of *Orientalism*, and in the Sprinker and Salusinszky interviews, implying that this is only fully possible in modern times and from a specific political standpoint.

73   Parry, 'Overlapping territories', pp. 29–30. Other examples can be found in *Culture and Imperialism*.

74   Melman, *Women's Orients*.

75   Said, *Culture and Imperialism*, pp. 28, 245–6.

76   See my critique of Rana Kabbani, Linda Nochlin and exhibition catalogues in Chapter 3.

77   Interview in Sprinker, *Critical Reader*, pp. 246.

78   *ibid.*, p. 244.

79   MacKenzie, *Propaganda and Empire*, pp. 255–7, revising the conventional view that the imperial ideology received a death-blow with the First World War.

80   MacKenzie (ed.), *Imperialism and Popular Culture* and *Popular Imperialism and the Military*.

2

The Orient and culture and imperialism

IN SO FAR as Said is a historian at all, he is a Whig. What he seems to imply is that until the late twentieth century, all western scholarship involving representations of other peoples is tainted by its viewpoint of political dominance. In the recent past, it has just become possible for scholars to operate in unmanipulative ways. In the present and the future, if certain principles are followed, principles that seem to deny ideology but embrace humanity, scholars may aspire to operate in libertarian and unrepressive ways. And the key to this intellectual Utopia is the slaying of the dragon of imperialism. Progress is possible and Said is its apostle. Where *Orientalism* hinted at this opportunity, *Culture and Imperialism* – which will be considered at the end of this chapter – is a manifesto for its achievement.[1]

It is perhaps this prescriptive Whiggism which has made Said's work so difficult for historians to handle. But since 1990 a number of writers working in the fields of what may loosely be called the cultural aspects of imperial history, in studies of travel writing, in historical geography, and in what is left of colonial discourse analysis, have issued a series of largely unconnected challenges to Said. Extending the work of the theoreticians considered in Chapter 1, they have revised his binary oppositions and produced a major critique of his oversimplifications of the imperial relationship. These works have highlighted mutual complicity and the interpenetrations of imperial and indigenous culture which

can produce reversals in apparent power relationships. They have emphasised a multiplicity of voices, differentiated by gender, ideology and religious standpoint, distinctions between surface simplicities and disguised
ironies, and the disfunctions between representation and agency. They
have also tended to stress the vulnerability of the dominant in a romantic
search for the extended and fuller self, as well as to resurrect the autonomy and ambiguities of great art, reflected in the displacements and
destabilising elements of the artistic product. To this can be added the
problems of Said's oversimplified conception of the 'Other' and his failure to recognise the powerful critique of home culture – particularly its
industrialism – that lies at the centre of so many representations of the
attractions of other life-styles.

Interestingly, many of these scholars are women. Most of them
retain a commitment to 'intellectual decolonisation', the 'decolonisation
of knowledge', the 'demystification of imperialism', as it has variously
been called. But they seek to revise and reinterpret what Mary Louise
Pratt has described as the 'totalising momentum' which, though unrelated in her account, describes well a conquering Orientalism. Pratt,
conventionally, sees travel writings from 1750 to the twentieth century
as illustrative of the global taxonomic project, based upon Linnaeus and
his followers. Using examples drawn from Africa and the Americas, she
underlines Gellner's notion, in a historical context, of 'world-levelling,
unificatory epistemologies'. Thus she acknowledges the power of ethno-
graphical, geographic, hydrographic and botanical description, the com-
mand expressed through naming, visually possessing and evaluating the
global scene. She echoes Said in enquiring how far travel and exploration
writing have '*produced* "the rest of the world" for European readerships
at particular points in Europe's expansionist trajectory', the extent to
which 'such signifying practices encode and legitimate the aspirations of
economic expansion and empire'.[2] But these thoughts are hedged about
with question-marks rather than certainties and she introduces several
destabilising concepts.

The first is the notion of the 'domestic subject' of empire (derived
from Spivak, but simply another term for a familiar idea, the reciprocal
effect of empire on the home population). 'While the imperial metropolis tends to understand itself as determining the periphery, . . . it habitu-
ally blinds itself to the ways in which the periphery determines the
metropolis.' The second is 'contact zone', the area where coloniser and
colonised intersect, not in a diffusionist or separate way, but 'in terms
of copresence, interaction, interlocking understandings and practices'.
And related to this is the well-worn ethnographers' usage, the 'transculturation' of her title. This is used as a substitute for 'acculturation' and
'deculturation', with their assumptions of overwhelming imperial power

to produce total cultural accommodation on the conquerors' terms. Transculturation describes the subordinated peoples' capacity to select and invent from the dominant culture, determining what they are pre-pared to absorb or reject.[3] Thus, perfectly familiar ideas here applied to the texts of travel writing and exploration make inroads on the power and autonomy of the discourse.

Dennis Porter has also used travel writings to indulge in a more fundamental critique of Said. As early as 1982 Porter offered a brief, readable and powerful (but largely ignored) revision both of Said's the-oretical position and of his handling of texts.[4] He argued that literary texts can distance themselves, that they are seldom univocal and that they incorporate textual dialogues between western and non-western cultures. In illustrating that such texts require to be set into their precise historical moment, he used Marco Polo's *Travels* and T. E. Lawrence's *Seven Pillars of Wisdom* to demonstrate the heterogeneity of such materials, their doubts and contradictions and their 'counter-hegemonic energies'.[5] Literary works use ideology, but transform it by putting it on display and, by implication, dissecting it. He concluded that Said failed to find alternatives to his hegemonic discourse because

> he overlooks the potential contradictions between discourse theory and Gramscian hegemony, he fails to historicize adequately the texts he cites and summarizes, finding always the same triumphant discourse where several are frequently in conflict. Second, because he does not distinguish the literary instance from more transparently ideological textual forms, he does not acknowledge the semi-autonomous and overdetermined char-acter of aesthetic artefacts. Finally, he fails to show how literary texts in their play establish distance from the ideologies they seem to be reproducing.[6]

In his important book, *Haunted Journeys*, Porter has used travel writings from the eighteenth to the twentieth centuries to highlight the mixture of emotions bound up in travel and the consequent grappling with other cultures. He discovers a certain continuity in travel writing in which travel is stimulated by the desire to 'fantasise the satisfaction of drives denied at home', to transgress against domestic socialised norms, and also by the conflict between guilt and duty, often expressed through the father–son relationship. To extend Porter's idea further, travel (at this elite and aesthetic level at any rate) can thus represent at one and the same time alienation from 'patria' and Utopia-seeking abroad together with filial duty and a concomitant denigration of the 'Other'. These apparently oppositional, but in reality mutually supportive purposes are expressed in mixes of poetic and practical or unofficial and official lan-guage, combining both discourse and anti-discourse. Using a combination of psychoanalytic and late Foucauldian ideas, he sees one function of travel writing as representing 'a form of experimentation at and beyond established limits'. In place of the 'obliteration of otherness' ... 'implied by radical discourse theory', 'self-transformation' can be achieved 'through a dialogic engagement with alien modes of life'.[7] In his consideration of travel writings from Boswell to Naipaul (famously, one of Said's *bêtes noires*), he sees this very twentieth-century idea as a useful analytical tool. Porter's work offers a valuable corrective not only to the Said monolith, but also to the disturbingly over-empirical works on travel by some historians.[8]

Porter explicitly concentrates on male travellers and suggests that his work is a contribution to masculinist studies. By contrast, Billie Melman identifies an 'alternative female discourse' on the Orient, a discourse, moreover, which is heavily fractured. Thus in her view there is not only a distinction in assumption and intent between male and female observers, but a 'multi-vocal, polyglot' discourse within the women's accounts. Women reflect the ambivalence, complexity and chronological transformations of Victorian attitudes, including female perceptions of their sexual and familial roles and their positions in respect of their class origins or essentially secular and missionary viewpoints. She also identifies a distinct movement in late Victorian times, associated with greatly increased travel opportunities, when racial ideas and social Darwinian concepts were brought to bear upon contemporary Middle Eastern peoples.[9] Melman roots her writers more clearly in their social context and historic period than any other scholar of Orientalism and argues that the female discourse reflects pluralities of class, gender and period much more than ideological conformity. Moreover, there are some hints of Porter's combination of 'duty and transgression' which suggest that there may indeed be considerable overlaps between the feminine and masculine traditions.

Following Peter Gay, and thus using a more emotional/intellectual than psychological paradigm, Melman sees the female encounter with the oriental 'Other' as part of the development of bourgeois sensibilities, the more progressive 'education of the senses'. As such sensibilities shifted and changed, they were 'richly manifested' in a multiple canon, in 'diverse texts and a "heteroglot" language':

> There is not *one focus* of power and knowledge about 'things oriental', but *diverse foci*, which, characteristically, are located outside the places identified with political domination, or economic expansion overseas. The voluntary and philanthropic organisation; the smaller missionary enterprise; the struggling 'new' scientific society, these are the typical places where the feminine interest in the Orient emerged.[10]

Western women set out to place oriental social practices in the context of their own experience, adapting and accommodating rather than establishing binary models, 'symmetrical oppositions'. However, Melman certainly does not go so far as to suggest that the women she studies were ideologically free, but concedes that 'the reconstruction of the Orient cannot and *should not* be separated from the construction of the notion of Empire and from modern imperialism' (again, her emphasis).[11] Yet, beyond placing her foci of feminine knowledge outside the locus of political domination, she never fully explores the relationships between social groups, intellectual and religious societies and imperialism. Agency and instrumentality are absent from her account. Nor does she attempt to range beyond the Middle East, which throughout her period was in any case subject only to the indirect imperialism of the West making archaeological, religious and economic inroads on the Ottoman Empire.

If Melman discovers a gendered heterodoxy in relation to the Orient, Lisa Lowe has argued for a profoundly heterogeneous Orientalism, 'engendered differently' not only by distinct national circumstances (as between Britain and France), but also by the 'social and literary circumstances' of particular historic moments.[12] Using four examples – the visions of Turkey and Persia by Lady Mary Wortley Montagu (who also features prominently in Melman) and Montesquieu in the eighteenth century; Flaubert's use of a North African Orient; the reception of E. M. Forster's *Passage to India*; and the visions of China as a Utopia by French intellectuals like Julia Kristeva and Roland Barthes in the 1970s – she rejects the 'totalising framework' and discovers 'multivalence', 'indeterminability' and 'heterogeneity'.[13] In some respects her work is even more profoundly ahistorical than that of Said. Whereas Melman sets changing attitudes into specific contexts and tries to explain them in terms of shifts in social, political and intellectual viewpoints, Lowe effectively collapses widely divergent historical periods in order to discover heterogeneity. Historians would surely find it unsurprising that writings drawn from the early eighteenth to the late twentieth centuries should exhibit a certain amount of contrasting assumptions and purposes. Whereas she has effectively identified instances of Porter's 'Utopia-seeking' to meet the needs of her various periods, she is so intent upon an assault on Said that she grossly oversimplifies his discourse theory into a 'discrete and monochromatic phenomenon'. In denying the existence of a 'master narrative' and asserting that works are 'not always expressions of European colonialism' she confuses linguistic form and cultural content, wholly failing to historicise adequately.[14]

However, within the first two of her individual sections, Lowe revises Said's monolith and fits her work into postmodernist theory by finding moments of instability, contradictory approaches, counter-hegemonies and resistances to domination, contestations and accommodations, examples (following Bhabha) of 'psychic shuttling' between the two cultures on the part of both supposedly dominant and subordinate people. Her account of Flaubert, in particular, is more concerned with his ambivalences, his self-conscious postures and critiques of such posturing. Whereas for Said Flaubert is a prime literary Orientalist, feminising and abusing the East, Lowe finds irony, aesthetic release and a critique of the West in his writings.[15] (It is indeed an interesting fact that Said seems wholly unconscious of irony in his various works.)[16] Lowe, akin to Pratt, views Orientalism as the means to a mutually interpenetrating transculturation, as a cultural ground on which western social and cultural weakness as well as oriental resistance can be played out in often subtle and implicit ways.

Sara Suleri similarly used a wide range of texts and periods to illustrate the complexities of 'The Rhetoric of English India'. Using Kipling's short story 'Naboth' as her starting-point, she ranges over Burke, Hastings, women writers of non-fiction, Kipling (specifically *Kim*), Forster, Naipaul and Rushdie to take issue with Said's binarism. She sees her texts as part of a 'mutual narrative of complicities', illustrative of the 'necessary intimacies that obtain between ruler and ruled'. These intimacies involve violence, mental as well as physical, which she dubs 'unpartitioned traumas between coloniser and colonised'. She sees the 'monolithic other' as obsolescent, a conceptual blockage. The imperial literary experience reflects a sense of joint loss, almost a narrative of mutual grief. When 'empire messes with identity' (a phrase of Spivak's) it does so both at the periphery and in the metropolis.[17] After all, as she might have argued, for even the most successful empire, as Kipling illustrated in 'Recessional', fear is ever the obverse of triumphalism.[18] For Suleri, the ultimate consummation of this joint endeavour, forged out of appropriation and precarious control, physical aggression and psychological terror, is the colonial gift of the nation. Nationalism represents the ultimate setting for the attraction/revulsion duality, emerging from imitation, even admiration, and adaptation as well as cultural loathing and revulsion at exploitation. Perhaps in some respects this is a distinctively Indian view, but the notion of negative and positive influences operating on both sides of the imperial equation will be fruitful for the examination of the operation of Orientalism in the European arts beyond the purely literary text.

Suleri's book is one of a considerable group of recent writings about Orientalism as it related to India. This has the effect of repatriating the word to its Anglo-Indian origins, sometimes in its new guise, sometimes in its older form discussed in Chapter 1, and sometimes in a combination of the two in which historical judgements become curiously reversed. Said himself noted Anglo-French Orientalism of the late eighteenth century at some length and, much influenced by Raymond Schwab's classic, *Renaissance Orientale,* acknowledged the achievements of Sir William Jones and his associates.[19] But none the less he saw them as constituting the origins of his Orientalist discourse. Jones had a passion for codification, to 'subdue the infinite variety of the Orient to "a complete digest"' (p. 78). But he implies that Orientalism proper was built by a 'later generation' (p. 122); what Jones and the other pioneers made available, 'the literary crowd exploited', enabling the Romantics to reconstruct the Orient (pp. 168, 22).

By contrast, Said made only one mention of James Mill and scarcely alluded at all to his fiercely anti-Orientalist (in the Jonesian sense) *The History of British India* of 1817. This has surprised some commentators. David Kopf has suggested that Said would have found more grist in the more dismissive writings of Mill and his utilitarian, evangelical and Whig allies.[20] B. J. Moore-Gilbert went so far as to reinterpret the very word 'Orientalism' by redefining it as criticism of and hostility to Indian culture, as represented by Mill and his successors.[21] Thus the description applied to the activities of a group of eighteenth-century scholars who sought to rediscover the languages, arts and laws of India comes to be identified with an ideological faction constituted of their sworn enemies and seeking to overturn all the policies associated with them. Nothing could better illustrate the problems of Said's conception of a continuous oriental discourse. In any case, both Kopf and Moore-Gilbert misunderstood Said's intention, which was to dissect a discursive Orient of exotic archetypes created by scholarship that often had the air of sympathetic understanding. Jones went to India; Mill did not. Said's Orientalists are generally those who created their supposedly mythic Orient out of personal experience. Hypercritical cultural dismissal was not a particularly useful contributor to his argument.

Moore-Gilbert indeed tried to resolve this problem of metropolitan and peripheral focus by identifying two Orientalisms in the nineteenth century. That constructed in Britain was in his view culturally more arrogant and, as the 1857 insurrection demonstrated, destructive of interracial peace. The Orientalism constructed in India, as exemplified among others by Kipling, made a more genuine attempt to understand India and its indigenous customs and polities. Kipling's admiration for the Indian princely states was apparently illustrative of the latter. The gulf between literary study and historical scholarship is neatly demonstrated by this extraordinary assertion. If ever there was a product of metropolitan administrative 'Orientalism' in the post-Mutiny period it was the survival and inflation of the princely states.[22] Indeed, through their invented traditions and fake, though supposedly representative Indianness, they constituted as classic an instance of a mythic and stereotypical Orient as could be found.[23] Far from representing a sympathetic understanding, they illustrated a re-feudalisation of large swathes of Indian society to stand over against the economic and social transformations of British rule. As we shall see in subsequent chapters, their 'traditional' and supposedly pre-industrial character was used as an aesthetic counterpoint to the revolutionary forces of economic imperialism.

Thus the old, clear-cut landmarks of the Orientalist–Anglicist debate have faded into something of an interpretative fog. The juxtaposition of the work of Ronald Inden and Javed Majeed confirms the dizzy swinging of signposts which has turned the well-trodden analytical path through Indian history into a labyrinth. Inden identified Mill's *History* as a 'hegemonic text' which served to oppress India with its 'essentialist vision' (a phrase derived from Said).[24] Mill contributed powerfully to the reduction of India to a set of essences which for the British reflected its static or retrogressive tendencies, its ancient and anti-modernising character. These included caste, the supposedly self-sufficient and immutable village, and divine kingship, which, together with the spiritual and imaginative India, constituted the Indian collective 'mind'. By distinguishing and suspending these in a scholarly solution, as it were, the British created 'imperial knowledges' which served to consolidate the intellectual 'imperial formation' through which India could be ruled. As a sociologist, Inden's professed objective is to re-distil and analyse these 'essences' together with the scholarly system of which they form a part – he seeks to expose examples well into the twentieth century, particularly in the work of A. L. Basham and his students – in order to create the opportunity for the contemporary 're-empowerment' of India and Indian scholarship.[25]

Javed Majeed has reacted to Inden by denying that Mill's *History* is a hegemonic text. Indeed for him it is not even a confident text, but, despite its language, a highly ambivalent one, just as both Bentham and Mill had a complex relationship with imperialism itself. Rather, Mill's work represents the close connection between imperial and domestic affairs, the 'self-reflexivity' of Indian studies. In the *History* Mill was criticising British society as much as Indian, and through it two intellectual traditions, radical and Tory at home, Anglicist and Orientalist in India, struggled to define each other. Mill rejected romantic Conservatism, its stress on the imagination, on poetry rather than prose. He distrusted notions of the 'gorgeous East', alleged riches that the British could exploit at will. He extended his domestic attack on aristocracy and landed wealth to support for the *ryotwari* system (taxing the peasantry directly) rather than the permanent settlement of Bengal. And with Bentham he doubted the economic advantage of India to Britain, seeing empire as a means of prolonging bad government at home. In his passionate belief in an enlightened present, particularly as represented in the power of education to remodel any society, Mill rejected a patriarchalist idiom in favour of regenerative bourgeois reform.[26]

If 'In India the ideology of the British establishment was writ large against an alien background', providing Mill with 'the necessary distance to fashion the tools and principles with which to launch an attack on it', there were none the less important consequences for the character of British rule there. Mill supported intervention rather than non-interference in native states; he sought a secular alternative to religious certainties; and he hoped for reform based on clear principles derived from systematisation. Thus Majeed implies that Mill's notorious ridicule of Indian society and culture was no more than a means of attacking the policies of his political opponents to an equally fossilised society at home. If Majeed sees *The History* as a much more ambiguous and heterogeneous work than previously thought, it is because he too is in the business of 'empowerment'. While Jones, a radical at home, became a conservative abroad (although he did desire to break the power of the pundits by securing direct access to Indian law), Mill, by staying at home, kept his radicalism intact. Whereas the conservative Orientalists emphasised tradition, cultural property and patriarchal rule, Mill offered the opportunity of a 'liberating critique'. Thus modernisers and reformers should look to Mill for their inspiration since his critique, by analogy, 'affords the possibility of changing the way we define ourselves in order to change our practices for the better'. Hence Majeed, overturning the orthodox view of modern Indian historiography that Jones is an infinitely more sympathetic figure than Mill, reinterprets *The History of British India* – and its subsequent use in the training of British officials for Company and imperial rule in India – as a liberating instance of 'transculturation'.[27] Though it is not entirely clear why Mill, had he wanted to write about home society, would not have done so directly, it is apparent that Majeed argues – as to a certain extent Suleri does – as a secular modernising nationalist.

Regardless of his standpoint, however, Majeed writes as a historian to historians. He thoroughly contextualises; he understands the complexities of contemporary politics; and he offers subtleties of interpretation in the place of black and white certainties. Like Suleri, he is implicitly concerned with 'the gift of the nation' and with identifying the origins of modernising influences. Thus the intolerant radicalism of Mill at least possessed the virtue of looking forward to a wholly new dispensation. Other historians have continued to find the more conservative approach of the Orientalist predecessors and rivals of Mill more attractive. They have demonstrated that the reputation of Sir William Jones has tended to overshadow the activities of many other Orientalists active in both India and Britain in the late eighteenth and early nineteenth centuries. Moreover, such Orientalism has never been adequately set into its

intellectual context; in particular, the influence of the conceptual framework of the Scottish Enlightenment has been either ignored or grossly
underestimated.

In an article which has been almost entirely ignored in the Orientalist debate, Jane Rendall has examined a number of Scottish Orientalists, almost all of them associated with the University of Edinburgh and
influenced by such luminaries as William Robertson, Dugald Stewart and
Adam Smith.[28] These writers (Alexander Hamilton, James Mackintosh,
William Erskine, John Leyden, Alexander Murray and Mountstuart
Elphinstone, among others) set out to understand Asian societies in
terms of the 'philosophical history' practised by the Scottish *philosophes*.
Rendall has identified the basic principles of this approach as being the
close interrelationship of all aspects of human life within a given society
(economics, politics, culture and social life); an evolutionary scale of
civilisation running from 'rudeness' to 'refinement'; the central importance of the mode of subsistence, as defined by Adam Smith's fourfold
division (hunting and gathering, pastoral, agricultural, commercial); and
the possibility of progress from one level to another, even if such progress
was generally slow, undirected, and even accidental.[29] But although these
writers were influential in the founding of the Bombay Literary Society
in 1804, and wrote articles in *Asiatic Researches* and *The Edinburgh
Review*, they represented an Orientalism retreating in the face of the
utilitarian and evangelical onslaught.

However, the ideas of the Scottish Enlightenment continued to
constitute an important philosophic basis for the Indian administrative
theory and practice of such prominent governors as Sir Thomas Munro,
Sir John Malcolm and Sir Mountstuart Elphinstone until the 1820s. In
a recent thesis, Martha McLaren has demonstrated the manner in which
the philosophical history, political economy, moral philosophy and approaches to government and religion of the leaders of the Scottish
Enlightenment influenced the ideas of Munro, Malcolm and Elphinstone
in relation to land tenure and revenue, the administration of law, economic change, and attitudes towards indigenous societies generally.[30]
The 'Munro system' (*ryotwari*, the direct taxing of peasants or ryots
rather than landlords as in the Bengali *zamindari* permanent settlement)
was immensely influential throughout southern and western India.
According to McLaren, the 'organising principle' of the writings and
administrations of these figures was 'the universality of human nature.
They did not see Indian and Western society in opposition to one another. Elphinstone complimented Malcolm on the "eminent degree" to
which his *History of Persia* demonstrated a "knowledge of human nature
and of Asia" – not of the nature of Asia'.[31] Of course, these very figures
were highly instrumental in the extension of British power in India, but

in their campaigns and the resultant establishment of administrations in conquered territories they would have seen themselves as no more than subscribing to the forces that drove societies forward from one stage to another. In their eighteenth-century secularism and mental scepticism they presented a very different intellectual front to that of pseudo-scientific racism in the later nineteenth century.[32]

Neither Edward Said nor his many followers and critics show themselves as fully aware (if at all) of the intellectual background of the Orientalists and other factions in the philosophic approach to Indian government. They neither acknowledge the influence of the Scottish Enlightenment nor recognise the onslaught upon it of philosophic radicalism in the nineteenth century. The complexities and oppositional force of such intellectual affiliations are generally lost upon them, as when Gyan Prakash, as recently as 1990, continues to use the tired language of 'binary opposition' and decribes Orientalists as construing Indians 'to be outside and opposite of self'. For him the 'essentialism . . . deployed in the formative phase of Orientalism outlived the early Orientalists'.[33] Here we have representation without roots, where a repeatedly used language has become a substitute for refined thought.

A wholly different sensitivity to intellectual and emotional complexity suffuses Nigel Leask's excellent book, *British Romantic Writers and the East*. In his study of the eastern-inspired works of Byron, Shelley, De Quincey and Coleridge, Leask recognises that the fascination of the Romantics with the Orient was rooted in both a sense of European superiority to the oriental Other and a recognition that aspects of the culture of the East also undermined such a claim. In their work, Leask finds not a 'closed system . . . hermetically sealed', but representations that are both determined and undermined by a considerable variety of cultural pressures, revealing 'anxieties and instabilities' rather than 'positivities and totalities'. Rightly recognising the complexity of the Other, he contrasts reactions to enemy Europeans, such as the French, with the sense of dependence upon, almost addiction to, economic and cultural characteristics of the East. In a particularly interesting passage, he also indicates the manner in which internal Others, like the Scots, redefined themselves – often in highly contrasting ways – in relation to empire, and particularly India. He similarly reveals the highly ambivalent attitudes of Romantic radicals to empire.[34]

Thus, for the philosophic radicals and some of their literary interlocutors, both allies and enemies, British imperialism of the 1820s and 1830s turned India into a 'laboratory of modernity', in which the revolutionary radicalism of the 1790s could become a global project and the overturning of the *anciens régimes* of the East might in the end justify their conquest. Those regimes were of course hailed by others as offering the gorgeous cloak of indirect rule, an imperial method developed in the late eighteenth century, experiencing something of a trough in the period between the 1820s and 1850s, but vigorously revived after 1858.[35] Thus, the extension of empire could be simultaneously hailed by Romantic conservatives, Whigs and radicals as part of a political and philosophical universalisation, disseminating new European ideas or feeding back old feudal allegiances. Hence common objectives and results could conceal powerfully antithetical discourses.

Of course on another level, the Romantics had highly individualised responses to their visions of the East, each a projection of their own fantasy worlds. At one and the same time, Byron feared, and sought to overturn, the triumph of Asiatic over Hellenistic values, Turk over Greek, while still suggesting that Islam contained a powerful potential for revolution. He envisaged and admired the possibility of complicated gender exchanges in an eastern setting, together with the prevalence of homoerotic love. Shelley, heavily influenced by Sir William Jones, dreamed not only of a continuation of the programme of the Enlightenment but also of the emergence of heroic Asiatic rebels (like the Assassins)[36] to carry forward the revolutionary agenda, while De Quincey and Coleridge, in their different ways, conceived the East as a repository of desirable hedonism, a source of opium therapy which at the same time heightened sensibilities and stimulated intellectual activity. But in each case, the attraction/repulsion duality was paramount. The relationship between West and East, riddled with stereotypes and fabricated constructs as it was, was viewed as profoundly interwoven: the Orient aroused anxieties and fears in almost equal measure with both imperialism itself and the social and intellectual conflicts of home. Thus essentialism becomes a highly movable phenomenon in which Self and Other become absorbed in common objectives and fears, ideals and neuroses. On the other hand, John Drew, in *India and the Romantic Imagination*, has tended to emphasise the idealisation of India in the work of Romantic writers and their hopes for the reinvigoration of the culture of home through contact with the East. If for Shelley and others the East represented an unseen power, an awesome presence, even a source of profound affinities between Celt and Indian, for the younger Coleridge (before scepticism took over), it offered a heightened awareness, an enlargement of meditative and imaginative states.[37]

One of the best instances of a literary historicism which is profoundly ahistorical is to be found in the work of Gauri Viswanathan, a student of Edward Said. She acknowledges neither the liberating nationalism of Majeed and Suleri nor the close interrelationship of economy, culture and society in the work of the radical writers and thinkers of the late eighteenth and early nineteenth centuries. She is concerned with

English education in India, but in divergent ways from those who have previously examined this phenomenon. She takes a perfectly conventional approach to the Orientalist–Anglicist debate by seeing both policies as pursuing the same objective, the furthering of state power through forms of acculturation. Eighteenth-century Orientalism constituted a sort of 'reverse acculturation'. As Warren Hastings himself put it, if the subjects cannot be persuaded to meet us on our culturally sympathetic ground, we must meet them on theirs.[38] His Anglicist successors claimed the same dual justification, that the policy furthered both the interests of the state and of humanity, but insisted that it could only be achieved on their ethnocentric meeting place. The Orientalists had striven to rule by using their linguistic skills to codify Indian laws, religions and imaginative literature. Abandoning respect for indigenous languages and associated texts, the Anglicists required a simple medium through which an alien morality and culture could be disseminated. They found it, according to Viswanathan, in the study of English literature. English literature offered the opportunity for a secular education, enabling the British to escape both the constraints of the Church at home and the accusation that they were meddling with indigenous religions in India. English literature would have a 'salutary, emancipatory influence because it released Indians from false consciousness and replaced outmoded styles of thought with enlightened concepts of justice and liberty'.[39]

More significantly, English literature could be used to obscure the naked realities of British power:

> The self-presentation of the Englishman to native Indians through the products of his mental labor removes him from the place of ongoing colonialist activity – of commercial operations, military expansion, and administration of territories – and deactualises and diffuses his material reality in the process. In a parodic reworking of the Cartesian axiom, the Englishman's true essence is defined by the thought he produces, overriding all other aspects of his identity – his personality, actions and behavior. His material reality as subjugator and alien ruler is dissolved in his mental output; the blurring of the man and his works effectively removes him from history. . . . The split between the material and the cultural practices of colonialism is nowhere sharper than in the progressive refinement of the rapacious, exploitative, and ruthless actor of history into the reflective subject of literature.[40]

This quotation has been allowed to run on because it reflects many of the problems with this kind of work. Viswanathan is primarily concerned not with social change or outcomes but with the discourse leading to the formulation of policy. She then imposes upon this discourse her own 'split between the material and cultural practices of colonialism', implying that early nineteenth-century Anglicists were consciously trying to obscure their 'rapacious, exploitative, and ruthless' activities beneath a cloak of literary study. Nothing could be further from the truth. The Scottish evangelical missionaries, whom Viswanathan discusses, were themselves the intellectual sons of Adam Smith. They would have seen no distinction whatsoever between an English education and the elevating effects of free trade and *laissez-faire* liberalism. Far from diffusing their material reality, they wished to concentrate it. Thought, personality, actions and behaviour were indivisible. What's more, as has been demonstrated in South Africa, their objectives were initially at odds with those of imperial rulers who either reflected older norms or were concerned with administrative quietude.[41] But neither administrators nor missionaries and educators, in this period at any rate, would have made any distinction between their economic and their spiritual and cultural missions.

Viswanathan makes interesting, but not wholly new connections between educationalists' attitudes to Indians and to the lower classes at home, but her contention that the practice and curriculum of an education in English literature were forged at the periphery, to satisfy the specific requirements of empire, and only later transferred back to the metropolis, is unproven. English literary study for the metropolitan masses was as likely to offer routes to an increase in political freedoms and economic liberation (and would certainly have been so depicted by the auto-didacts of the day) as to hegemonic submission in an alienating social and economic system. In any case, the formulatory discourse, overlaid by her own highly contentious, anachronistic and fundamentally ahistorical exegesis, answers few historical questions of real interest. The most basic – did it work? – is not even formulated, let alone answered.

Said includes an admiring reference to Viswanathan in his book, *Culture and Imperialism*.[42] And indeed there is much about this book which is equally problematic for historians. Here he broadens the perspectives of *Orientalism* to embrace the European cultural expressions of a global imperialism as well as to consider the 'fundamental liberationist energy' (p. xxiii) of the nationalist and post-colonial resistances to western empire. Not surprisingly, perhaps, it is a much more sprawling and less focused work. Moreover, he makes even higher claims than before: he seeks to demonstrate that imperialism was central to the cultures of the British, the French and, later, the Americans, and that the very origins and development of modern literary forms like the novel are to be found in the spatial extensions, narrative character and power relations of empire.

This book has been more vilified than admired.[43] Those who share some of its ideological perceptions have praised it as a work of remarkable erudition drawing on an extraordinary range of sources derived from literature, music, philosophy and history. Others have seen it as taking the polemics of *Orientalism* yet further, particularly in its excoriation of American policy and the Gulf War in its lengthy concluding section. But polemics aside, this work is again both 'supremely historicist' and supremely ahistorical. From the point of view of the historian, the erudition is frequently misplaced, offering tangential quotation rather than central argument.[44] Moreover, it sets up phalanxes of heroes and villains among both historic figures and modern scholars presumably according to whether they comply with some 'libertarian and unrepressive' norm which is itself often anachronistic.

As in *Orientalism*, he seems to deal in truisms that have been the stock-in-trade of historians for many years. He refuses to see culture as 'antiseptically quarantined' from its worldly affiliations. Culture is a theatre where political and ideological causes engage each other and politics are not checked like coats at the door. The past and present are interconnected and, although he never explicitly says so, claims of objectivity are themselves the tools of power, invariably wielded by the political Right. Moreover, he sees the barriers of excessive academic specialisation turning into cultural barricades (in both an ethnic and intellectual sense). This is perhaps a useful restatement of interdisciplinarity and transcontinental awareness, a further blast of a necessary scholarly trumpet against the petty nationalisms and highly partisan 'objectivities' of politicians who seek to extend the frontiers of the state into education while claiming to be rolling them back and upholding freedoms, who when extolling the virtues of literature always deal in the canonical facade rather than the analytical foundations, which they deeply distrust. But Said's worldly affiliations are far too closely defined.

Imperialism, again a continuing and unfinished phenomenon, is the prime conditioning element of all western culture in the past two centuries. In one of his favourite musical metaphors, he calls for a 'contrapuntal' reading of literature, a counterpoint that has to be heard at various levels. Each cultural artefact can only be understood in terms of its 'Other', the negative against which it defines itself. English literature (and later French and American) can only be fully analysed in the light of western power, the geographical and economic relations of empire. Finally, twentieth-century culture can only be comprehended against a background of response, the capacity of the non-western world to speak back and reassert its cultural autonomy. It is hard to gainsay that such a counterpoint is indeed important, though many might dispute that it is the central one worth noticing in all of modern culture.

Where the metaphor begins to break down, however, is in relation to the visibility or audibility of the contrapuntal lines. The juxtaposition of melody in musical counterpoint is explicit. In literature and the other arts it is apparently capable of becoming merely a trace element, barely mentioned, yet implicitly vital to the entire message of the work. In works like *Mansfield Park, Jane Eyre* and *David Copperfield*, where empire enjoys apparently marginal references, these are in reality central to the structures of their plots. The 'massive appropriations' of British power make the narratives of these novels work, since by these means limitless possibilities are held out to the British bourgeoisie, liberating energies and ambitions, creating the linear perspectives central to the novels' drive.

Said goes further. Even those works that do not mention empire at all can be seen to fit the same criteria. Metropolitan space becomes a metaphor for global power: social relations and conflicts represent wider racial contacts. Here we have a mythic counterpoint in which one melody is supplied and the other has to be contrapuntally inserted in one's brain. Moreover, the themes of state identity and Otherness are precisely defined. To take the British case, Britain and English literature are always discrete entities defining themselves in relation to global (and therefore racially different) Others. Said fails to notice that the building of empire is first an internal process, with internalised Others, and second that the Others of nineteenth-century European nationalisms are more likely to be rival Europeans, arguably more important in the definitions of culture and national character than imperial possessions and peoples. New national histories, idealised pasts, myths, sagas and heroic figures were marshalled in these cultural formations and played a central role in the aesthetic artefacts of the period. This is not to deny the importance of the imperial relationship nor to decry the power of racial stereotyping. But it does suggest that the European counterpoint is made up of a more complex set of motifs – not least the leitmotif of class – than Said allows.

Such a single-minded contrapuntalism leads Said into wilful misunderstandings. His reversal of the true significance of Verdi's opera *Aida* will be examined in Chapter 6 and this reflects again his lack of an adequate contextualisation not only of aesthetic artefact and its author, but also of his sets of heroes and villains. Indeed, his ascription of virtue and vice has a distinctly fundamentalist ring to it. Nothing better demonstrates Said's lack of subtlety and sheer failure of comprehension of the intellectual history of the nineteenth century than his treatment of John Ruskin and J. A. Hobson. Ruskin is excoriated as an imperialist and racist in contradistinction to Hobson's laudable and honourable anti-imperialism.[45] Yet Hobson was a fervent admirer of Ruskin and in his book *John Ruskin: Social Reformer* and several articles described himself as a disciple of the great art critic and sage.[46] It has even been suggested that Hobson derived some of his economic theory from Ruskin, particularly his ideas on underconsumption.[47] Another disciple was that scourge of the British and patron saint of Indian nationalism, M. K. Gandhi. In his *Autobiography*, Gandhi declared himself to be a follower of Ruskin. When he read *Unto This Last* in South Africa it had a galvanising effect on him, influencing the manner in which he ordered his own household and developed his ashrams:

> I believe that I discovered some of my deepest convictions reflected in this great book of Ruskin, and that is why it so captured me and made me transform my life. . . .
>   The teachings of *Unto This Last* I understood to be:
> 1. That the good of the individual is contained in the good of all.
> 2. That the lawyer's work has the same value as the barber's, inasmuch as all have the same right of earning their livelihood from their work.
> 3. That the life of labour i.e. the life of the tiller of the soil and the handicraftsman is the life worth living.
>   The first of these I knew. The second I had dimly realised. The third had never occurred to me. *Unto This Last* made it as clear as daylight to me that the second and third were contained in the first. I arose with the dawn, ready to reduce these principles to practice.[48]

Thus Ruskin's homely economics, in the hands of Hobson, fed the critique of the export of capital and working-class underconsumption which produced the major assault upon the theory of imperialism in the twentieth century, while his social message, anti-industrialism and environmentalism inspired the leading theorist not only of the return to communal living and craft production, but also of anti-imperial passive resistance. As it happens, in a postmodernist, environmentalist, and post-industrial age, Ruskin's thought is currently the subject of a major rediscovery and reassessment. His imperialism reflected his desire to see his ideas applied on a global scale. It represented his acceptance (even radical prefiguring) of the dominant political ideology as one context in which his quasi-socialist message could strike home.

By contrast, Hobson's critical concern with the export of capital and his underconsumptionist theories have little to do with Said's vision of racially liberal anti-imperialism. Indeed, his fierce anti-Semitism (which goes unmentioned) runs directly counter to it. What's more, Said pays no attention to the lively discussion of Hobson's theories which has exercised historians throughout the twentieth century, nor does he notice the influential, right-wing critique of imperialism by Joseph Schumpeter. Indeed, nothing better represents the naïveté and lack of sophistication of the left-wing literary critics than this inability to handle historiography. The Marxist Fredric Jameson, for example, cheerfully uses the Hobson–Leninist economic theory of imperialism as a given, while exhibiting no understanding of the historiographical progression in which these ideas must be set.[49] Such intellectual atavism and analytical crudity perform a grave disservice to the very political stance which they presume to represent.

It is perhaps this glaring divide between an alleged historicism and the complex historiographical understanding (which is the historian's stock-in-trade) that has led to the relative absence of historians from the Orientalist debate. Edward Said and the literary theorists have a tendency to 'pick and mix' ideological fragments of historical interpretation which simply do not add up to any sort of coherent whole. Perhaps this is why Stephen Howe was forced to 'the somewhat depressing conclusion' that 'imperial history and colonial discourse analysis, the traditional chroniclers and the cultural theorists, apparently speak mutually incomprehensible – worse, reciprocally despised – languages'.[50] There is much in this, though 'traditional chroniclers' hardly seems an apposite description of the majority of serious historians (a few renegades have appeared on the Right) who have long since abandoned a partisan and narrative tradition for the strongly analytical and self-critical bent of recent imperial historiography. The problem of translation lies not in a conflict between description and deconstruction, but between modes of analysis that occupy such different linguistic and mental spheres that so far no Rosetta Stone has been found to connect the two.

Indeed radical scholars who might be expected to be sympathetic to Said, and who have themselves been influenced by Gramsci, have had difficulties with the notion of an unchallenged western dominance and a Manichaean set of binary oppositions in the colonial cultural confrontation. Historical geographers have also begun to reassess Said's 'imaginative geographies', his use and misuse of Foucault and his ignorance of or lack of interest in the wider social relations of geographical knowledge, including its production and consumption.[51] Above all, it is difficult for historians and geographers to find in all this work a single instance in which cultural artefacts are directly influenced by specific events, or themselves have bearing on individual decision-making or developments in the European imperial relationship with particular territories, although such connections abound. Although Said is so concerned with cultural narrative, he himself offers no narrative thread which the historian can follow.

Moreover, the worst excesses of colonial discourse analysis are at odds with fundamental tenets of historical procedures. The historian is necessarily concerned with explaining change over time, with the interrelationship of ideas and events, with the social, economic and intellectual milieu in which sources are produced. The historian seeks to tie analysis to a firm empirical base, to specific episodes, particular individuals and territories, definable socio-economic contexts in the historical record. For most of those outside the Marxist tradition – and for some within it – the mode of explanation is highly particularist. The historian seeks out unities of period, place, and often person, even when dealing with broader time-spans. Of the works surveyed above, only those of Melman and Majeed would fit such criteria, and the former has very little to say about the theory, practice or events of imperial history.

While historians, who inevitably felt uncomfortable with a 'discourse' which, however complex, had a supposedly unchanging intention and effect over a century and a half, may welcome some of the recent revisions, none the less for them too much of this work seems to circle around an intellectual superstructure wrenched from its empirical base.[52] Moreover, the historian trades in the ironic and the unwitting, what has sometimes been dubbed 'incidental causality'. To take some examples derived from the Indian Empire, historical interpretation has been full of the unanticipated: Britain's economic and social policies forging it into Marx's 'unconscious tool of history' (interpreted in turn in a different way by subsequent Marxist and non-Marxist commentators);[53] education policies designed to produce collaborators turning out resisters instead;[54] oriental studies of the late eighteenth and early nineteenth centuries helping to produce the Bengali intellectual renaissance which fed into Indian nationalism at the turn of the nineteenth and twentieth centuries;[55] Macaulay's 1830s vision of English education leading to the demand for English freedoms proving more prescient than the 'illusion of permanence' generated by the British later in the century.[56] Paradox has long been the stock-in-trade of the historian whose discipline breeds a certain cynicism. Modern practitioners are much less attracted to the illusion of 'balance' or 'progress' than by the seduction of the unexpected. The unpredictable and unplanned outcome often appeals more than the master design.

But for the discourse theorist the paradox, the irony and the unexpected tend to be destructive. Colonial discourses are seen to emanate from the search for power, to reflect those relations of power, and to perpetuate the exercise of that power. Consequently, their work implies both moral judgements and prescriptive programmes. Historians, on the other hand, have never been confident about the predictive and practical purposes of their discipline, even if most of them have sensibly recognised the impossibility of escaping value-laden language. Further, the theorists fall into all the pitfalls the historian constantly warns students, the public and himself to avoid: reading present values into past ages; passing judgements on entire previous generations; failing to discriminate intention from effect; missing the multiple readings emanating from the conflict between authorial intention and audience expectation. Historians can be lumpers and splitters, enthusiastic builders and sceptical doubters (sometimes in one and the same person). By definition, discourse theorists must lump. The imperative of deconstruction is construction, building unwieldy piles out of the ruins of dismantled texts.

Above all, the historian seeks accessibility. The historian's craft is blessed with a certain degree of public interest. The finest historians seek to wear their scholarship lightly, to infiltrate ideas and searching analysis into a good story. Above all, the historian is interested in a clear and readable style, a supple English in which jargon is kept to a minimum. By contrast, some of the discourse theorists cloak themselves in an invented language, embroidered in lengthy sentences of great opacity, and indulge in tautology akin to a repeated abstract design in which complex filigree is more important than symmetrical pattern. No one outside the field would read them for pleasure, and they appear to use an esoteric argot in order to communicate essentially with each other. No wonder that the historian, secure in the conviction that the finest thought can be expressed in the simplest of language, has found it difficult to penetrate the often arcane cabalism of the discourse theorists. As their influence wanes (including with Said himself), they have become little more than an unexplored and largely ill-defined intellectual cul-de-sac.

The arts of empire and Orientalism require a different approach to their understanding, a clearer periodisation, a closer relationship to event, mood, fashion and changing intellectual context, an effort to comprehend authorial influence and audience reaction, and above all the multiple readings to which they can be subjected. The rest of this book represents an initial and perhaps excessively bold attempt at a new understanding of imperial cultural history in several of its artistic manifestations. The manifold examples of Orientalism in the arts will be tested against the debate between a monolithic binary discourse and the more complex intertextuality identified by some recent historical and literary commentators. Orientalist preoccupations will also be set into the debates between conservatives and radicals in the arts and will be discussed in relation to the generation of innovative styles.

Notes

1   In *Culture and Imperialism* Said issues a cry for a new critical consciousness rooted in a global and anti-nationalist identity: 'The fact is, we are mixed in with one another in ways that most national systems of education have not dreamed of.' See, *inter alia*, p. 401.

2   Mary Louise Pratt, *Imperial Eyes: Travel Writing and Transculturation* (London, 1992), p. 5.

3   Pratt, *Imperial Eyes*, pp. 6–7 and *passim*.

4   Dennis Porter, 'Orientalism and its problems' in Francis Barker *et al.* (eds), *The Politics of Theory* (Colchester, 1983), pp. 179–93.

5   Porter, 'Orientalism', p. 187.

6   *ibid.*, p. 192.

7   Dennis Porter, *Haunted Journeys: Desire and Transgression in European Travel Writing* (Princeton, 1991), pp. 5–9.

8   John Pemble, *The Mediterranean Passion* (Oxford, 1987).

9   Billie Melman, *Women's Orients* (London, 1992), introduction and conclusion and pp. 101, 111, 149, 182, 193. Melman is particularly interesting on changing attitudes towards nomads: see 'Ethnography and empathy', pp. 296–305. Although Pemble hints at different attitudes resulting from social Darwinian ideas later in the nineteenth century, he never works these out in relation to the Mediterranean world.

10   Melman, *Women's Orients*, p. 315.

11   *ibid.*, p. 316.

12   Lisa Lowe, *Critical Terrains: French and British Orientalisms* (Ithaca, 1991), p. ix.

13   Lowe, *Critical Terrains*, p. x.

14   *ibid.*, p. 5.

15   Compare Lowe on Flaubert, pp. 1–4 and *passim* with Said in *Orientalism*, pp. 188–190, 309.

16   Two examples of Said's inability to cope with irony will suffice. See his misreading of Orwell in *Orientalism*, pp. 251–2 and his misunderstanding of Ernest Gellner in his letter to the *Times Literary Supplement*, 19 March 1993, p. 15 and Gellner's response, 9 April 1993, p. 15.

17   Sara Suleri, *The Rhetoric of English India* (London, 1992), pp. 1–12.

18   As Francis Bacon (1561–1626) put it in 'Of Empire' (by which he meant power), 'It is a miserable state of mind to have few things to desire and many things to fear.'

19   Raymond Schwab, *La Renaissance Orientale* (Paris, 1950), trans. Gene Patterson-Black and Victor Reinking as *The Oriental Renaissance: Europe's Rediscovery of India and the East, 1680–1880* (New York, 1984). The page numbers that follow are from Said's *Orientalism*.

20   David Kopf, 'Hermeneutics versus history', *Journal of Asian Studies*, XXXIX (1980), pp. 494–506.

21   B. J. Moore-Gilbert, *Kipling and 'Orientalism'* (London, 1986).

22   See, for example, Thomas R. Metcalf, *The Aftermath of Revolt* (Princeton, 1965).

23   Bernard S. Cohn, 'Representing authority in Victorian India', in Eric Hobsbawm and Terence Ranger (eds), *The Invention of Tradition* (Cambridge, 1983).

24   Ronald Inden, *Imagining India* (Oxford, 1990).

25   Inden, *Imagining India*, pp. 77, 263–70.

26   Javed Majeed, *Ungoverned Imaginings: James Mill's The History of British India and Orientalism* (Oxford, 1992).

27   Majeed, *Ungoverned Imaginings*, Chapter 4, pp. 123–50, especially pp. 128, 148. See also pp. 158, 174.

28   Jane Rendall, 'Scottish Orientalism: from Robertson to James Mill', *The Historical Journal*, 25 (1982), pp. 43–69.

29   Rendall, 'Scottish Orientalism', p. 43.

30   Martha McLaren, 'Writing and Making History, Thomas Munro, John Malcolm and Mountstuart Elphinstone: Three Scotsmen in the History and Historiography of British India' (Ph.D. thesis, Simon Fraser University, 1992).

31   McLaren, 'Writing and Making History', p. 183.

32   McLaren, Chapters 7–11; Christine Bolt, *Victorian Attitudes to Race* (London, 1971); Douglas A. Lorimer, *Colour, Class and the Victorians* (Leicester, 1978). For further discussion of the influence of the Scots and the Scottish Enlightenment

on empire, see John M. MacKenzie, 'Scotland and the Empire', *International History Review*, XV (1993), pp. 714–39.

33   Gyan Prakash, 'Writing post-orientalist histories of the Third World: perspectives from Indian historiography', *Comparative Studies in Society and History*, 32 (1990), pp. 383–408, especially pp. 384–5.

34   Nigel Leask, *British Romantic Writers and the East: Anxieties of Empire* (Cambridge, 1992), pp. 2, 6, 9, 87 and *passim*.

35   For a recent account of the origins of the indirect rule system, see Micheal H. Fisher, *Indirect Rule in India: Residents and the Residency System, 1764–1857* (Delhi, 1991).

36   Leask, *Romantic Writers*, p. 78. See also Edward Burman, *The Assassins* (London, 1987).

37   John Drew, *India and the Romantic Imagination* (Delhi, 1987).

38   For recent and contrasting discussions of Hastings's policy, see Gauri Viswanathan, *Masks of Conquest: Literary Study and British Rule in India* (London, 1989), pp. 28–30 and J. L. Brockington, 'Warren Hastings and Orientalism' in Geoffrey Carnall and Colin Nicholson (eds), *The Impeachment of Warren Hastings* (Edinburgh, 1989), pp. 91–108.

39   Viswanathan, *Masks*, p. 17.

40   Viswanathan, *Masks*, p. 20.

41   See, for example, Andrew Ross, *John Philip (1775–1851): Missions, Race and Politics in South Africa* (Aberdeen, 1986).

42   Said, *Culture and Imperialism*, pp. 48, 130.

43   See the reviews listed in notes 22 and 24 of Chapter 1; also Fred Inglis, 'A peregrine spirit with an eye for eagles', *The Times Higher Education Supplement*, 5 March 1993, pp. 25, 27.

44   See, for example, his curious misuse of R. E. Robinson's collaborationist theory, pp. 316–17. See also my review in the *Journal of Historical Geography*, 19 (1993), pp. 101–6.

45   Said, *Culture and Imperialism*, pp. 94–5, 123–6, 196–7, 290–1.

46   J. A. Hobson, *John Ruskin: Social Reformer* (London, 1898); 'Ruskin and democracy', *Contemporary Review*, 81 (1902), pp. 103–12; 'Ruskin as a political economist' in J. Whitehouse (ed.), *Ruskin the Prophet* (London, 1920).

47   James Clark Sherburne, *John Ruskin, or the Ambiguities of Abundance* (Cambridge, Mass., 1972).

48   M. K. Gandhi, *The Story of my Experiments with Truth* (Ahmedabad, 1929), Vol. II, pp. 106–8. The chapter is entitled 'The Magic spell of a book'. Just as there is a rediscovery of Ruskin in the West, so is there a revaluation of Gandhi's thought in India, in the wake of the environmental and urban problems produced by Nehru's policies of industrialisation and self-sufficiency.

49   Fredric Jameson, 'Modernism and imperialism' in Terry Eagleton, Fredric Jameson and Edward W. Said, *Nationalism, Colonialism and Literature* (Minneapolis, 1990), pp. 43–66, in which he takes the theory of capitalist imperialism as read and makes no acknowledgement of the considerable debate and dissent which it has engendered. To be locked into the Hobson–Leninist interpretation in 1990 seems, to say the least, bizarre, curious even for a modern Marxist.

50   Stephen Howe, 'When the sun did set', *The Times Higher Education Supplement*, 13 November 1992, p. 17.

51   Felix Driver, 'Geography's empire: histories of geographical knowledge', *Society and Space*, 10 (1992), pp. 23–40.

52   Said's *Culture and Imperialism*, extensive work as it is, reflecting wide, but often misdirected, reading in historical sources, makes very few references to actual imperial events.

53   This quotation is taken from Karl Marx's articles on the Indian Mutiny, published in the *New York Herald* in 1857.
54   Bruce McCully, *English Education and the Origins of Indian Nationalism* (New
     York, 1942) and Anil Seal, *The Emergence of Indian Nationalism: Competition
     and Collaboration in the Later Nineteenth Century* (Cambridge, 1971).
55   David Kopf, *British Orientalism and the Bengal Renaissance: the Dynamics of
     Indian Modernisation, 1773–1835* (Berkeley, 1969).
56   Francis G. Hutchins, *The Illusion of Permanence: British Imperialism in India*
     (Princeton, 1967).

I   Ludwig Deutsch (1855–1935), *The Emir's Guard*. While the figure here has less of the handsome swagger of the same artist's several depictions of *The Nubian Guard*, nevertheless it is a dignified image, conveying pride in beautiful fabrics, weaponry and architectural detail.

Rudolf Ernst (1854–1932), *The Musician*. The oriental musician was a favourite   **II**
subject of Ernst: this version is of a black singer, reclining at ease amidst a riot
of abstract patterns in carpet, fabrics and architectural detail. While the figure
is not as handsome as in other Ernst paintings, it is far from being ugly and
reveals the honour accorded the black musician in Middle Eastern society.

3
Orientalism in art

FOR MANY, Orientalism is essentially an art-historical term. In this guise it often has a relatively restricted meaning, relating to the paintings of a specific group of nineteenth-century and mainly French artists who took North Africa and the Middle East as their subject-matter. This usage is generally attributed to Théophile Gautier, who travelled in and wrote about the East, and was an admirer and critic of their work until his death in 1872. 'Orientalism' came under critical attack from the 1870s, as Impressionism superseded Realism, but it had a remarkable power of survival: in the 1880s and 1890s it re-established itself as an exceptionally popular form, surviving until the inter-war years. Thus, like the cultural and linguistic Orientalism of eighteenth-century India, the word normally had a positive resonance. During the past fifteen years, the period of the rediscovery of Orientalist painting, the term has sometimes been extended to the very large number of artists who produced representations of the Orient, including South Asia and the Far East, between the eighteenth and the twentieth centuries. But positive connotations have now mixed with negative as radical art historians have critically revalued the work of Orientalists in the light of Said's literary model.

The number of artists dubbed 'Orientalist' is considerable. One standard work examines no fewer than 148, by no means an exhaustive collection.[1] The major gallery in London which deals in this work lists

100 artists whose paintings pass through its hands.[2] In addition to these
better known examples there were many amateurs, architects and military men (whose work is, for example, well represented in the Searight
collection, now lodged at the Victoria and Albert Museum in London)
as well as trashy imitators who apparently found a ready market with
nineteenth-century travellers eager to purchase souvenirs of their journeys.[3] Among the more important artists, some were very nearly special-
ists; others devoted a large proportion of their *oeuvre* to the Orient;
while a few turned to oriental subjects only briefly. Some never visited
the East; others travelled extensively; and a few settled for longer periods. Sometimes, oriental subjects were painted before they went; paintings and sketches were made on the spot; but large numbers were worked
up after they had returned. As James Thompson has argued, the East
was a major preoccupation of nineteenth-century painting, an East which
was, in turn, 'Imagined, Experienced, Remembered'.[4]

While the best known of the Orientalist painters were French,
there was a considerable group of English exponents of eastern themes,
including several Pre-Raphaelites, as well as an extensive Scottish school.
Indeed, the form was so popular that practitioners emerged in Austria,
Belgium, Germany, Hungary, Ireland, Italy, Malta, the Netherlands, the
Ottoman Empire, Poland, Russia, Spain, Switzerland and the United
States. It has been truly said that all of these painters were united the-
matically rather than stylistically.[5] In no sense do they constitute a 'school'.
Yet they require stylistic analysis as much as thematic, for many of the
artists drawing inspiration from the East were stimulated technically as
well as visually. Moreover, the extraordinarily long life of 'Orientalism'
ensured that it passed through a variety of phases, phases that can be
demarcated by subject-matter, style, ideology and national affiliation.
Further, many of the artists had associations with other art forms (such
as architecture, crafts, textiles or photography) which in turn influenced
them and were influenced by the Eastern experience.

The 'Orientalists', perhaps more than any other group of painters,
have been subjected to extremes of admiration and vilification. The
extraordinarily buoyant market of the nineteenth century stimulated excess
production, which produced its inevitable reaction in the twentieth century. Indeed, some artists became so unfashionable that galleries sold off
their holdings, prices plummeted, and the whereabouts of many paintings were lost. In the 1970s and 1980s, the almost inevitable revaluation
– in both critical and market terms – began to take place. A series of
exhibitions, most notably in Munich in 1972, London in 1978 and
Rochester, New York in 1982, brought them back to public notice.
Separate aspects of painterly Orientalism were explored in London
(Leighton House and the Barbican), Brighton, Birmingham, Bristol and

several French provincial galleries, and the process culminated with the Royal Academy Exhibition of 1984 (also at the National Gallery of Art, Washington, DC) and the quirkily stimulating exhibition at the National Gallery of Ireland in Dublin (also at the Walker Art Gallery, Liverpool) in 1988.[6] Orientalism was set into a much wider historical and cultural context in British exhibitions on the China Trade (1986), on British rule in India ('Raj', 1990–91), and on Lord Macartney's China embassy of 1797 (1993).[7] A further, broadly-based reappraisal of Orientalism took place in Preston, Hull and Oldham in 1992.[8] In 1985, Coral Petroleum Inc. of Houston, Texas, which had loaned eighteen pictures to the Washington show, capitalised on the publicity by selling off sixty-one of its Orientalist paintings through Sotheby's, New York.[9] By this time, the Mathaf Gallery in London had established the new commercial acceptability of Orientalist art, enjoying, in particular, a considerable market in the Middle East. This gallery exhibited in an Islamic centre in London, and began to publish its catalogues in Arabic.[10]

But if Middle Eastern buyers appear to find in Orientalist paintings acceptable images of the world they have lost, neither critical rehabilitation nor a bullish (camelish?) market has been given a free run. Said referred to painting only in passing in his *Orientalism*, but his modes of analysis have been brought to bear on the Orientalist canon by Rana Kabbani and specialist art historians, most notably Linda Nochlin and Marcia Pointon.[11] Over the past ten years, the vast field of Orientalist painting has become the scene of skirmishes between traditional art historians, primarily concerned with aesthetics and positivist approaches to representation, and radicals influenced by Said. In 1983, Linda Nochlin argued that art history had to be repoliticised.[12] In her view, Orientalist paintings had to be analysed in terms of imperial ideology and hegemonic approaches to the East.

As Nochlin has put it, art history finds it difficult to move out of its celebratory mode, and it is certainly true that several of the exhibition catalogues and standard works on Orientalism carefully ignore the ideological dimension.[13] Thompson's catalogue for the Dublin Exhibition meets the controversy head on, and this makes it quite the most stimulating of all the exhibition guides.[14] With the Preston/Hull/Oldham show, entitled (with a self-conscious use of the lower case) 'fine material for a dream', we reach the highest point of the Said/Nochlin approach. No other exhibition extended the Orientalist canon so far or interpreted images from the eighteenth to the twentieth centuries in such mercilessly racist contexts or relentlessly hegemonic modes. Contributors to the catalogue saw Orientalism as inexorably rooted in racism, as portraying fantasies of all that the artists hated and feared, creating essentialist images of an East that was both evil and servile.[15] Its organisers sought to

display the ways in which the Orientalist vision continues to be perpetrated in modern advertising and popular culture, and contrasted the
work of modern Asian artists and photographers, burdening them with
the need to counter the European visual appropriation of the East.

Thus, for Nochlin and her followers, oriental painting is suspect
because its messages and its uses mark it out as the product, reflector and
tool of imperialism. Visions of the Orient were highly selective, creating
oriental archetypes through which the 'Otherness' of eastern peoples
could be readily identified. Tyranny, cruelty, laziness, lust, technical
backwardness, languid fatalism and cultural decadence generally, offered
a justification for imperial rule and a programme for its reforming zeal.
The ethnic diversity of oriental paintings conveys a set of racial concepts,
particularly through the juxtaposition of black and lighter-skinned people, while the treatment of women is the clearest indicator of attitudes
towards women in the nineteenth century. The 'licked finish' of the mid-
century Realists is an illusory device presenting ideologically charged,
iconic images as an objective reality. The careful depiction of repaired
tilework, the decay and crude repair of buildings were used as indicators
of a decadent civilisation. Moreover, the Orientalist canon is marked by
its absences. According to Nochlin, Europeans are visually absent but
psychologically present because they constitute the all-seeing, all-
powerful gaze. Westernising influences are also absent, as the violence
and expropriation of the imperial thrust is cloaked in a highly selective
and essentially destructive nostalgia. Orientalist images imply timelessness, the absence of the historical dynamic of progress that represents
western superiority. Yet its idealised vision also excludes squalor, disease
and low life.[16] Thus the East is symbolically constructed in order to be
dominated, devised to be ruled.[17]

In pursuing this case, Nochlin makes an instructive selection of
paintings. Delacroix's *Death of Sardanapalus* becomes both an indicator
of the monumental indifference to human life which is the supposed
characteristic of the East and an indication of the artist's psycho-sexual
neuroses in relation to contemporary attitudes to women. Gérôme's
Snake Charmer hints at mysterious deviance. Regnault's *Summary Execution under the Moorish Kings of Granada* reflects the western construction of the irrational violence of the East. Racial as well as sexual
statements are made through the repeated juxtaposition of lighter-skinned
odalisques and black slaves in bath and harem scenes (in Gérôme's *Moorish
Bath*, for example), while women again become abused personifications
of the East in the many treatments of the slave market (Gérôme's *The
Slave Market* of the early 1860s is her prime example). Resisters and
collaborators among the indigenous rulers are portrayed in romantic, but
moralistic ways (Delacroix's *Moulay Abd-el-Rahman, Sultan of Morocco*

contrasted with Chassériau's portrait of Kalif Ali-ben Hamet). Thus
Orientalism seeks to combine visual beauty with moral disapprobation.

Nochlin's conclusion is highly suggestive:

> Works like Gérôme's, and that of other Orientalists of his ilk, are valu-
> able and well worth investigating not because they share the esthetic
> values of great art on a slightly lower level, but because as visual imagery
> they anticipate and predict the qualities of incipient mass culture. As
> such, their strategies of concealment lend themselves admirably to the
> critical methodologies, the deconstructive techniques now employed by
> the best film historians, or by sociologists of advertising imagery or analysts
> of visual propaganda, rather than those of mainstream art history.[18]

This statement contains some surprising assumptions: that 'great art' is
somehow above such techniques, that popular culture, notably film, can
never aspire to high art, and, finally, that all Orientalist art exists on an
entirely different plane from that considered by 'mainstream art history'.

Nochlin, and other exponents of the Said model, have one thing
in common. They write about imperialism, but they are not imperial
historians. It is true that Nochlin throws in the odd imperial event, the
occasional French law, to provide an air of spurious realism to her imperialism, but generally 'imperialism' is a somewhat nebulous, even
impressionistic concept. In reality, imperial attitudes are seldom consistent: it is, for example, a glib assumption that collaborators are always
going to be portrayed (in print as well as visually) more positively than
resisters. The British invariably took the opposite view, as the portrayal
of the Zulu neatly illustrates. It is of course the case, as the Manchester
University Press 'Studies in Imperialism' series is concerned to point out,
that imperialism must be seen as an intellectual and cultural phenomenon as much as an economic, political or military one, but that is not
to say that it should be regarded in an imprecise and undifferentiated
way, somehow free of the chronological dynamic that is the stuff of
historical study. It will not do to pick and mix artists from different
points in the nineteenth century and portray them as locked into a set of
racial and imperialist assumptions. The durability of the oriental obsession, from at least the late eighteenth to the early twentieth centuries,
must raise doubts that its 'deconstruction' can be anything other than
highly complex, producing different results at varying periods, as well as
opposing dualities among artists and even within the single artist's work.

Moreover, as with all popular culture, the market must be thoroughly understood. The Orientalists were remarkably responsive to market
conditions. They were themselves fascinated by the East, as we shall see,
but they also reflected the shift from aristocratic to bourgeois patronage

that constitutes such an important aspect of nineteenth-century art. Many of them had royal and aristocratic patrons, but these generally provided the cachet which helped to increase bourgeois sales, rather like the royal warrant. It is instructive too that an important, perhaps the principal market for their work, at both royal and bourgeois ends, was in Britain. A number of the French artists moved, at least temporarily, to England. Several Orientalists, particularly a Viennese group, had contacts with Queen Victoria and, more particularly, with her son the Prince of Wales.[19] Following the royal lead, their works were bought by industrial and commercial *nouveaux riches.* American millionaires also seem to have become important purchasers of these paintings.[20]

The success of a number of the artists was dependent upon the French dealers Goupil and Gambart, who fed their works in the appropriate directions, and also increased their fame through the judicious use of photographs and engravings. Engravings became a significant aspect of the income of several artists, some of whom found themselves trapped into the provision of repetitive, but saleable images. It is for this reason that there are invariably extant many variations on the same theme or even the same picture. Occasionally, a dealer might ask an artist to be directly responsive to taste – for example, Fromentin was told that horses sold better than camels, and he appears to have stressed the equine thereafter.[21] It was partly this popular fashion for Orientalism that ensured its longevity even after it had come under critical attack, but this taste inevitably changed even as artists' attitudes and techniques developed.

Some Orientalist artists set up studios in the East, in Cairo for example, and sold portraits, street scenes and topographical studies (often with monuments) as souvenirs to travellers. Others painted local royalty and dignitaries and sometimes sold the results to their sitters. By the end of the century, westernising tendencies led the Ottoman Empire to attempt to create its own school of painting in occidental style, including its own 'Orientalism', of which perhaps Hamdy Bey was the most celebrated exponent. In addition some of the Orientalists were book illustrators whose work reached a much wider audience through engravings. With cheaper printing in the later nineteenth century, these works were more widely available than the very expensive books of prints that were produced in the first half of the century. Orientalist images also found their way into popular magazines, advertising and eventually into the cinema. Thus the market was both socially and geographically diverse, although the receptiveness of certain classes in Britain and the United States is clearly significant.

What were these consumers looking for? To answer this question we have to relate Orientalism to wider cultural and historical trends. Orientalism can, perhaps be divided into five principal phases. The first

1   David Roberts (1796–1864), *The Gateway of the Great Temple at Baalbec*, 1843. Roberts has been accused of denigrating contemporary Middle Eastern society while glorifying ruins. His figures, however, are painted with some sympathy and are designed to demonstrate the enormous grandeur of the ancient remains.

consists of imagined images of orientals created in the eighteenth century by those who had seldom, if ever, seen the real thing. William Hogarth's *A Procession through the Hippodrome*, Gavin Hamilton's portrayal of Wood and Dawkins discovering Palmyra and the illustrations for Johnson's *Rasselas* and Beckford's *Vathek* are good examples. The second divides into two streams, the tradition of topographical and archaeological 'realism' symbolised by Dominique Vivant Denon (1747–1825) and David Roberts (1796–1864) and the energetic, vibrant Romanticism of Alexandre-Gabriel Decamps (1803–60) and Eugène Delacroix (1798–1863), more concerned with atmospheric power than accuracy. The third is characterised by the realism, detailed minutiae and alleged ethnographic precision of Horace Vernet (1789–1863), who made the transition from an exuberant Romanticism to detailed Realism in the 1830s, Eugène Fromentin (1820–76), Jean-Léon Gérôme (1824–1904) and the latter's pupils and followers, together with John Frederick Lewis (1805–76) on the British side. In the fourth, developing in the last decades of the nineteenth century, we find some reaction to Impressionism (in both negative and positive terms), but we also find new thematic concerns. The Orient becomes less glamorised, more varied, with a greater range of subjects and moods, often more reflective, in some ways more concerned with mutual understanding. Arthur Melville (1855–1904) is a good exemplar of this period. Moreover, eastern artefacts become less a set of stage props and begin themselves to influence western crafts and design. Some of the painters of this period – Frank Brangwyn (1867–1956) is an excellent example – have a real concern with the rediscovery of the values of craft production and heroic individual labour in reaction to the industrial system. The fifth phase is more technical than thematic. Painters come to be specifically influenced by eastern art, particularly that of the Far East, while the avant-garde (artists like Kandinsky, Matisse and Klee) found abstract inspiration in the geometrical intricacy of Islamic art.

If these phases are matched to the imperial experience, we find a curious counterpoint. It may be true that French Orientalism was inspired first by Napoleon's Egyptian expedition of 1798, the army of *savants* he took with him, the creation of the *Institut* and the publication of the great official *Description de l'Egypte* preceded by Denon's more personal *Voyage* and second, by the invasion of Algeria in the dying days of the Bourbons in 1830.[22] The French continued to expand and posture in Algeria in the days of Louis Philippe and Napoleon III, but their next direct act of territorial aggrandisement came with the annexation of Tunisia in 1881. The British, on the other hand, lacked major formal acquisitions until their invasion of Egypt in 1882, undertaken by a Liberal administration which, though eager to withdraw, found itself trapped. Moreover, the Egyptians themselves had attempted to expand their imperial presence in the Sudan, the Red Sea and even the East African coast. The conclusive European push into North Africa was to come only in the years immediately preceding the First World War, with the French acquisition of Morocco, the Italian of Libya and, in 1914, the declaration of the British protectorate in Egypt. The Ottoman Empire, so often depicted as the sick man, in fact expanded its power in Syria and the Levant, Palestine and Arabia in the late nineteenth century, and the British and French only acquired authority there through the mandates granted in 1919.

It may be that throughout this period, following Napoleon's dramatic and bloody defeats of the Mamluks, the Europeans were confident of their technical and cultural superiority, which could so readily be transformed into economic and military mastery. But although the French became embroiled in imperial adventure in limited areas of North Africa, often as a diversion from domestic instability, the British remained unsure about either the necessity or the efficacy of establishing direct controls. Dominance of strategic positions such as Gibraltar, Malta, and from 1878 Cyprus, seemed a perfectly adequate means of controlling trade routes. Their policy throughout the century was the protection of the Ottoman Empire against the predatory designs of rivals, in other words the maintenance of the balance of power. Even in the case of Egypt, where the opening of the Suez Canal in 1869 inevitably increased their concerns, they would have preferred the maintenance of some kind of indirect international supervision. Imperial responsibilities elsewhere, particularly in India, kept British hands full.

Two interesting points immediately arise from this chronology. The first is the distinction between French and British Orientalism. The British never indulged in the grandiose gestures of Delacroix and other French artists. With the exception of a few grand canvases by John Martin (who never visited the East) and David Roberts, their approach was generally more pragmatic and low key. Second, the paintings which convey the strongest gestures to an imperial ideology precede the direct imposition of European rule in North Africa and the Middle East, with the sole exception of the French in Algeria. The high point of the 'new imperialism' in the period between 1890 and 1914 coincides with the shift of Orientalist painting into more radical techniques, not so much associated with imperial ideology as with the new crafts-based anti-industrialism of the western arts. Thus, there is little evidence of a necessary coherence between the imposition of direct imperial rule and the visual arts. There is very little evidence that the purchasers of Orientalist paintings bought them as emblems of imperial power, as illustrations of the onward march of westernisation and technical progress, or as images of a condign cultural destruction and disappearance.

Moreover, the Orientalism of the Middle East and North Africa seems to be strikingly distinct from the other imperial art of the period. It is hard to avoid the conclusion that the Orientalist canon was influenced more by the proximity of the Islamic Near East, its ancient, biblical and classical associations, and the increasing tourist potential of the Mediterranean region than by direct imperial rule. Indeed, when other imperial art is considered, it is apparent that Orientalism celebrates cultural proximity, historical parallelism and religious familiarity rather than true 'Otherness'. It is surely for this reason that several artists initially sought out the East in Europe. David Roberts and J. F. Lewis, Georges Clairin (1843–1919) and Henri Regnault (1843–71), among others, visited Granada and portrayed the architecture and culture of Moorish Spain before they ventured further afield.

While there are copious representations of British imperial possessions throughout the world, of which those of Australia and the Pacific, India, and even South Africa are perhaps best known, none of these areas has a tradition of painting attached to it of the 'Orientalist' sort.[23] Some Orientalists of the late nineteenth and early twentieth centuries went to India (Lear, Horsley, Swoboda, Tornai, Menpes), and one (Talbot-Kelly) to Burma, but most of the artists of the outer imperial possessions were (in art-historical terms) lesser figures, and many of them were amateurs. Most of the well known eighteenth and nineteenth-century figures associated with India, the Pacific and Africa were topographical, architectural or taxonomic artists, illustrating landscape, exotic structures, and botanical or zoological specimens, without any pretension to the high art of the salon. They have to be positioned either in the scientific tradition of the oceanic explorations of the Enlightenment or the extension of the tradition of picturesque water-colouring, engraving and lithography to Asia and the Pacific.[24] As Bernard Smith has argued, they worked within a tradition of scientific draughtsmanship, illustrating natural phenomena (including atmospheric conditions) of all sorts. Practical considerations, like the need to produce accurate coastal profiles, were a vital influence upon the art of some of them, but they also searched for characteristic or typical landscapes to illustrate the geographical varieties of the globe. Their work has come to be highly valued in recent times, but none of them enjoyed the fame, the powerful dealers and rich patrons of the Orientalists, and few of them were hung in the Royal Academy, the French salon, major exhibitions and galleries, as so many of the Orientalists were. Their work was rendered familiar through illustrated books.

These artists of the wider world also indulged in human taxonomies. In their portrayals of South Sea islanders, Indians, Australian aborigines, Maoris and Africans, they moved from Arcadian noble savagery in the eighteenth century to a grittier racial imagery in the nineteenth. Indeed, as racial hierarchies were distinguished in the course of the nineteenth century, the Semitic peoples were considered to be on a distinctly superior plane to that of many other peoples, including other orientals. This type of hierarchy is even apparent in popular writings and in school textbooks.[25] Moreover, if, as seems to be the case, Orientalist representations of Arabs become more sympathetic in the late nineteenth and early twentieth centuries, this fits oddly both with the more pronounced character of racial thinking in that period and with the fact that direct imperial controls had only just been established throughout the region.

This is not to imply that the artists were in any sense neutral observers. They never are. There is no such thing as the innocent eye or the objective lens. Several artists were members of official diplomatic, scientific and military expeditions. Some were present at acts of imperial aggression. Some extolled the virtues of French rule in North Africa and bought property there to capitalise upon it themselves. One at least (Vernet) referred to North Africa as a potential gold mine for the French.[26] Many of them participated in that ultimate imperial act, the acquisition of booty, antiquities of all sorts, the robbing of tombs and buildings, sometimes paid for, invariably not. Lord Leighton's tiles and inscriptions in his Arab Hall at his home in Holland Park. London, were after all acquired in such a manner.[27] Thus, as Nochlin has put it, some of the artists distinguished between visual beauty and moral quality. The moral superiority of the West, able to preserve while the East destroyed, justified such plunder.

However, Nochlin goes further and suggests that there is a more subtle form of destruction. The picturesque derives its fascination from its apparent transience.[28] For the viewer, its picturesque power is heightened because of its implied doom. The suggestion seems to be that the artists, in seeking out the picturesque, were agents in its destruction. Direct forms of plunder cannot be gainsaid, and this is no place to go into the arguments about preservation, the character of cultural flattery, the extension of knowledge, the representation of one culture to another, and so on. But the suggestion that artists were implicated in the retreat of customs and cultures in the face of major world processes merely by portraying them is surely going too far. When Delacroix wrote in his diary that 'Economists and Saint-Simonians would have a lot to criticise here with respect to the rights of man before the law, but the beautiful abounds here'; 'This is a place completely for painters', he was surely implying that artists have different criteria from economists and Saint-Simonians.

In any case, some form of destruction is the inevitable concomitant of all scholarly and artistic activity. Archaeology is a conscious act of destruction in order to understand and preserve; the collection of oral traditions and oral evidence is also destructive, since it forms patterns and creates emphases that ultimately destroy the pure source of the testimony. Each new phase in every art is an act of destruction, since it destroys an area of innocence, creating a route forward which renders others redundant or inadmissible. Creation has ever been the obverse of destruction, particularly obvious and poignant for the architect or the landscape gardener. To suggest that the artist should not portray cultural forces that are in retreat, disappearing customs or classes, is a counsel of despair.

Indeed the wild enthusiasm, the sometimes delirious responses of artists to North Africa and the Middle East should surely be accepted as genuine and unfeigned. W. J. Müller (1812–45), who described himself as half-Arab, revelled in the bazaars and street scenes of Cairo, which he viewed as pictures out of Rembrandt.[29] Richard Dadd prophetically described the excitement of Middle Eastern scenes as being enough to turn the brain.[30] Dehodencq similarly found that Morocco drove him out of his senses,[31] while Wilkie and a host of other artists were reduced to ecstatic reveries by Constantinople.[32] Gérôme made no fewer than seven visits to Egypt between 1857 and 1880, waxing lyrically about all that he saw.[33] Of course the Orientalists could not escape involvement in the intellectual, economic, social and political forces of their day, whether by positive or negative responses. No generation can. In that respect, there is nothing unique about imperialism. But although developing commercial and political contacts, technical changes and relative power balances made the East more accessible; it was not solely or specifically imperial rule that drew artists there. As we have seen, there was no similar flood to other, more directly controlled imperial territories. European artists flocked to North Africa and the Middle East because Europe seemed to offer little more to explore, because these new regions were relatively close, because they represented an extraordinary range of ancient cultures, the origins of several world religions, including their own, and dramatic topographical, architectural and cultural features. Some of the same excitement of discovery and displaced sense of familiarity must have impelled the purchasers of their work.

Moreover, if Orientalism is linked to the full range of art forms, an alternative 'deconstruction' presents itself. The essence of Romanticism lay in violent and turbulent imagery. The central element of the 'sublime' was defined as involving a frisson of fear. Nature, like genius and the individual human psyche, was wild and potentially uncontrollable. Hence the fascination with volcanic eruptions, storms, disasters, massacres and the wildest of animals, with ruins, murder and the Gothic novel.[34] The swirling, energetic and sometimes violent images of Delacroix in fact tell us a good deal more about Romanticism than they do about

the 'construction' of the East. The East, and more particularly the ancient world, happened to be one convenient location of violent imagery.

Animal violence helps to illustrate this point. The destructive power
and ferocity of the lion was a source of great fascination to animal artists.
Yet the cruelty of its massive frame, bared fangs and claws in no way
diminished its heroic grandeur, a prime symbol of human power. The
horse, on the other hand, has always indicated refinement and sensibility,
breeding, grace and speed, linked to a slightly unpredictable character:
an elemental force tamed by humans, but remaining always on the edge,
never wholly sure of its domestic status. The juxtaposition of the lion
and the horse therefore brought together two partly contrasting images,
the one almost supernaturally wild, the other not quite tame. Rubens
conjoined them. Stubbs depicted animals in a clinically taxonomic way,
but he also produced terrifying Romantic images, including his painting
of a lion on the back of a horse. The Orientalists took up the theme, and
lions and horses abound in their paintings. But the 'Orient' was largely
incidental, merely a theatrical backdrop to an established violent imagery.[35]

Such paintings are strikingly ambivalent. The lion is terrifyingly
violent, yet admirable in its muscular truth to its own nature, its will to
survive. Nineteenth-century art is full of such violence: the pictures of
animal conflict mirror and justify human violence, both in relation to
nature, through the ubiquitous hunting scenes, and to fellow humans in
war. Such work is common among artists, like Sir Edwin Landseer, who
seldom touched the Orient.[36] In fact, in looking at Orientalist painting,
we require not a theory of 'Otherness', but a theory of cultural cross-
reference. European artists projected on to the East not only the fantasies and fears of the West, but also aspirations, renewed values and
wished-for freedoms. Paradoxically, they often sought to portray not the
strikingly different, but the oddly familiar.

To the critics of Orientalism, this may seem like a fantastical claim.
Yet the paintings are full of contemporary European obsessions. Mark
Girouard has ably chronicled the recreation of the medieval chivalric
code in Britain, through the novels of Sir Walter Scott, the Westminster
Hall banquet of 1821, the Eglinton Tournament of 1839 and a host of
other manifestations.[37] The oriental canon is packed with chivalry, an
endless parade of equestrianism, of Arab knights bearing their long muskets
like lances, sometimes in repose, sometimes hurling themselves across
the desert towards some unseen foe, occasionally in single mounted conflict as in the tournament. Time and again the resonances are not just
Saracenic (and of course a renewed interest in the Crusades played a
significant part in this), but chivalric. After all, 'chevalier arabe' is a common title of French paintings. There is just such chivalric content in the
swagger of Gérôme's *Arnaut of Cairo* or his *The Rose*, which completely

recreates a medieval image (woman on balcony, 'knight' on fine steed below) in an Islamic setting.[38]

Hunt scenes also evoked chivalry: Fromentin and others often painted Arab falconers at a time when hawking was returning to popularity in Europe. It was understood that the Normans in Sicily had picked up the practice from the Arabs, and turned it into the medieval courtly pursuit *par excellence*. But the Arabs enjoyed all forms of hunting and shooting, and this made images of their hunts all the more acceptable when it was becoming the favoured pastime of European royalty, aristocracy and *nouveaux riches*. It comes as no surprise to find that many of the Orientalist painters were themselves fervent hunters.[39] Equestrianism was inseparably bound up with this and, as the Orientalists endlessly pointed out, the Arabs were supreme horsemen. Such images underpinned the anachronistic cavalry mentality in Europe which was to survive into the twentieth century.

But the Arab horse meant something more than this. Since first introduced in the eighteenth century, it had contributed a vital strain to English bloodstock. Horse-racing was a central aspect of British leisure, a common bond among the classes, as Frith's painting *Derby Day* was

Horace Vernet (1789–1863), *The Lion Hunt*, 1836. A classic depiction of men,   **2**
horses and lions pitted against each other.

3   Georges Washington (1827–1901), *The Standard Bearer*. A chivalric image,
discovering a medieval resonance in contemporary Arab lands. Many Orientalist
artists revealed this delight in depicting horses, antique saddles and finely clad
expert riders in bright landscapes.

concerned to point out. In the second half of the nineteenth century
strenuous efforts were made to renew that Arab strain with new bloodstock
from the East. The couple who were celebrated among the leading
Arabists of the late nineteenth century, Wilfrid Scawen Blunt and Lady
Anne Blunt (the granddaughter of Lord Byron), established a stud of
'arabs' at Crabbet Park, which was the finest of its day. They scoured the
Middle East for new stock.[40] Fine bloodstock was synonymous with
'breeding', including a certain amount of controlled and beneficial 'in-
breeding'. The most admirable human Arabs were seen as reflecting such
'breeding' too, particularly as they practised marriage customs which
emphasised kinship, just as the British aristocracy did. Thus the highly
bred, highly strung, but swift and courageous horse was itself a symbol
for human 'breeding'. The noble Arab chieftain, astride his equally noble

Arab horse, was a paradigm for the purchasers of his Orientalist image. For the owners of such pictures, these images did not so much celebrate a doomed world, dominated to be destroyed, but a world they yearned to regain.

There can be no doubt that depictions of horsemen and the hunt were designed to make statements about masculinity. The active, powerful, dominant western male imagined he found in the East a model. It comes as no surprise therefore to find that smoking-rooms, billiard-rooms, clubs and messes were often given an oriental atmosphere through design, decoration or accessory. Rana Kabbani's examination of the sexuality of the Orientalist paintings is telling, but her suggestion that oriental males 'are almost always portrayed as predatory figures. . . . They are mostly shown as ugly or loathsome' is grotesque.[41] On the contrary, they are often portrayed (as in countless paintings of Gérôme and others) as a masculine ideal. Similarly, the contention of Nochlin and others that black people are always ugly in Orientalist painting is also hard to sustain. There is a handsome, muscular splendour about *The Nubian Guard* of Ludwig Deutsch (1855–1935), a haughty pride to the *North African Man in Travelling Costume* by William Collins (1862–1951), a gorgeous elegance with finely rendered skin and features to Gérôme's *Black Bashi-Bazouk*, and an idealised winsome beauty to *A Nubian Girl Standing beside the First Cataract of the Nile* by Prisse d'Avennes (1807–79).

There can be no doubt that these paintings appear to celebrate the separation of male and female spheres in the Arab world, and hold up this ideal for emulation. However, Joanna de Groot has stimulatingly reinterpreted the portrayal of gender and the feminisation of the East in both texts and images of the nineteenth century. She rightly doubts the concept of a binary Other in these portrayals, reinterpreting male viewers (or voyeurs?) as seeking to explore and deal with their own identities. Thus the feminising of the East reflected a necessary attraction and close connection with European males' inner needs. Through the East, men were rediscovering and renegotiating their capacity to handle emotion, personal expression and intimacy, so often repressed in the European context.[42] Yet it may also be, as I have suggested, that through the chivalric image painters were attempting to recreate the ritualised and curiously ambivalent gender and sexual relations of the Middle Ages.

The rediscovery of medieval chivalry and the social and ritual aspects of the hunt reflected the extraordinary cultural eclecticism of the nineteenth century. If the Orientalist paintings are timeless, it is because timelessness was precisely the quality sought and found in the East. Here was an opportunity for history painting in a modern setting, and history painting had of course been seen as the highest accomplishment of art. Delacroix saw Algerians as having the classical grace of ancient Romans;[43]

other artists viewed the peoples of the Middle East as having stepped straight from the pages of the Bible;[44] while others again found an essentially medieval inspiration. It is true that some, like David Roberts, sought to moralise on past and present, ancient grandeur and modern decadence, but many looked at continuities, seeing images of a purer past which European culture was seeking to emulate, a quasi-feudal past of personal relationship, loyalty, hospitality, female protectiveness (at least in the harem setting) and the settling of scores by a swift, clean vendetta.

In other words, the fascination of the East lay in the manner in which it offered an atavistic reaction to modern industrialism, with its urban squalor, moral and physical unhealthiness, mass demoralisation, social discontents and the transfer of loyalties from the individual to the labour organisation with its politically explosive potential. Moreover, as Martin Wiener has shown, British industrialists and commercial *nouveaux riches* strove for gentrification.[45] While some aspects of this interpretation are controversial, there can be no doubt that industrial wealth was rapidly translated into country estates, country pursuits and solace in rural social relations. These seem to have been among the very people who provided a ready market for oriental paintings. While reactions to the Middle East were complex and often contradictory, admiration for the peasant or desert life and a consequent rejection of the urban became increasingly the norm. Blunt undoubtedly saw an opportunity to recreate personalised, feudal relations as one of the attractions of his property outside Cairo. He also increasingly extolled the virtues of the fellahin.

If timelessness was an attraction for an age undergoing rapid and racking change, then so was cleanliness. The central point about the desert was that it was perceived as morally and physically clean. Quite apart from the biblical resonances of retreat for spiritual renewal, the restoration of courage and purpose, the desert represented a great purifying force. It had the power to cover over past civilisations, as it had buried or nearly buried so many Egyptian monuments. It lacked the putrefying stench of industrial civilisation: its vultures picked carcasses clean, and its sands, blown by hot desert winds, covered over in a constant act of renewal, creating new and fantastic shapes. Its personal relations were similarly speedily renewable. They reflected old values, shorn of the festering social discontents and endless litigiousness of the West. Its peoples were quick to offence and swift in revenge, rapidly averting wider conflict. However different the reality, the desert iconography was, *pace* the Orientalist critics, idealist rather than decadent. To demand squalor is entirely to miss the point.

Many of the Orientalist artists sought out the desert and its peoples. J. F. Lewis and Frederick Goodall (1822–1904) found Cairo too

urban and escaped to the desert whenever they could. Goodall, Adolf
Schreyer (1828–99) and Gustave Guillaumet, among others, were fascinated by the Bedouin. A whole clutch of French artists, including
Théodore Chassériau (1819–56), Eugène Girardet (1853–1907) and
Paul Lazerges (1845–1902), found the coast and cities of North Africa
far too Frenchified and were ever eager to head for the purer cultural
wells of the south.[46] They were followed in the twentieth century by
Wyndham Lewis.[47] Most, being culturally conservative, viewed with dis-
favour the encroaching characteristics of western civilisation. As the century wore on, and imperial power was intensified, some artists, such as
Leopold Carl Müller (1834–92), Gustav Bauernfeind (1848–1904),
Maurice Bompard (1857–1936), Etienne Dinet (1861–1929), Franz
Kosler (1864–1905) and others did portray squalor, beggars, the rough
interiors of peasant homes, and physiognomies that displayed the harsh-
ness of desert life, its hunger, disease, and unremitting toil.[48] Moreover,
the Orientalist canon does include images of western tourists, French
soldiers and battle scenes.[49]

Two other areas of Middle Eastern life were invariably handled
with genuine respect. One was religion, and the other was the related
concern of learning and education of the young. For many artists, visions
of the Orient provided a direct route into the world of the Bible, and
scenes were repeatedly given biblical referents. F. Goodall claimed to see
a Holy Family in every Arab village.[50] Others had a genuine respect for
Islam. J. F. Lewis, J-L. Gérôme and many other artists were impressed
by the manner in which religion entered the fabric of everyday life. As
Paul Lenoir put it, here was 'real religious faith', a lesson to the West
in religious constancy and simplicity.[51] Indeed, far from highlighting
architectural decay and religious barbarity, as the Orientalist critics have
suggested, Gérôme actually 'restored' buildings known to be crumbling
and consciously excluded elements that would be seen as superstitious or
barbaric, as in his *Prayer in the Mosque of 'Amr* of c.1862.[52] The work
of countless artists abounds in scenes of piety and of muezzin calling
worshippers to prayer, images that offered opportunities for satisfying
architectural compositions combined with a religious message that seems
more obviously positive than negative. Although the critics of Orientalism
have professed themselves as seeing messages of languor and laziness in
the images of scribes penning letters and boys studying in Koranic schools,
such paintings can equally be read as showing respect for learning and
literacy suffused by religious belief.

When artists turned their attention from God to Mammon, from
religion, learning and the desert to the market, they displayed their
fascination with the pattern, colour and texture of the materials of eastern crafts. Carpets are everywhere, reflecting a European passion since

4   Hamdy Bey (1842–1910), *A Young Emir Studying*. Something of a polymath, Osman Hamdy Bey one of the most distinguished of eastern Orientalists, spent his career in Constantinople. He was trained in France by, among others Gérôme, but while following their realism and attention to detail, his paintings often convey a mood of quiet reserve. Here, learning and contemplation are exhibited amidst gently understated oriental fabrics, architectural detail and 'props'.

5   Gustavo Simoni (1846–1926), *At the Art Dealer's Shop*. The artist revels in carpets, fabrics, metalwork, firearms and musical instruments. It is an idealised image, but is intended to convey both the craftsmanship and connoisseurship of the East.

the sixteenth century. These rectangles of striking patterns and subtle colours presented a considerable artistic challenge, but they also offered the opportunity for human statements. People bargain over them, admire them, mend them and sit upon them. There was indeed a great exhibition of oriental carpets in Vienna in 1891, and artists rated them highly.[53] Moreover, fabrics, silks, cottons and woollen stuffs are carefully distinguished, their capacity to take dyes and display differing colours examined and perhaps exaggerated. The character and light-reflecting propensities of different metals, in the hands of craftsmen, present another challenge, the varied and satisfying shapes of pots and jugs, swords and daggers, firearms and smoking utensils its reward. Tiles and wooden lattices, *mashrabiyyah*, are lovingly portrayed, not only because they presented technical problems of pattern, texture and light, but also because they represented architectural adornments that could be, and were being adopted in the West.

In their fascination with crafts the Orientalists unknowingly answer the modern critics. They do not depict the superiority of industrially produced items. They do not make moral statements about the backwardness of craft production. On the contrary, some of them were actively involved in the movement associated with William Morris to re-create in Britain a craft alternative to the perceived soullessness of the industrial product, and they brought cartloads of eastern crafts home with them. As with chivalry, the hunt, the horse and social relations, the East had preserved older forms to renew western inspiration. The utensils of the coffee-house, so beloved by W. J. Müller and others, the work of the coppersmith and the carver in wood, all offered a return to craft values. Such a return was celebrated at the Colonial and Indian Exhibition of 1886 when craftspeople were brought from India. Rudolf Swoboda prepared portraits of many of them, old and young, men and women, and they now adorn the Durbar Hall corridor of Queen Victoria's Osborne.

Many of the Orientalist paintings were displayed at the exhibitions and international expositions that were such a feature of the nineteenth century. As we shall see in Chapter 4, these exhibitions were often obsessed with the East in their architecture and their displays. Among these, eastern crafts and craftsmen at work were invariably prominent. In their tobacco kiosks, coffee-rooms and tea-shops they connected these commodities to the East and often sought to create an oriental atmosphere. Here the East was surely associated with pleasant products, and the relationship of the Orient with ease and leisure had entirely positive connotations. For the British particularly, the pipe became a symbol of reflection, solidity, repose after action. Not for nothing was the 'smoking-room' often designed in oriental ways. Perhaps we should be sceptical of the idea that when Orientalists depict eastern coffee-shops, smoking, languor even, they are constantly making moral statements about Arab laziness. It is just as likely that they are making statements about the uniform and frenetic character of western urban existence.

It is equally unlikely that when they depict oriental games they are suggesting that Asian people are immature.[54] Nineteenth-century British society, after all, was supremely a society of sports and games. Ackerman is surely right when he sees Gérôme's *The Chess Players* as the 'glorification of an honest recreation' and one, moreover, requiring mental power and concentration.[55] Interestingly, Gérôme also depicted women playing chess in his *Almehs Playing Chess in a Café*, although it is true that they appear to be receiving advice from a male onlooker. In each of these paintings, the colour and texture of eastern fabrics and the simplicity and elegance of the products of eastern crafts are emphasised. This fascination with craft production overlaid the different and often conflicting artistic periods. It comes as no surprise to discover that a major show of Orientalists (including the work of the Impressionist Auguste Renoir, 1841–1919) was held in Paris in 1893 to coincide with an exhibition of Islamic arts. Another such exhibition took place in Munich in 1910.[56] As will be re-emphasised in the succeeding two chapters, a concern with eastern arts and crafts far transcended debates about western style and was just as likely to infuse radical as conservative approaches.

The British sought escape from a drab industrial world in shows and theatrical displays of all sorts. Flaubert described Egypt as having the air of an immense theatre set, and indeed one of the great attractions of the East was its theatricality. David Roberts, Adrien Dauzats and Jules Laurens (1825–1901) were trained as painters of theatre sets. Later in the century, Orientalists like Clairin, Jean-Joseph Benjamin Constant (1845–1902) and Frank Brangwyn were employed to decorate theatres, opera houses, hotels and other major public buildings in France, Britain and the United States. The nineteenth-century theatre was characterised by its spectacular productions, its melodrama, and its creative eclecticism.[57] Moreover, a favourite subject of the highly popular panoramas and dioramas of the period was eastern cities and antiquities.[58] Carlo Bossoli (1815–84) was an Orientalist painter who also worked on panoramas. The East provided ample scope for all of these theatrical and visual spectacles.

Indeed, viewing Orientalist paintings as an extension of the theatre offers an important key to unlocking meaning. Panoramas, dioramas, landscapes, monuments and battle scenes offer spectacle in plenty. Pictures of slave markets, and other sexually charged images, can be related to melodrama, which invariably involved aspects of female honour or fall from grace. The Victorians were eclectic in all things, and that may well include sexual experience, imagined or real. As Rana Kabbani has suggested, 'the nineteenth century, a conspicuously consuming era, thirsted for variety in its sexual depictions as it craved a variety of products in its markets'.[59] There is indeed a good deal of evidence to suggest that this was the case, particularly in European responses to the sexual opportunities of empire.[60] But this must be seen in terms of a complex duality. In slave market and harem scenes, the Orientalists may make moral statements, or at least permit of this as one possible reading, but they also hint at fantasy and freedoms, an escape from the stifling mores of the West, even if, as is undoubtedly true, the freedoms were male, and involved the further subjection of women. Nudity in Orientalist paintings had a striking and titillating immediacy when compared with the nudity associated with myth or classical times. Stage nudity had, perhaps, to await the twentieth century, but the treatment of women and the spectacle of women within the proscenium arch, particularly in the later nineteenth century, progressively broke the bounds of respectability, ironically at a time when it became socially more acceptable to be an *habitué* of the theatre.

Rana Kabbani concludes her examination of the depiction of women in Orientalist painting by suggesting that: 'Such portraits, in wishing to convey the East, described more accurately, Europe. They portrayed the repressiveness of its social codes, and the heavy hand of its bourgeois morality. The gaze into the Orient had turned, as in a convex mirror, to reflect the Occident that produced it.'[61] But was it so unwitting? Were not Orientalist artists consciously making statements about their own society? Nochlin and Kabbani are highly selective in order to make their points. By looking across a wider range of Orientalist paintings, cultural cross-references become clearer. The Orientalists cease to be radical, imperialist, morally sententious or wildly fantasist. They become culturally conservative, atavistic even, holding up societies to their own to be emulated as much as condemned. Rather than portraying repressive social codes or heavy-handed bourgeois morality, some of them surely mounted an attack on both, albeit in the process betraying their particular brand of nineteenth-century dominant masculinity.

Indeed, what emerges most powerfully from the memoirs and descriptions of journeys written by Orientalist painters is the kind of duality that has been identified in other travel writings.[62] All such works contain a mixture of positive and negative comments, reflecting genuinely held views, the physical and psychological ups and downs of travel, and the responses of the moment. Moreover, there is plenty of evidence that such a mix of attitudes was by no means restricted to the East. Descriptions of the eighteenth-century Grand Tour abound in xenophobic remarks as well as ecstatic discoveries.[63] Among Orientalists, David

Roberts neatly reflects this. He described southern Spain as the 'wild, unpoached game reserve of Europe' for artists and collectors, and regarded the Alhambra as 'unrivalled in the world'; yet he abominated Spanish Catholics and their clergy. Similarly, in Rome, he was astounded by the rich visual splendours of the city and its ceremonies, while abhorring its popery.[64] It may be argued that he always celebrated remains, never contemporaries, but this is not borne out by his many admiring remarks about Arabs and Nubians, although he tended to be condemnatory of Islam. His was a peculiarly Calvinist vision.

W. J. Müller exhibited a similarly powerful duality for that real litmus-test of attitudes from the abolitionist West, the slave market. Müller wrote that 'The scene is of a revolting nature, yet I did not see, as I expected, the dejection and sorrow I was led to imagine'. He went on to describe the manner in which purchasers removed all the clothing of female slaves (as depicted by Gérôme) and pronounced Abyssinians and Circassians to be very beautiful. The negresses were less appealing on account of the large quantities of malodorous tallow fat which they placed in their hair and which melted down their bodies. 'Yet in this place did I feel more delight than any other part of Cairo; the groups and the extraordinary costume can but please the artist. You meet in this place all nations.'[65] Was Müller being callous, or was he perhaps responding to the absence of dejection and sorrow with the realisation that Islamic domestic slavery was of a very different order from the transatlantic trade and the plantation variety?

Thus, the Orientalist painters expressed both sublime fear and a sense of liberating themselves and their art; both admiration for the outward forms of alien religion and anxieties about its inner meanings; both fright at cultural difference and an admiring fascination with characteristics their own society had repressed. Above all they held out a programme for renewal to their own highly urbanised, excessively industrialised and overripe societies.

Yet if there should continue to be debate about this theory of cultural liberation – substituting a society of personal relations, natural responses, hunting, equestrianism and craftsmanship for urban industrialism – there can be no doubt at all that the East provided for artists a technical liberation. As we have seen, metals, fabrics, ceramic and wooden architectural ornament presented considerable challenges of texture, pattern and colour. So did light. For the fierce light of North Africa and the Middle East reversed northern values. It washed out colours, banishing vibrant tints to the shadows. Moreover, the physical difficulties of painting in the East inspired particular responses. Holman Hunt may have painted in the Dead Sea with a brush in one hand and a rifle in the other (though flies and inquisitive passers-by were the more normal problems), but most artists adopted rapid sketching techniques, so that with the help of sketches made on the spot, the painting could be recollected and recreated in the tranquillity of the studio. Moreover, the particular character and speed of execution of water-colours made them particularly amenable to eastern subjects. Water-colouring was invariably seen as a distinctively English technique, and some French and Italian artists sought English masters to tutor them. The East helped to extend the incidence and language of the water-colour.

By the end of the nineteenth century, the East was still offering untold technical inspiration to painters who had moved well beyond the Romantics and Realists of an earlier generation. The vibrant school of artists which emerged in Scotland in the last quarter of the century (most of them constituting 'the Glasgow boys') put themselves at the forefront of European art, helping to create Post-Impressionist styles, partly through contact with the East. Arthur Melville visited Egypt and the Middle East in 1880–82 and produced a fine series of both oils and water-colours which were inspired by the strong contrasts of powerful light and shade, colour and pattern. In his *Arab Interior, Turkish Bath* and, above all, *Awaiting an Audience with the Pasha*, he recreated in a fresh and radical form the long-standing fascination with the abstract patterning of shutters, light, architecture and carpets, as well as with the drama and ritual of Arab life. He achieved what Billcliffe has described as a remarkable stylisation and syncopation of compositional rhythms.[66] Sir John Lavery visited Morocco, while George Henry and E. A. Hornel went to Japan in 1893–94, bringing back a strikingly innovative series of oils and water-colours which contributed to the extensive fascination with Japanese arts in the Glasgow of the period.[67]

While India offered opportunities to artists for a long continuation of the tradition of the picturesque (as in the work of Edward Lear) and an obsession with the grandeur and magnificence of the durbar, pursued by artists as varied as Frederick Christian Lewis (in India, 1839–49, 1851–55, 1863–66 and 1874–75)[68] and Mortimer Menpes (who painted the Delhi Durbar of 1903),[69] it was still to North Africa that twentieth-century artists turned. Kandinsky and Klee both travelled there, developing their sense of colour and design. In a whole succession of paintings. Matisse continued the nineteenth-century fascination with the odalisque down to the 1930s. Wyndham Lewis also journeyed into the interior of Morocco in the 1930s, writing and drawing as he did so.[70] In this work some of the angularity and machine-like components of the vorticist movement clearly survives. Quite apart from the influence of sub-Saharan African art on twentieth-century artists, which lies beyond the scope of this study, we can see North Africa as a continuing source of inspiration for the abstract expressionists, fauvists, and in a different way, a leading vorticist. Thus the artistic interest in the Orient far transcends the obsessions of the allegedly conservative nineteenth-century schools. And in each case the artists looked for technical inspiration in the context of what were often seen as alluring social values and craft and design traditions.

Hence we find a great paradox. For the modern critics of Orientalism, the Orientalists portrayed the decayed and backward civilisations of the East in order to render them more amenable to the economic, cultural and political transformations of imperialism. To display their moral disapprobation, they used an outdated realism and clung to it long after 'high art' had moved on. But if Orientalism is read in alternative and more convincing ways, as a series of reactions and lessons to the artists' own societies, as a means of extending the language of art through the experience of other climates and other artistic and architectural traditions, as movements which need to be set into a much wider chronological context, we arrive at a very different conclusion. The nineteenth-century Orientalists were not culturally radical and technically conservative; they were culturally conservative and technically innovative. Far from offering an artistic programme for imperialism, they were finding in the East ancient verities lost in their own civilisation. Many of them set out not to condemn the East, but to discover echoes of a world they had lost. For their twentieth-century counterparts this lost world involved hidden emotional states, the psychological drama of abstraction or of designs of whirling movement or deconstructed geometrical elements. Yet again the East offered inspiration for a radical movement to refresh itself anew at deep wells of colour and light, pattern and design.

Notes

1   Lynne Thornton, *The Orientalists: Painter–Travellers, 1828–1908* (Paris, 1983).
2   The Mathaf Gallery, London, founded in 1975.
3   Bryony Llewellyn, *The Orient Observed: Images of the Middle East from the Searight Collection* (London, 1989).
4   James Thompson, *The East: Imagined, Experienced, Remembered, Orientalist Nineteenth-Century Painting* (Dublin and Liverpool, 1988), p. 18.
5   Thornton, *Orientalists*, p. 13.
6   Catalogues include The Fine Art Society, *Eastern Encounters: Orientalist Painters of the Nineteenth Century* (London, 1978); The Fine Art Society, *Travellers beyond the Grand Tour* (London, 1980); Donald A. Rosenthal, *Orientalism: The Near East in French Painting, 1800–1880* (Rochester, NY, 1982); Mildred Archer and Ronald Lightbown, *India Observed: India as viewed by British Artists, 1760–1860* (London, 1982); The Fine Art Society, *The Travels of Edward Lear* (London, 1983); Patrick Conner, *The Inspiration of Egypt: its Influence on British Artists, Travellers and Designers, 1700–1900* (Brighton, 1983); Mary Anne Stevens, *The Orientalists: Delacroix to Matisse, European Painters in North Africa and the Near East* (London, 1984); Bryony Llewellyn and Charles Newton, *The People and Places of Constantinople: Watercolours by Amadeo, Count Preziosi* (London,

1985); Peter A. Clayton, *David Roberts' Egypt*, Weinreb Architectural Gallery (London, 1985); Sarah Searight, Bryony Llewellyn *et al.*, *Romantic Lebanon: the European View, 1700–1900* (London, 1986); Helen Guiterman and Bryony Llewellyn, *David Roberts* (London, 1987); Francis Greenacre and Sheena Stoddard, *W. J. Müller 1812–1845* (Bristol, 1991); Llewellyn, *Orient Observed* and Thompson, *The East*. The Birmingham Exhibition, 'J. F. Lewis and the Orientalists', took place in 1988. The Fine Art Society proclaimed itself as having held seventy exhibitions of Orientalist interest in its hundred-year history, *Eastern Encounters*, p. 5. See also Michelle Verrier, *The Orientalists* (London, 1979).

7   Patrick Conner, *The China Trade, 1600–1860* (Brighton, 1986); C. A. Bayly (ed.), *The Raj, India and the British, 1600–1947* (London, 1990); the Macartney Exhibition was at the British Museum and did not have a catalogue.

8   *fine material for a dream . . . ? A Reappraisal of Orientalism: 19th and 20th Century Fine Art and Popular Culture Juxtaposed with Paintings, Video and Photography by Contemporary Artists* (Preston, Hull and Oldham, 1992).

9   Sotheby's, *Important Orientalist Paintings from the Collection of Coral Petroleum Inc.* (New York, 1985).

10   Mathaf Gallery, *Lands Without Shade: the Orient Through Western Eyes*, an Exhibition at the Zamana Gallery (London, 1985).

11   Linda Nochlin, 'The Imaginary Orient', *Art in America* (May 1983), pp. 118–31, 187–91; Marcia Pointon, *Bonnington, Francia and Wyld: an Exhibition at the Victoria and Albert Museum* (London, 1985).

12   Nochlin, 'Imaginary Orient', p. 119.

13   Almost all of those cited in note 6 above ignore 'imperialism' and ideological approaches. Stevens, *Orientalists*, mentions Said's approach, only to reject it as 'too simplistic', p. 19. The stance of the various exhibitions is interestingly implied by the illustrations on their covers. The Royal Academy chose Renoir's *Girl with a Falcon*, a great painting and marginal to the Orientalist school. (The back cover, Bauernfeind's *Market in Jaffa*, fitted the Orientalist canon better, though it is not an ideologically charged painting.)

14   Thompson, *The East*. See in particular his acute criticism of Marcia Pointon's Nochlin-style deconstruction of a Wyld water-colour on p. 162.

15   See, for example, the unpaginated 'Reappraising Orientalism: a personal statement' by Amrit Wilson in *fine material for a dream . . . ?*, where Orientalist art is seen as the product of xenophobia and race and cultural hatred.

16   Nochlin, 'Imaginary Orient', pp. 127–9. This notion of absences is true of many other periods and forms of art. To give but one example, the twentieth-century art of the English rural idyll attempted to convey timelessness, an absence of social change, of mechanisation, of modern transportation, and above all of the industrial city. In the inter-war years artists travelled around by car, but the car did not appear in their pictures. Artists like the brothers John and Paul Nash and Graham Sutherland were themselves devotees of speed and movement, but produced timeless, peaceful rural views. Even the railway posters of the period pursued the same timeless rural images, where horse-drawn ploughs predominated over the, by then common, tractor.

17   Rana Kabbani, *Europe's Myths of Orient: Devise and Rule* (London, 1986).

18   Nochlin, 'Imaginary Orient', p. 189.

19   Thornton, *Orientalists*, p. 20 and entries on individual artists like Wyld, Schreyer, Haag, Fortuny, Benjamin-Constant, Wilda, Rosati and Kosler, Preziosi, Swoboda (the younger), L. C. Müller and Lamplough all sold to the Prince of Wales and other members of British and European royal families.

20   Benjamin-Constant, Fromentin and Schreyer enjoyed good American sales, while Charles Gleyre (1818–74) worked for the rich American John Lowell. The Maltese Shranz family made a living by drawing views of Turkey, Egypt, Syria and Palestine

for wealthy travellers. Preziosi followed in this tradition, Llewellyn and Newton, *Constantinople*, p. 6.

21   Stevens, *Orientalists*, p. 132. The message to Fromentin that horses sold better than camels came from his dealer Beugniet.

22   Vivant Denon, *Voyage dans la Basse et la Haute Egypte* (Paris, 1802), trans. as *Travels in Upper and Lower Egypt* by A. Aiken (London, 1903); *Description de L'Egypte etc.* (Paris, 1809). Peter A. Clayton, *The Re-Discovery of Ancient Egypt: Artists and Travellers in the 19th Century* (London, 1982).

23   Such artists include William Hodges, Thomas and William Daniell, Sydney Parkinson, John Webber, P. G. de Loutherberg, George Chinnery, James and William Fraser and, in Africa, Thomas Baines. See, among many other sources, Archer and Lightbown, *India Observed*; Bayly, *Raj*; Mildred Archer, *Early Views of India: the Picturesque Journeys of Thomas and William Daniell* (London, 1980); Mildred Archer and Toby Falk, *India Revealed: the Art and Adventures of James and William Fraser, 1801–1835* (London, 1989). See also *Art and the East India Trade*, a catalogue of a Victoria and Albert Museum exhibition (London, 1970) and C. F. James, *An Artist on the March: Paintings of India, Abyssinia and Kashmir by Colonel Cornelius Francis James, 1838–1889* (St Peter Port, 1989).

24   Bernard Smith, *European Vision and the South Pacific* (New Haven, 1985, first published 1959). See also Bernard Smith, *Australian Painting 1788–1960* (Melbourne, 1971) and *Imagining the Pacific* (New Haven and London, 1992).

25   John M. MacKenzie, *Propaganda and Empire* (Manchester, 1984), pp. 184–5; Christine Bolt, *Victorian Attitudes to Race* (London, 1971).

26   Thornton, *Orientalists*, p. 46. Vernet was an artist who did depict the violence of European upon North African. See, for example, his *The Battle of Somah*.

27   Guidebook to Leighton House, Holland Park, London.

28   Nochlin, 'Imaginary Orient', p. 127.

29   Greenacre and Stoddard, *Müller*, p. 11.

30   Quoted in Thompson, *The East*, p. 54.

31   Quoted in Thornton, *Orientalists*, p. 104.

32   Llewellyn and Newton, *Constantinople*, introduction; Wilkie quoted in Thompson, *The East*, pp. 157–8.

33   Gerald M. Ackerman, *The Life and Work of Jean-Léon Gérôme* (Paris, 1986), p. 44 and *passim*.

34   Christopher Thacker, *The Wildness Pleases* (London, 1983).

35   There are many such paintings, but see as examples Delacroix's *Chasse au Tigre*, Vernet's *Chasse au Lion*, William Strutt's *The Terrible Scare* and Alfred de Dreux's *The Combat*.

36   Richard Ormond, *Sir Edwin Landseer* (London, 1982). A discussion of hunting and animal violence in painting can be found in John M. MacKenzie, *The Empire of Nature* (Manchester, 1988), pp. 31–4.

37   Mark Girouard, *The Return to Camelot* (New Haven, 1981).

38   Ackerman, *Gérôme*, pp. 95, 132, 261.

39   W. J. Müller, Vernet, Gérôme and Fromentin are four examples. There are many depictions of the hunt and of its results, as in Gérôme's *Pelt Merchant of Cairo*. Ackerman, *Gérôme*, pp. 80–1.

40   Elizabeth Longford, *A Pilgrimage of Passion: the Life of Wilfrid Scawen Blunt* (London, 1979), pp. 129, 142, 168, 413.

41   Kabbani, *Europe's Myths*, p. 79; Nochlin, 'Imaginary Orient', p. 126.

42   Joanna de Groot, '"Sex" and "Race": the construction of language and image in the nineteenth century' in Susan Mendus and Jane Rendall (eds), *Sexuality and Subordination: Interdisciplinary Studies of Gender in the Nineteenth Century* (London, 1989), pp. 89–128.

43   Thornton, *Orientalists*, p. 38.

44   Malcolm Warner, 'The question of faith: Orientalism, Christianity and Islam' in
        Stevens, *Orientalists*, pp. 32–9.

45   Martin J. Wiener, *English Culture and the Decline of the Industrial Spirit, 1850–
        1980* (Cambridge, 1981).

46   See the entries on these artists in Thornton, *Orientalists*; Stevens, *Orientalists* and
        Thompson, *The East*. Charles Gleyre also found Cairo oppressive because there
        were too many painters there and sought to escape into the desert, *fine material
        for a dream . . . ?*, p. 7. Ackerman (p. 92) has described Gérôme's *Arabs Crossing
        the Desert* as a masterpiece of heroic stoicism.

47   Wyndham Lewis, *Journey into Barbary*, ed. C. J. Fox (Harmondsworth, 1987).

48   See the entries on these artists in Thornton, *Orientalists*.

49   Such European presences are to be found in the work of William Simpson,
        Francis Spilsbury, David Roberts, Horace Vernet and Adrien Dauzats, among
        others.

50   *fine material for a dream . . . ?*, p. 9.

51   Quoted, *ibid.*, p. 14.

52   Stevens, *Orientalists*, p. 142. See also Ackerman, *Gérôme*, p. 132.

53   Delacroix remarked that 'the most beautiful pictures I have seen are certain
        Persian carpets', quoted in Robert Irwin, 'The Orient and the West from Bona-
        parte to T. E. Lawrence' in Stevens, *Orientalists*, p. 26.

54   *fine material for a dream . . . ?*, p. 14.

55   Ackerman, *Gérôme*, pp. 50, 52, 99.

56   Thornton, *Orientalists*, p. 21. The Paris exhibitions coincided with the found-
        ing of the *Société des Peintres Orientalistes Français* in 1893, reflecting the late
        nineteenth-century comeback by the Orientalists.

57   Michael Booth, *English Melodrama* (London, 1965) and *Victorian Spectacular
        Theatre, 1850–1910* (London, 1981).

58   Ralph Hyde, *Panoramania! The Art and Entertainment of the 'All-Embracing
        View'* (London, 1988) lists many 'Orientalist' panoramas. See also John Sweetman,
        *The Oriental Obsession: Islamic Inspiration in British and American Art and
        Architecture, 1500–1920* (Cambridge, 1988), pp. 157–8.

59   Kabbani, *Europe's Myths*, p. 70.

60   Ronald Hyam, *Empire and Sexuality: the British Experience* (Manchester, 1990).

61   Kabbani, *Europe's Myths*, p. 85.

62   Dennis Porter, *Haunted Journeys: Desire and Transgression in European Travel
        Writing* (Princeton, 1991).

63   Jeremy Black, *The British and the Grand Tour* (London, 1985).

64   Katharine Sim, *David Roberts RA, 1796–1864: a Biography* (London, 1984), pp.
        61, 70–4, 79–80, 278. See also Helen Guiterman, *David Roberts RA, 1796–
        1864* (London, 1978) which contains extracts from Roberts's diaries and letters.

65   Greenacre and Stoddard, *Müller*, p. 120.

66   Roger Billcliffe, *The Glasgow Boys: the Glasgow School of Painting 1875–1895*
        (London, 1985), p. 116. In an interesting connection with musical and theatrical
        developments of the period, Melville also painted *The Javanese Dancers*, 'a bril-
        liant impression of whirling angular figures in loose crimson garments' (p. 295).
        See also Chapters 6 and 7.

67   Billcliffe, *Glasgow Boys*, pp. 222, 255–64. See also Elizabeth Cumming, *Glasgow
        1990: Art and Design* (Amsterdam, 1992).

68   Sweetman, *Oriental Obsession*, p. 154.

69   Mortimer Menpes, *The Durbar* (London, 1903).

70   Lewis, *Journey into Barbary*.

4

Orientalism in architecture

THIS CHAPTER and the next deal with the related areas of architecture and design, the exterior and interior forms of the European response to the Orient in the structural and decorative arts. Yet the influence of the East on each seems on the face of it very different in both scale and quality. While there are numerous examples of Orientalist architecture, together they never really constitute a movement. They seem to be the product of stylistic fads and fancies, explorations of the exotic possibilities of the architecture of other cultures. The sheer range of eclectic experimentation, together with the critical debates about climatic and cultural, religious and geographical suitability which it stimulated, prevented the emergence of a continuing and influential set of oriental forms which might have seriously modified European architecture. In the nineteenth-century 'battle of the styles' between Gothic and classical, the Orientalist interest constituted a set of relatively minor, geographically distant and virtually unrelated skirmishes.[1] Yet there was some serious discussion of the significance of the example of the East and a wildly syncretic Orientalism became particularly prominent in the architecture of leisure.

With the decorative arts, however, the influence of oriental forms, motifs and colourings, together with the practices and techniques of Asian craftsmen, became increasingly influential as the nineteenth century wore on. Eastern styles, however modified in the process of transfer,

become central to the development of interior decoration, fabrics, carpets, ceramics, metalwork, jewellery, even furniture, and the interest of
designers in the Orient reveals a capacity to transcend the work of a
single generation, feeding into repeated waves of creative reaction.
Throughout this movement, the oriental approach to crafts and design
is extolled to a remarkable degree, with very little cultural and racial
relativism, although it is of course also subjected to severe criticism,
particularly by John Ruskin. These interests often feed into the revulsion
against industrial, machine-made products (an animus paradoxically shared
by Ruskin) which is so characteristic of the second half of the nineteenth
century. Thus, while the Orient seemed to have little influence on overall
architectural form, interest in the motifs and materials of its arts and
crafts transformed decorative elements, interior design and the contents
of buildings. Architects as exponents of a high art appeared merely to
flirt with the East, while designers passionately embraced it.

Yet this distinction should not be carried too far. As we shall see,
many architects attempted to match craft work and contents with architectural form, at least for individual rooms. Architects turned to the East,
albeit a perceived Orient, to express changing attitudes and moods, fresh
functions and new pastimes. What started out as a means of flattering
the sensibilities and extending the range of experience of the aristocracy
was ultimately transferred to leisure pursuits for the masses, in what I
call 'demotic Orientalism', an architecture for popular culture. Moreover, there were serious debates about the character and attractions
of aspects of eastern architecture and some architects of distinction
genuinely extended the language of western styles through a remarkable
creative eclecticism. This stimulation from eastern ideas was greatly extended in the twentieth century, both through the development of radical new ideas and the re-emergence of creative pastiche in postmodernism.
Moreover, on another level, an Indian form, the bungalow, became a
central aspect of an architectural global culture, carrying all before it in
the twentieth century. It became a favoured living space, first as a seaside holiday home and later as one of the characteristic expressions of
suburbia.

Tasting the architecture of the Orient: gardens, rooms and experimental buildings

There have been repeated essays in an Orientalist architecture since the
seventeenth century. These have been concerned with imitation and
adaptation, with the creation of mood, and in so far as they depict the
Orient they do so indirectly. But while the form is strikingly different
from written or pictorial description, such architectural expressions are

not of course ideologically neutral. The character of the adaptation, in presenting a culturally filtered analysis of the original, carries its own message. Above all, ideas about the East are conveyed through function. The setting and/or use of an eclectic or exotic building makes statements (which some may see as no more vague or indirect than those conveyed by the written word or the visual arts) about the society that allegedly contributes it. Whether such statements are negative or positive lies partly in the eye of the beholder, but the technique of cultural cross-referencing once more aids understanding.

A number of scholars have examined the influence of chinoiserie, Indian, ancient Egyptian and Islamic styles in the West, but as historians of art and architecture they have been principally concerned with aesthetic influences and judgements, and until recently they have tended to ignore more modern expressions of oriental influence, particularly in exhibitions, railway stations, theatres, cinemas and the architecture of the seaside, piers, bandstands, towers and ballrooms.[2] Their works tend to concentrate on the taste of the aristocracy and upper middle classes between the late seventeenth and nineteenth centuries, with 'one-off' buildings, temporary structures or rooms. Their interest wanes when oriental styles become democratised. Yet it is 'demotic oriental' forms which are in many ways the most interesting, in some cases the most enduring, and certainly the most suggestive of messages and ideas.

As we have seen, the striking fact about Orientalism in architecture is that until the later nineteenth century it seems to have had such little fundamental influence. Until that time we apparently find a number of temporary fashions being pursued by a few architects to the aristocracy, controversial ideas much haggled over, major movements frequently expected, but never quite materialising. Part of the problem was the sheer range of oriental models and the manner in which their reputation tended to fluctuate according to contemporary events and cultural attitudes. Thus we find Chinese styles provoking considerable interest (and also a strenuous critique) in the late seventeenth, eighteenth and early nineteenth centuries; by the 1840s, after the First China War, they are in decline and by the 1860s, after the Second, they are virtually eclipsed. Japan takes over as a Far Eastern inspiration and exemplar. The ancient Egyptian had some application to public monumentality and private rituals, but generally it was too heavily bizarre for wider use. An Egyptian craze, particularly in interior design and decorative arts, was prominent at the turn of the eighteenth and nineteenth centuries and was renewed in several subsequent decades, but in many respects it was another 'revival' which never became fully animated. Many notable examples can still be singled out, but until the twentieth-century cinema, only a minority of the population ever beheld a building with Egyptian influences.

John Sweetman has rightly argued that Moorish and Islamic styles were more influential, and it is certainly true that they were applied to a greater range of buildings and rooms.[3] They could be more effectively blended with major European forms (classical and Gothic) and Indian elements and became particularly important in the later nineteenth century as the architectural language of both exhibitions and leisure. Nevertheless, the notion that British rule in India should produce a significant switch to Indian styles, whether Mughal or 'Hindu', was never translated into reality. Humphrey Repton's idea that the Indian might become an important, even national style for the British was fiercely resisted, despite its appropriateness in relation to imperial power and growing economic realities, and some major 'Indian' projects were never executed.[4] The Indian Museum was never built and appropriate buildings like the Imperial Institute (which received a high proportion of its funding from India) and the India Office generally avoided cross-cultural architectural allusions, except in their sculptures and some aspects of decoration.[5] It was only in India in the late nineteenth and early twentieth centuries that truly hybrid styles were formed out of Gothic, Byzantine, 'Saracenic', Mughal and classical, in railway stations and at New Delhi.[6]

But what messages did each of these complex and internally disparate styles convey? Although substantial Chinese 'houses' appeared at Drottningholm and Potsdam in the 1750s and 1760s, as the climax of a process developing from the Trianon at Versailles, the first Orientalist buildings in Britain were exotic additions to garden 'furniture'. Chinese 'temples' and pavilions, often bearing only a remote similarity to the real thing, were built in the eighteenth century at Stourhead, Stowe, Studley Royal, Alton Towers, Shugborough, Woburn, Wroxton, Blair in Scotland, and elsewhere. The Duke of Cumberland, second son of George II, built a Chinese pavilion at Virginia Water, together with an elaborate junk known as 'The Mandarin'. Many of these had been inspired by Sir William Chambers's *Designs of Chinese Buildings, Furniture, Dresses, Machines and Utensils ...* of 1757. Chinese 'rails' (trellis fences) and bridges became a feature of the 'jardin anglo-chinois', the attempt to create the picturesque and irregular, yet intimate characteristics of Chinese gardens. The open latticework, which was seen as distinctively Chinese, lent itself particularly to the construction of aviaries, which became another addition to the accoutrements of the great houses of the period.

If the Chinese craze reflected fascination with a contemporary culture, the spell of ancient Egypt represented interests that were geographically closer, but more distant in time. Obelisks, pyramids, sphinxes and 'Egyptian' mausoleums appeared on English estates (and occasionally town squares and cemeteries) from the beginning of the eighteenth

III   Ludwig Deutsch (1855–1935), *At Prayer*. Mosques, prayer and devotions were a common subject for Orientalist painters. It is hard to see such paintings as denigrating their originals, however idealised the images may be. On the contrary, the figure has a handsome and pious dignity, in which the centrality of religion amidst the fine detail of oriental design is intended to convey a sense of a reverential world the West has lost.

Ludwig Deutsch (1855–1935), *The Scribe*. The scribe is depicted as a learned   **IV**
and dignified individual, surrounded by examples of oriental design, furniture
and leather book binding. Critics of Orientalist painting have suggested that
damage to architectural detail was used to indicate a decadent culture. While the
doorway exhibits such damage, there seems very little that is decadent about
other elements of the image. It is much more likely that the painter was authen-
tically illustrating the kind of damage which could undoubtedly be seen on
Middle Eastern buildings.

V   The Arab Hall in Lord Leighton's
house in Holland Park, one of the
many Islamic interiors of Victorian
England. He recreated the cool
repose of a Middle Eastern interior
with tiles (inset, right) and architectural features brought back
from the East.

Arab Interior by Arthur Melville (1855–1904), a study in the geometrical patterns of the *mashrabiyya* allowing filtered light into a sumptuous interior.   **VI**

century, and interest in the style was re-emphasised by Napoleon's invasion in 1798 and Nelson's victory at the Battle of the Nile. Egyptian forms now took on a patriotic ambience[7] although, bizarrely, a Chinese pagoda and bridge were put up in St James's Park as part of the Nile celebrations, only to be burnt down when set alight by fireworks. Indeed, it may be that there was almost an alternation in Chinese and Egyptian taste in the eighteenth century, the one expressing delicacy and refinement in asymmetry and fluidity of line, the other grandeur, stark geometrical forms and solidity. Obelisks and other 'Egyptian' monuments became almost commonplace in the nineteenth century, including the major 'Egyptification' of the decorative design and street furniture of the Embankment in London after the arrival and erection of Cleopatra's Needle in 1877–78. At Biddulph Grange (Staffordshire) in the 1850s James Bateman brought together Egyptian and Chinese gardens, although the latter was much easier to express in botanical terms.[8]

Indeed, this distinction represents a significant difference in respect of these garden structures. Many, particularly the Egyptian, were divorced from any attempt at an equivalent landscape or botany. For climatic reasons this was also true of Islamic structures like the 'Moorish temple' at Wroxton, the 'mosque' at Stourhead, and the various 'Turkish tents' which enjoyed an extensive, but necessarily brief vogue. At Kew Gardens in the 1760s, Sir William Chambers, who had travelled extensively in the East, built his great pagoda (which survives), his 'mosque' and 'alhambra' (which have disappeared). At Kew these represented exotic architectural expressions of the plant taxonomy which was its central purpose, but even here there was little attempt to place these structures within appropriate botanical contexts.

It would be wrong, however, to see these structures as merely exotic appendages, garden arabesques, as it were. Nor were they simply adding to a developing architectural taxonomy, rendered in time with increasing accuracy. They reflected a developing interest in the elegant pursuit of alfresco leisure: gentle walks within an intimate and tamed, yet picturesque and intriguing landscape, heightened by structures associated with water, islands, rocks and animals; entertainments and meals taken in Turkish tents or other more stable pavilions; the display of rare animals, birds, shrubs and other plants. Thus the garden became a sort of outdoor 'cabinet of curiosities', increasingly controlled and classified as the eighteenth century wore on. Although the vogue for chinoiserie passed through phases – Chinese rococo to the 1770s, a fresh burst of interest associated with the Macartney embassy to China and its associated publications in the 1790s, and a brief resurgence of fascination at the time of the first China War, 1839–42 – the existing buildings in the better known gardens provided a perennial interest. Moreover, with increasing botanical exploration Chinese, and later Japanese structures could indeed be placed in appropriate contexts. Chinese and Japanese gardens extended the form, mood and plant design of gardens in ways that were supposed to mirror those of other garden-loving cultures, although the British examples were always botanically more eclectic, particularly once the plants of the Himalayas became better known.

Thus, whereas oriental monuments and structures had first been introduced into formal and alien landscapes, they were later used as an integral part of a liberated aesthetic, romantic and sublime, both wild and tamed. The oriental garden and its associated pieces of Orientalism represented a liberation from the formalism of Palladianism, the heavy luxuriance of the baroque, the rigidities of the formal garden or the extensive pseudo-wildness of its landscaped successor. Oriental forms offered the irregular and asymmetrical as a relief from the rigidities of classical rules. Thus the Orient offered an alternative court of aesthetic appeal, as it was to do in so many of the arts from the Romantic period. It represented a foil, an alter-ego, even an id, attractive precisely because it threw off the restraints of accepted conventions. If it revealed strikingly new, even outrageous forms and fresh moods through which the out-doors could be enjoyed, it also offered an extended language of materials. Wood could be used in original and interesting ways; tile, ceramics and textiles could be incorporated into structures to offer a new richness of decoration and texture. And these structures could be married to natural, or artificially natural features, hydrographic and geological, botanical and sculptural.

Leaving botanical correctness on one side, the idea took more popular forms at the celebrated gardens and other places of entertainment on the south bank of the Thames, where it was carried through into the nineteenth century and could be enjoyed by a wider cross-section of the social classes of the capital. In the Vauxhall, Ranelagh and (later) Cremorne gardens, Orientalism could be linked to new forms of spectacular entertainment, the use of lights and fireworks, reconstructions of events, pictures and pageants, botanical and zoological wonders, as well as the outdoor enjoyment of food, music and dancing. Vauxhall boasted a pseudo-Chinese arcade (in fact it was mainly Gothic), a Turkish tent and a rotunda that was occasionally described as resembling a great Persian pavilion. Painted pictures of Indian scenes could be viewed from the windows and verandahs of the latter. Ranelagh had a Chinese pavilion and kiosk; Cremorne a pagoda. They were more or less approximations, but they were named as such and the association of the relevant culture with gaiety and leisure was clearly indicated. Thus the oriental features of the popular as well as the great private gardens were not just excrescences, quaint and supposedly objective representations of

another culture, but the means to a liberation of something more than
fresh aesthetic potential for the West. The East, however much it may
have been a fabricated East, was used as an aid to unlock fresh personality traits, a richer imaginative expression, a wider scope for leisure and
entertainment. Illuminated and pyrotechnic entertainments occurred without oriental references, and could have developed, of course, outside
eastern contexts, but Orientalism remained an important mood-former,
an essential part of the total picture.

By Victorian times, the municipal public park became the national
expression of the garden movement, often displaying exotic plants and
landscapes, as well as eastern-inspired monuments, furniture and buildings, such as bandstands, 'kiosks' and conservatories or palm-houses.
The relationship of many of these to the East was often relatively obscure, but through rooflines, domes, ironwork, statuary and the palms
themselves, it was clear that a generalised exotic Other, vaguely related
to the East, was being conveyed. In some places, however, particularly
at the seaside, more specific Chinese or Japanese gardens were created.
Thus the park and its associated structures became a public expression,
albeit less well focused, of what had previously been in the private domain. These later 'demotic' forms blended with the architecture of leisure, entertainment and recreation, rational or otherwise, as expressed in
exhibitions, theatres, cinemas, seaside piers and ballrooms, examined later
in this chapter.

But if Orientalism came to be closely associated with leisure, recreation, entertainment and the refreshment of health, it seldom assaulted
the major architectural structures of the period. It is tempting to argue
that the classical houses and palaces of the eighteenth century and the
great public buildings of the nineteenth century represented a serious
indoor world, the world of business, government, rationality, learning
and culture, while the outdoor park with its wildly eclectic structures
acted at its foil, irrational emotion, undisciplined leisure, occasional wild
abandon. Thus the private and municipal estates represented the inner
and outer worlds of metropolis and empire. This glibly seductive interpretation, however, does not work. There was far too much aesthetic
interpenetration between the two. The park, far from representing an
exotic Other, was integral. It was malleable: like the human personality,
tastes and experiences that it was intended to reflect, it was capable of
development and often was, from generation to generation.

If great buildings remained classical or, later, Gothic, they did so
with their Moorish, Egyptian, or Indian rooms, their Chinese wallpaper,
their proudly displayed ceramics and ivories, their 'Chinese' Chippendale
furniture, 'japanned' work, screens and chests, musical intruments and
cased clocks. Indoor accessories and outdoor features could represent

new facets of cultural experience and artistic enjoyment, but we still need some explanation for the fact that the basic form of cities, of public and private buildings, remained stubbornly western. This was partly because of the powerful criticism levelled against the oriental fads. The fashions for chinoiserie, Egyptian and Moorish styles were strongly attacked. There were those who abused Chinese architecture and design, as lacking rules, intellectual distinction or aesthetic appeal. Its products suffered from a superfluity of ornament, a self-indulgence of form, an eccentricity of purpose; they were frivolous, light and insubstantial, entirely unsuitable for the business of serious architecture. The Egyptian was seen to be too monumental and bombastic, both inappropriate to the climate and pagan in form. The Moorish and Indian were likewise climatically alien and spiritually threatening, although both were to become acceptable when used for individual rooms (like libraries and billiard-rooms) or buildings with specific functions, like baths or masonic lodges.

Even without such critics, however, it is hard to see how oriental architectural styles could have successfully assaulted western forms. It is very doubtful that Chinese characteristics – as perceived by the West – such as multiple roofs, curvaceous ogee rooflines, the treatment of external surfaces, lightness of design, open fretwork, and eccentric fenestration, could ever, in practical terms, be applied to major buildings. They were amenable to picturesque experimentation in gateways, lodges, dairies and workers' cottages, but in nothing more substantial than these. Objections to their application to more extensive works were as much practical as aesthetic. The wholesale use of Egyptian forms, with their extremes of monumentality, angularity, density of stone, flat roofs and lack of fenestration, also seemed impractical, except in very rare cases such as the Egyptian Hall in Piccadilly, built by William Bullock in 1812. It was supposedly a free adaptation of the temple of Hathor, adorned with statues of Isis and Osiris, a sphinx, pylons around the fenestration, Egyptian bulbous columns and capitals, and a prolific use of meaningless hieroglyphs. It was much criticised when it opened, but it succeeded in drawing attention to itself, particularly when it housed the exhibition of sculptures and artefacts from Giovanni Belzoni's Egyptian expeditions in the early 1820s. Other examples included the Egyptian houses at Hertford and Penzance, the Civil and Military Library in Devonport (all dating from the 1820s and 1830s) and Temple Mills at Leeds of 1842, where flax production – with its association with the ancient world – was sited in adaptations of the temples at Edfu and Dendera.

These objections did not seem to apply so powerfully to some of the forms of Indian and Islamic architecture, even if open courtyards and reception halls, loggias and blank walls seemed wholly unsuited to a northern climate. Christopher Wren had expressed interest in the principles

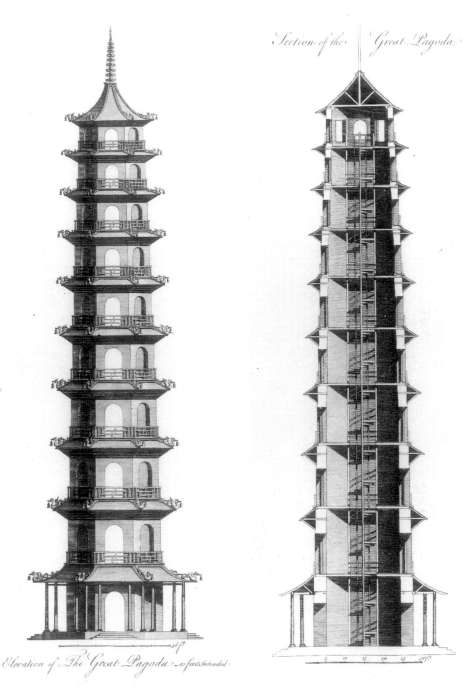

Section of the Great Pagoda

Elevation of The Great Pagoda as first Intended

6   The Great Pagoda at Kew, elevation and section, the only survivor of Sir William Chambers's eclectic group of buildings at the royal gardens, dating from the 1760s. Though never emulated in scale, it set a fashion for Chinese and other garden architecture designed to match both celebratory moods and exotic botanies.

of the Islamic dome and in the course of the eighteenth century the architecture of the Islamic and Hindu East became better known and understood. The nabobs of the East India Company constituted a group of patrons who were likely to make cultural references to the sources of their new wealth and status or be reminded of the settings in which they had secured fame and fortune, although in reality very few of them did. After the visits of Thomas Hodges and Thomas and William Daniell to India in the 1780s and 1790s, the publication of their magnificent sets of engravings of Indian buildings might have been expected to stimulate fresh interest.[9] But given the increasingly important position of India in the British economy, in British public life, and therefore in the British cultural experience, once again it is the relative paucity of Indian buildings, rather than their abundance, that is striking.

There were Indian garden temples, pavilions or 'minarets' at Preston Hall in Scotland, Muntham, Sussex, Melchet Park, Wiltshire, and the Scottish home of the East India Company general, Sir Hector Munro, at Novar.[10] He also built an extraordinary folly, the gates of Negapatam, on a hilltop at Evanton, Easter Ross. George Dance the Younger rebuilt the Guildhall in London with a 'Hindu Gothic' façade in 1788, employing pointed and cusped arches together with 'minarets'. Samuel Pepys Cockerell added a Mughal dome to the eccentric classicism of Warren Hastings's Daylesford House, Gloucestershire, in the 1780s. Later, Colonel Robert Smith, who had been an engineer in Bengal, built 'Indian' houses for himself at Paignton and Nice in the 1850s. But the only major essay in the Indian country house in England was Sezincote, the extraordinary confection of Sir Christopher Cockerell, designed by his brother Samuel Pepys Cockerell in about 1805, in Gloucestershire. Significantly, the Sezincote guidebook proudly proclaims that the house is the 'only Moghul building to have survived in Western Europe'.[11] It was built with a tent-room, a temple to Surya, brahmin bulls, and gardens influenced by Thomas Daniell, whom Cockerell knew well, and Humphrey Repton.

Sezincote almost certainly had a considerable influence on the development of ideas for the Prince Regent's 'Pavilion' at Brighton, where, significantly, the plans for William Porden's Chinese building were abandoned in favour of Nash's striking 'Indian' structure, which harmonised with Porden's earlier stable-block. At the Brighton Pavilion the perceived appropriateness of the various oriental styles was perfectly represented in the marriage of an Indian exterior to a Chinese interior, flaunting lurid Chinese colour combinations, an excess of gilding, and a vast collection of chinoiserie furniture, accessories and ornaments.[12] It is hard to imagine what Indian soldiers made of it when it was considered culturally appropriate as a nursing-home for the wounded of Indian regiments during the First World War.[13]

If at the Brighton pavilion an oriental exterior cloaked an incongruously different eastern interior, many western buildings harboured exotic rooms. Some important examples over a lengthy period include Thomas Hope's set of oriental interiors (Indian and Egyptian) at his Duchess Street mansion, dating from the 1790s and opened to the public; James Playfair's Egyptian billiard-room at Cairness House, Aberdeenshire of 1793; Egyptian halls at Stowe and Craven Cottage; and the remarkable Egyptian chapter-room of the freemasons' lodge in Queen Street, Edinburgh, dating from the beginning of the twentieth century. Henry Holland's Chinese drawing-room for the Prince of Wales at Carlton House, dating from the 1790s, was one of many such rooms which continued to be inserted in country houses throughout the nineteenth century. Lord Armstrong's Cragside, built between 1869 and 1884,

7   Bullock's Egyptian Halls, Piccadilly, by P. F. Robinson. A classic instance of the influence of Egyptian ruins newly rediscovered in the West. The Halls were used for many appropriate functions and, before demolition early in the twentieth century, briefly became a cinema.

contained Bamboo and Japanese rooms, and Norman Shaw blended Gothic and oriental throughout the decoration of the house. William Burges provided an astonishing Arab Room at Cardiff Castle (restored 1866–85) and contributed a wealth of Saracenic and Moorish detail to Knightshayes Court (1869–71). George Aitchison created Lord Leighton's Arab Hall at Leighton House in Holland Park between 1887 and 1879, using tiles, stained glass and screens collected from throughout the Middle East. A remarkable Moorish smoking-room was created for Rhinefield, Hampshire between 1888 and 1890, influenced by the Alhambra; other such rooms included the billiard-room at Newhouse Park, St Albans, Hertfordshire, the smoking-room of the Berkeley Hotel in Piccadilly, London, both dating from the 1890s, and the Turkish room at Sledmore, Yorkshire for the Arabist, Sir Mark Sykes, as late as 1912–16, while the Powell-Cottons had an Indian-style oriental drawing-room at Quex House, Birchington, Kent. These are but the most striking of a succession of oriental rooms to be found throughout nineteenth-century country houses. The tradition was continued in the Moorish court at Port Lympne in Kent in the 1920s.[14]

Towards the end of the century the grandest examples of oriental halls were the striking essays in the Indian style such as the billiard- and smoking-rooms at the Duke of Connaught's Bagshot Park (dating from the second half of the 1880s) and the durbar room or dining-room at Osborne (1890–92), both designed by Lockwood Kipling with details executed by his school of Indian craftsmen at Lahore, or the interiors of the Maharajah Duleep Singh's Elveden, with Lord Iveagh's durbar hall, famously 'the coldest room in England', added between 1899 and 1903 by Sir Caspar Purdon Clarke. The durbar hall at Osborne (immensely popular with visitors, but summarily dismissed by architectural historians),[15] was later filled with the gifts of the Indian princes to the royal family and its associated corridors and vestibule are adorned with portraits not only of princes, but of the host of Indian craftspeople who attended the Colonial and Indian Exhibition of 1886, some of whom worked on its decoration. But the Indian extension at Knebworth, the home of the former Viceroy, Lord Lytton, planned in the 1880s, was never built, neatly symbolising the various unexecuted projects in the Indian style. These included the extraordinary scheme for Gravesend in the 1830s which incorporated buildings and bathing ghats intended to imitate the Ganges at Benares, and the grandiloquent and ethereal design of 1910 for an Indian Museum on London's Embankment by Robert Fellowes Chisholm, who had designed several 'Saracenic' buildings in India. The only major building in London to be given a vaguely Indian exterior in the late nineteenth century was the National Training School for Music (1874), later the Royal College of Organists.[16]

Specific listings serve to underline the fact that Orientalist buildings (as opposed to rooms) were a comparative rarity. But there were some types of buildings and rooms which were more common for two reasons: first because they represented a powerful cultural cross-referencing in which form and function satisfactorily blended, and second because they served to confirm the gendering of space which was a characteristic of nineteenth-century country houses and public buildings. One example was the shop which was able to draw attention to itself through oriental frontages, while also referring to the frequently used loan-word 'bazaar' (which had Persian origins). During the so-called Egyptian revival there were a number of Egyptian shop-fronts and, once Owen Jones had followed David Roberts and other artists in unveiling the glories of the Alhambra, several 'Moorish' shops appeared in central London. They were fiercely attacked by Ruskin. Shopping arcades, like those other iron and glass structures, palm-houses and railway stations, were built with Moorish arabesques and patterns in the ironwork, windows and balustrades. Such ironwork was often cast at the appropriately-named Saracen Iron Works, whose own foundry at Possilpark in Glasgow conveyed the appearance of a mosque with minarets and whose displays at international exhibitions were notably Orientalist in form. The Saracen company supplied the world, including of course the British eastern empire: for example, it manufactured some magnificent ironwork for the Durbar Hall in Mysore.[17]

Bathhouses were an obvious instance in which the form of the building and the activity which took place within it led inexorably to the Turkish prototype. The tiles, columns, alcoves and benches celebrated in the works of so many Orientalist painters became the identifying features of both private and municipal bathhouses throughout Europe. Magnificent examples included the Turkish Baths at Jermyn Street, St James's in London, designed by George Somers Clark and completed in 1862, the Oriental Baths in Cookridge Street, Leeds, by Cuthbert Brodrick of 1866, the Drumsheugh Baths, Edinburgh, by Sir J. J. Burnet of 1882, and the surviving Turkish Baths at Harrogate, opened in 1897 when the Yorkshire spa was at the height of its popularity.[18] All of these contained, in varied combinations, domes, arches, coloured glass, lanterns, spandrel and cornice decoration and tilework heavily influenced by the Islamic world.

Islamic forms were also sometimes associated with learning (many Orientalist painters depicted those aspects of Islam which linked religious teachings to scholarship and the training of the young). The Royal Panopticon in Leicester Square, opened in 1854, was a domed structure featuring detail from mosques in Cairo and was devoted to exhibitions of scientific machinery, crafts and trades, paintings and sculpture. Thus it represented the marriage of arts, crafts and technology. While the Oriental and Turkish Museum at Hyde Park Corner, converted from the pagoda-like building which had been used for Chinese exhibitions, was never very successful, Sir Matthew Digby Wyatt's recreation of part of the Diwan-i-Kas audience chamber of the Red Fort at Agra as the sculpture hall of the East India House Museum (1858) was much visited. Occasionally, as in Thomas Ambler's work in St Paul's Square, Leeds in the 1870s, Turkish detail was used for warehousing and associated buildings.

The less exalted tearooms, smoking-rooms and billiard-rooms, whether in private houses, the high street, exhibitions or hotels, also frequently related their function to either the geographical source of the product, the 'femininity' or 'masculinity' of the activity, or the concept of leisure as proclaimed in oriental cultures, particularly the Islamic. To

The dining-room at Osborne House by John Lockwood Kipling and Ram Singh, built between 1890 and 1892 and drawing on the craftsmanship of those involved in the Colonial and Indian Exhibition of 1886.   8

a certain extent entire cultures were 'gendered' in this way. There were no Chinese smoking-rooms or billiard-rooms. In reserving the Chinese style for garden pavilions, drawing-rooms and dairies there was a clear implication that feminine spaces could be appropriately decorated in forms derived from an 'effeminate' culture.

9   The Royal Panopticon in Leicester Square, London by Thomas Hayter Lewis, 1854. Here a 'Moorish' Islamic style, with detail based on that of Cairo mosques, was undoubtedly designed to convey an atmosphere of learning as well as entertainment. Originally designed for exhibitions of scientific machinery and demonstrations of crafts and trades, with paintings and sculptures in galleries and basements, it was subsequently used as a setting for lectures and displays and eventually became a theatre.

Popular culture and Orientalism

The argument about gendered spaces and associated oriental cultures should not, however, be taken too far. In the second half of the nineteenth century we encounter the rise of 'demotic Orientalism' and this occurred in precisely those areas, the great exhibitions, places of recreation and instruction like the Crystal Palace at Sydenham, the theatre, seaside piers and other buildings, and in the twentieth century the cinema, where gender distinctions (at least in terms of use) were being rapidly broken down. The building boom in these types of structures can be attributed to a combination of factors: the search for appropriate rational recreation, the growth of the middle class and of distinctions within that social group, particularly the emergence of a large lower middle class, the rise in disposable income among almost all social groupings, the considerable expansion of the leisure and entertainment industries, and the rapid growth of transport systems and specialist seaside resorts. What's more, all these developments took place at a time when the 'new imperialism' was developing into a powerfully popular ideology.

Exhibitions were, as we shall see, important showcases of oriental crafts and products, but they were also often housed in buildings that were well adapted to the creation of specific geographical courts. The Crystal Palace of 1851 contained just such courts, of which the Indian was the most celebrated. When the Crystal Palace was moved from Hyde Park to Sydenham in 1854 the idea was developed further. A number of architectural spaces in different styles and periods were created. As well as Greek, Roman, medieval and Renaissance courts, there were several oriental examples, including Chinese, Byzantine, Egyptian and Alhambra, the latter two designed by Owen Jones. These are interesting choices, with Indian notable by its absence. The 1862 London Exhibitions displayed Indian crafts, but the exhibition building was strongly classical. A large Indian Pavilion by Sir Caspar Purdon Clarke was built for the Paris Exhibition of 1878 and at the Colonial and Indian Exhibition in London in 1886, Purdon Clarke again provided an Indian Palace with a durbar hall, approached through a courtyard entered by the magnificent Gwalior Gateway donated by the Maharajah Scindia of Gwalior. Indian craftsmen worked within this complex, which was intended to convey the impression of a 'royal residence' in 'feudal India'.[19] Thus, Asian craftsmanship was celebrated within the context of the anti-modernising tendencies of some aspects of British social and political policy in India.

Indian pavilions, together with other external signs of Orientalism, reappeared at the Paris Exhibitions of 1889 and 1900, but it was in Glasgow in 1888 that a major international exhibition was housed in unashamedly Orientalist buildings.[20] The Glasgow architect James Sellars, who normally worked in classical forms, chose an oriental style because it could be readily rendered in wood, the medium of these temporary buildings. He brought together an amalgam of Byzantine, Moorish and Indian influences and the exhibition was swiftly dubbed 'Baghdad by the Kelvin'. Onion domes dominated both a triumphal arch and the Gray Street entrance, while the main building had a polychromatic frontage and powerful dome with minarets. The oriental theme was continued in a Doulton Indian Pavilion, a bazaar-like Indian court, the Saracen Foundry's display of ironwork, Indian and Ceylon tearooms, a 'Moresque' royal reception room and a substantial tobacco kiosk, with a smoking-lounge replete with divans. There was even a Bungalow restaurant (which was decidedly not a bungalow) where patrons could eat curries served by Indian waiters.

The Glasgow 1901 Exhibition was also dominated by an industrial hall in the form of a vaguely eastern palace (it was treated as such by the populace, although it was intended to be 'Spanish') and boasted an

10   The Glasgow International Exhibition, 1888, the Royal Doulton 'Indian Pavilion', strikingly Orientalist to match the design of the building and the supposed origins of its ceramic products.

Indian theatre in Mughal style. Oriental designs appeared in many of the other exhibitions of the period, although they were primarily used for specific products, particular national pavilions, 'native villages' or fun-fairs. It has been suggested that in the case of the Chicago Columbia Exhibition of 1893, a distinction was made between the serious aspects of the celebration of nationhood, trade and industry, where the principal buildings were classical, and the fun-fair, where Orientalism was permitted to reign supreme.[21] However, two reservations need to be entered about such an apparent distinction in architectural norms. First, the vast majority of visitors probably found the fun-fair a good deal more attractive. Second, when the architect Louis Sullivan castigated the exhibition for its architectural conservatism, he himself contributed a building which had distinctly oriental references.[22]

European exhibitions, however, like those in Glasgow, seldom made such distinctions. Exhibition Orientalism reached its apotheosis in the exhibitions run by the impresario Imre Kiralfy. In a sequence of annual imperial and international exhibitions he promoted a highly popular Orientalist spectacle. At the White City, to which he moved his operations in 1908, the centrepiece of the exhibitions was the 'Court of Honour', a sequence of Orientalist palaces in gleaming white stucco set around a lake, with elaborate colonnades, terraces, kiosks, *chattris*, lanterns, balustrades and steps, vaguely reminiscent of the palaces of Rajasthan, with a hint of Fatehpur Sikri. There were also fountains, a cascade and a canal, clearly linking such hydrographic features to an eastern paradise, all particularly effective when lit at night. Major Orientalist buildings included the Congress Hall, Indian Palace and Ceylon Village. As at other exhibitions, there were many subsidiary features, connected with specific products or entertainments, which took Orientalist forms. Additional buildings, like the Kyoto Pavilion, in appropriate style, were erected for the Japan–British Exhibition of 1910.

It may be that Kiralfy's exhibitions were viewed essentially as fun-fairs, but he did ensure that the Orientalist style could be taken no further. It is noticeable that the Coronation Exhibition at the Crystal Palace in 1911, a rival to Kiralfy's Coronation show at the White City, avoided Orientalism in favour of a more 'imperial' classical approach. While some Orientalism could be detected at Bradford (1904), exhibitions at Dublin (1907), Edinburgh (1908), and Liverpool (1913) were essentially classical or 'Renaissance' in flavour. Furthermore, the Glasgow Exhibitions of 1911 and 1938 largely abandoned Orientalist styles and adopted, respectively, a nationalist Scottish baronial approach and undiluted Modernism. Although the style of the 1924–25 Wembley Empire Exhibition was primarily classical, a number of Orientalist buildings were constructed to house the exhibits of the appropriate imperial territories.[23]

This did, however, represent a decline in Orientalism in exhibition design, although it was to continue as a prominent style in cinema architecture.

As James Sellars suggested in Glasgow in 1888, it may be that the style suited temporary buildings, but it is equally possible that exhibition design interacted with that of other leisure forms, particularly theatres and seaside structures. The Orientalist style not only drew attention to itself, but became inseparably associated with leisure and recreation. It had other advantages. Here was a striking profile, make up of domes and minarets, which was visible from afar, and which stood out from existing buildings. Thus, like the more stolid Egyptian Hall in Piccadilly, and on a much larger scale, it confidently identified itself and cried out to be visited. It offered brightness and colour, together with a satisfactory combination of dominant forms and ornamental detail. Fourth, the oriental could be associated with craft displays and with specific products, such as tea (which had of course relocated itself from China to India and Ceylon), tobacco, porcelain, decorated ironwork, carpets, chocolate and (later) rubber. Thus, for visitors, the exhibitions offered a sense of occasion, drama, achievement, and fun all rolled into one. They surely must have viewed the form as striking and attractive, for even dominant peoples do not disport themselves in that which they despise.

There is, however, an intriguing paradox when halls of industry or machinery and 'courts of progress' are rendered in an Orientalist style. The exhibitions were major displays of western progress in industry, technology, transport and commerce, imported commodities and crafts, the arts, as well as major fun-fairs. The combination did not seem to be in any way incongruous to the Victorians and Edwardians, for many of the features of the showground element were themselves transport and technological marvels. They represented the idea that leisure and recreation had come of age, in the sense that they were themselves implicated in industrial production and business techniques. At first sight, perhaps, the Orientalist form represents a paradigm of colonisation and modernisation, with the 'forces of progress' inhabiting exotic surroundings. It is, however, equally possible that such juxtapositions illustrated the possibility of creative amalgamation between the modern and the exotic, in design values, in all forms of ironwork, for example, and engineering structures such as bridges and piers.

By the twentieth century, Orientalism had certainly become the language of pleasure and relaxation. Whereas only a minority of the population would have seen Orientalist structures or architectural features and examples of eastern-inspired design in the eighteenth and early nineteenth centuries, by the end of that century, leisure and recreation, 'escapism' and personal fantasies were invariably expressed in Orientalist forms. This was, moreover, a movement to be found throughout Europe, the Americas, and the European imperial territories, from Copenhagen's Tivoli Gardens to Melbourne's St Kilda fun-fair, from the cinemas of Hollywood to Cape Town and Auckland. In Britain, the statistics of buildings associated with leisure and entertainment are striking: between 1850 and 1950 over 900 theatres were built in London alone; by 1940 there were 5,500 cinemas in Britain (some former theatres, but the majority custom-built over the past three decades); cities like Liverpool and Glasgow boasted 118 and 130 cinemas respectively at the peak of their influence; between 1813 and 1957, 84 seaside piers were built in England, Wales and the Isle of Man (a figure which would considerably exceed 100 if piers in Scotland and Northern Ireland are added). To these we must add tower buildings, ballrooms, bandstands and 'kiosks' of all sorts. The great majority of theatres and cinemas were neo-classical or Modernist (particularly Art Deco) in design, but those with Oriental-ist exteriors and, more likely, interiors were hard to miss. Orientalism could be found in a sliding scale from some features of exterior or interior design through 'eastern' interiors set in neo-classical buildings to a full-blown marriage of exterior shell and internal decorations. In sea-side architecture, Orientalism virtually predominated.

The various Orientalist fashions were reflected in the interior de-sign of British theatres.[24] In 1812, for example, the rebuilt Theatre Royal, Drury Lane, appeared with 'Chinese' canopies over its boxes (subsequently removed), the Adelphi had a 'pagoda' as part of its inte-rior decoration. The Grand Theatre, Clapham Junction, built in 1900 and soon converted into a cinema, was a late example of theatre chinoi-serie, with pagoda boxes guarded by dragons and a ceiling dome deco-rated as an inverted willow-pattern plate. (At a much later stage, and in a very different entertainment form, the BBC at Savoy Hill had a Chinese studio, apparently used for musical performances, decorated throughout – even to the light fitments – in a chinoiserie manner.[25]) But it was 'Moorish' design, loosely based on the Alhambra and popularised by Owen Jones, which was most frequently used. In 1858, the Panopticon in Leicester Square (see above) was sold on as a theatre and, reopening as the Alhambra Palace, had its Moorish decoration re-emphasised. It was subsequently converted into a music-hall, was burned down in 1881 and was rebuilt in an even more strikingly Alhambresque form (it was demolished in 1936). The Tivoli music-hall in the Strand, though roughly 'French Empire' in external style when opened in 1890, boasted a Palm Room, an Indian buffet and Japanese and Arabian private dining rooms. 'Alhambras' and 'Tivolis' appeared across the British Empire, often though not always, Orientalist in form.

The most celebrated of the late Victorian and Edwardian theatre architects, Frank Matcham, who was responsible for the design of some 150 theatres between 1886 and 1910, developed eclectic Orientalism to its highest point, combining onion domes (often as the canopies of boxes), Alhambresque filigree decoration, cusped arches, and massive elephant heads by the proscenium (as at the Belfast Grand Opera House, but at other theatres too). Sometimes he even added chinoiserie features for good measure.[26] Glasgow illustrated its continuing adherence to Orientalism, and no doubt its close connections with empire through shipbuilding, locomotive construction and other aspects of heavy engineering through the building of the Palace Music Hall in 1903, a Mughal-style theatre by Bertie Crew, which subsequently became a cinema. No British theatre, however, was as elaborately 'Mughal' as the astonishing Broadway Theatre in Denver, Colorado.

Few theatres were Orientalist in external appearance, though occasionally, as at the Concert Hall at the Surrey Zoological Gardens, Turkish 'kiosks' or minaret-like features appeared as roof elements. With cinemas, however, both external and internal Orientalist features were used to highlight the fact that this was a medium of fantasy, romance and escapism.[27] The prototypes of these styles inevitably occurred in the United States, where they reached phantasmagoric heights never quite achieved in Britain. As well as Sid Grauman's Egyptian and Chinese cinemas in Hollywood, dating from the early 1920s, there were Peery's Egyptian Theatre in Ogden, Utah, the Roxy 'Temple of Solomon' in New York, the Beacon, a 'bit of Baghdad in Upper Broadway', the Hindu 'Oakland' in Oakland, California, the 'Buddhist' Beverley Theatre, Los Angeles, and the 'Hindu' and 'Jain' Loew's in New York, the last three all dating from the period 1928–30. Equally striking Orientalist cinemas were built in Paris, Berlin, Stockholm, Cape Town and Auckland, New Zealand, where the interior of the Civic Theatre was built as a free adaptation of an Indian rock-cut temple. Thus the patrons entered their world of fantasy through mysterious (but much more opulent) spaces reminiscent of the Caves of Elephanta in Bombay Harbour.

Both the Globe Cinema, Putney and the Electric Theatre in Paddington (of 1911 and 1912 respectively) had Mughal external appearances, including oriels and *chattris* rendered reasonably accurately. The Palace, Southall, was built in a Chinese style with ogee tiled roofs decorated with dragons, while the Royal in Uxbridge was said to be a piece of cinematic chinoiserie with doors that were almost Burmese in inspiration. A number of cinemas had Egyptian exteriors, like the Carlton in Islington, the Streatham Astoria, the Pyramid and the Riviera, both in Manchester, the Scala in Liverpool or the Govanhill Picture House in Glasgow. The Pyramid at Sale, Cheshire, by Drury and Gomersall which opened in 1933, was a remarkable exercise in stylistic consistency. Behind the Egyptian frontage, the interior was decked out in lotus-flower and papyrus detail, with a winged solar disc above the proscenium arch. Even its organ had an Egyptian-style console. It has often been said that this outbreak of a new Egyptian revival was related to the opening of the tomb of King Tutankhamun and the world-wide publicity which it received.[28] It is true that 'Egyptian' cinemas tended to appear in the late 1920s and early 1930s, but there is also a certain continuity in the style. Cinemas clearly made reference to Bullock's Egyptian Hall of 1812, which at the end of its career actually showed films before it was demolished in 1905. Moreover, an architect's drawing for an ideal Egyptian-style interior dates from around 1916.[29]

But it was the Alhambresque style which reigned supreme in cinema Orientalism. Now the names of cinemas often matched their styles, as in the Alhambras, Granadas and occasionally 'Orients' to be found around the country. Odeons, Tivolis and Hippodromes, despite the Greek and Roman origin of the names, were also to be found in Moorish style. The Palace, Portsmouth, unusually, had a Moorish exterior, but the great majority reserved their Alhambresque detail for their interiors. These cinema styles continued right through the inter-war years and were swept up into the concept of the 'atmospheric' which was introduced from the United States in the late 1920s. In the 'atmospherics', effects were produced by complex and ingenious lighting, rendered possible by advances in electricity, and stage-set decorations. These were able to produce elaborate and exotic atmospheres without the vast expense of solid decorations and gildings of the earlier cinemas. It comes as no surprise to find that the favourite tune of cinema organists was Ketèlby's 'In a Persian Garden', rendering cinematic Orientalism even more promiscuous.

The cinema and Orientalism: the Pyramid at Sale, Cheshire.   11

The architectural writer P. Morton Shand, an exponent of Modernism, castigated cinema architects in Britain for pastiches which he saw as the enemy of style. He argued that cinema architects should look to the Continent for examples of ways in which technologically advanced entertainment could be expressed in an equally modern form.[30] By the second half of the 1930s, cinema architecture seemed to have found a striking contemporary idiom through the appearance of the Art Deco style, which swept the country, particularly through the extension of the Odeon chain. Even Art Deco, however, had affinities with oriental detail in design, and Art Deco exteriors sometimes cloaked Orientalist interiors.[31]

Yet there was a long tradition of associating Orientalism with highly modern developments. For more than a century Orientalist design had often been considered appropriate for engineering works. Brunel, for example, rendered the gateway to the Clifton Suspension Bridge in Egyptian style. Although plans for an 'Egyptian' railway station in Britain were never executed, 'arabesques' were often a feature of ironwork in train sheds and other iron and glass buildings, while tunnel portals were occasionally orientalised. In Glasgow, the railway station at the Botanic Gardens was provided with minarets, no doubt to indicate that it was a station more likely to be used for pleasure than for business.

But it was the Chain Pier at Brighton, opened in 1823, which signalled a new form for which Orientalism would be ideally suited, the seaside pleasure pier. (It was not, however, the first pier which was built at Ryde in 1813–14.) The Chain Pier was again Egyptian in inspiration, but piers would more generally adopt Chinese, Moorish and Turkish references. The pier had a number of elements amenable to this kind of treatment: it required a gateway; there were often a series of kiosks breaking up its length; later there would be a building or buildings towards the end or at a half-way point; the detail of seats, railings, lighting brackets and of course the ironwork of the structure itself could adopt oriental patterns. A very high proportion adopted such motifs: Chinese pagoda roofs and other decoration at Hunstanton (1870), St Leonard's (1891) and St Annes (1885); Moorish/Mughal (but often with chinoiserie detail) at Brighton West (1866) and Palace (1891), Blackpool North (1863) and Central (1868), Eastbourne (1872), Southsea (1878), Morecambe West (1896), Bangor (1896) and Dover (1910), to name but a few. At Penarth, as late as 1927, Mughal features were incorporated which may well have been inspired by Lutyens's New Delhi. Pier theatres were often constructed in an Alhambresque style and Orientalism could also be found in ballrooms and seaside buildings like the Rhyl Pavilion and the striking palace and casino which fronted the ill-starred Morecambe Tower, which was never completed.[32]

Some may argue that the implication of this plethora of recreational

Orientalist architecture is clear, that the architecture of the East, as adapted and perverted by the West, was seen as suitably gaudy and frivolous for these purposes. The creators and consumers of Orientalist architecture were thus reasserting that it was not 'serious'; in intellectual and aesthetic terms it was light, insubstantial, a confection suitable for off-duty moments, a pastiche source of humour, transient and expendable. Those who used and abused it did so out of a sense of superiority, which could make fun of the serious architecture of the East, taking temples, mosques and palaces in vain. The use of such styles therefore made statements to the users of these buildings about the cultures that had contributed them, that they were not to be taken entirely seriously, that their religious and dynastic buildings could be cheerfully converted for sacrilegious pleasures as emblems of conquest, power and cultural superiority.

But there are a number of problems with such an interpretation. First, there were many buildings serving similar purposes which were built in classical or Gothic styles, so that the oriental was inseparably associated with western experimentation for the same purposes. In any case, the Orientalist styles were so wildly eclectic as to create, in effect, a wholly new form. Allusions to specific cultures were largely squeezed out of the creation of a style that was seen to be grand, mysterious, fantastic and opulent all at once. Piers were seen as riding over the sea, distant, ethereal, a sort of promenading magic carpet. Second, we should be careful not to demean the vogue for these new forms of leisure, particularly working-class leisure. They were big business, part of the coming of the mass market, and as a major source of recreation, refreshment and pleasure a means of the liberation of working-class time. Thus they constituted something of a revolution in pastimes and taste, and many of those who participated were, if only dimly, aware of the fact. Moreover, some of them set out to contribute to the efforts to offer 'rational amusement', a middle-class concern, to the working classes. Third, some of the oriental vehicles had eminently serious objectives, particularly in the exhibitions, which were intended to be showcases of both the creative achievements of the West and the craftsmanship of the East. Finally, these forms, curiously, were associated with progress and modern technology. This was particularly true of the exhibitions, but in a sense it was even more true of engineering (including the audacious piers) and the cinema. Here the most modern of technologies were revealed to be liberating rather than soulless, elevating and escapist rather than oppressive. The objective was to combine the strikingly modern with a timeless mood.

Whether the users of these buildings knew that they were having their emotions tugged and their pleasures heightened by an Egyptian or

Moorish ambience is of course a moot point. Some will have been aware of the allusions, no doubt, and many will have associated them with some of the exotic entertainments which they encountered within these 'dream palaces'. Sometimes, it is true, the veil upon racial prejudices appeared to slip. The guide to the Glasgow International Exhibition of 1901, referring to the Indian theatre, suggested that 'India is still considered the nursery of the arts of humbug, and the Indian wondermaker maintains his position as the arch mystifier of the world'.[33] By modern standards this seems to be a very explicit statement, but words have changed their meaning, and in an entertainment context this may be no more than a rather strong way of saying that 'India is the home of illusion and illusionists'. Some considered that these eclectic styles undermined Modernism, although cinema architecture reflected the manner in which the two could coexist, particularly in the shape of Art Deco. In a postmodernist age, when so many of the theatrical, cinematic and seaside pleasure domes have been destroyed, some of these examples of creative eclecticism have come to be appreciated afresh – particularly the work of Frank Matcham.

Architectural debates and eclecticism

To understand the development of oriental influences in the twentieth century, it is necessary to backtrack to examine the debates about eastern architecture conducted in the later nineteenth century. Through the work of Owen Jones (examined in greater detail in the next chapter), James Fergusson and others, there was a continuing – and often respectful – debate about oriental building styles. In a lecture before the Royal Society of Arts in 1866 and in his major two-volume work on the history of Indian and Eastern Architectures of 1876, James Fergusson examined the lessons of such buildings for the West.[34] Of course he reflected Victorian cultural and historical preconceptions. He erroneously believed that Indian architecture had been influenced by conquerors from the Greeks onwards and became involved in a heated and unpleasantly racist debate with the Bengali scholar Rajendralal Mitra on this point.[35] He valued the Aryan above the Dravidian; decline and decadence were abiding themes. But he described architecture as a stone book, a means whereby Indian history could be unlocked and elucidated. Above all he saw lessons in Indian, Arab and Moorish architecture (but he was dismissive of the Chinese) for the contemporary western architect. The best of Indian architecture represented the total integration of religion, art and civilisation – exactly the ideal the Victorians were striving for – and the perfect fusion of form, beauty and purpose. In arguing that the West should escape from the groove of the classical and the Gothic, he

suggested that architects should follow the underlying principles of eastern architecture. They should not copy actual examples, but seek out its
marriage of structure, form and ornament, its pursuit of the forms and
principles of nature, rather than the representation of them, and discover
the appropriateness of Indian, the grandeur of Arab, and the refinement
and elegance of Moorish architecture.

Fergusson's views were, of course, always controversial. But Egyptian and Indian elements were used to come to the rescue of Greek
revivalism and as a result their claims to be considered as serious architectural styles were enhanced. Generally, 'Hindu' and 'Muslim' forms
seemed to blend most effectively with Gothic, and later in the century
a major movement of 'Gothic Saracenic' was to develop in India. But in
Scotland, where the Greek revival survived longer than elsewhere, some
extraordinarily original blending of styles took place. Classical revivalism
remained a significant architectural force in Scotland for a variety of
reasons. It remained the architectural language of learning and the arts,
through the work of Hamilton and Playfair in Edinburgh, and later
James Sellars, among others, in Glasgow. Moreover, it was well adapted
to the requirements of Presbyterianism. A non-liturgical church, in which
the sermon was the principal aspect of worship, required, in effect, auditoriums for its services. The classical shape was as well adapted to the
needs of the Church of Scotland and the breakaway and nonconformist
churches as it was to the concert hall or art gallery. Finally, the terraces
and tenements of the rapidly growing Scottish cities were also amenable
to classical forms.

But this concentration on the classical needed to be lightened and
varied if it was not to ossify in form and stultify its consumers. In
Alexander 'Greek' Thomson (1817–75), Glasgow produced an architect
who wedded his classicism to a variety of eclectic elements, notably
Assyrian, Egyptian and Indian.[36] He linked Greek forms to towers which
had oriental references in form and in detail. He used the pylon to frame
doorways and fenestration to great effect, and he was even capable of
combining Egyptian motifs with Indian-shaped domes. He brought these
elements together in a number of churches, most notably his masterpiece, the St Vincent Street Church, which survives, and the remarkable
Queen's Park Church, a casualty to bombing in the Second World War,
described by Gomme and Walker as 'one of the unhappiest architectural
losses in Britain'.[37] It has even been suggested recently that it should be
reconstructed.[38] He succeeded in overcoming Presbyterian scruples to
the extent of providing his churches with richly coloured, sumptuous
interiors, full of oriental detail (though his clients at the St Vincent
Street Church jibbed at frescoes and took the decoration out of his
hands).[39] Commercial buildings (like the Egyptian Halls, Union Street),

12 The remarkable creative eclecticism of Alexander Thomson, the Glasgow architect now recognised as a major figure of the nineteenth century. Here classical, Egyptian and other Orientalist features combine in the majestic St Vincent Street Church of 1859.

monumental terraces and villas also received the strikingly original
Thomson treatment. In them he was able to use the Egyptian column,
powerful trabeation and acanthus decoration to great effect. He may
even, in his later years, have been influenced by Japanese design in his
handling of wooden detail in one of his great terraces. He certainly had
a long-standing interest in Japanese art.

Thomson never travelled, but he knew Fergusson's work on oriental architecture well and in demonstrating the extraordinary flexibility
of oriental motifs in their application to a variety of different building
types, he was breaking with what he regarded as the dry scholarship of
the classical revival. He disapproved of Ruskin's views on architecture,
which he saw as inimical to the architectural profession, and sought to
return to some of the basic architectural forms. Deeply religious himself,
he had a considerable interest in African exploration and missionary
work, yet he was prepared to draw inspiration from all structures ranging
from the African hut ('the embryo Parthenon') to the Hindu temple. In
lectures and writings he extolled the virtues of Egyptian architecture,
its stability, proportion, stillness, monumentality, duration and sense of
sequential space.[40] Moreover, like most of the greatest architects, he had
a deep sense of natural history, of botanical forms and the building
techniques employed by animals. Despite its monumentality, he was
searching for an architecture that grew out of nature and human history.
Thomson was unquestionably one of the eclectic geniuses of the nineteenth century.

Other architects sought to rediscover through architecture what
they saw as the purity, ornament and craftsmanship of the Middle Ages.
To help them achieve this end they searched through the design traditions of other societies in order to discover contemporary inspiration.
William Burges (1827–81) attempted to combine both Moorish and
Japanese elements in his Gothicism, while E. W. Godwin (1833–86) and
W. E. Nesfield (1835–88) adapted Japanese motifs to lighter architectural styles such as the revived 'Queen Anne'.[41] Charles Rennie Mackintosh (1868–1928) is often seen as representing a striking Modernism,
but he was also highly eclectic. He was prepared to design in Gothic,
classical and oriental styles (for example his unexecuted design for the
Glasgow Exhibition of 1901),[42] but his most striking contribution was
to combine the robust strength of the Scottish vernacular with an un-
cluttered handling of interior space, light walls and dark furniture re-
lieved by brightly coloured art-nouveau elements and stained glass, pierced
wooden screens and metalwork which, though highly original, owed
most to Japanese inspiration.[43] With his designs for Miss Cranston's
tearooms (he created four between 1897 and 1912), he brought together
these orientalised elements with an activity, tea-drinking, inseparably

associated with the Orient. This was particularly true of his Chinese room for the Ingram Street establishment. All this helped to make Glasgow, as one contemporary described it, 'a very Tokio for tea rooms'.[44] However, the Japanese influences upon Burges, Godwin, Nesfield, Mackintosh and others relate more to design than to architecture and will be touched on again in the next chapter.

Though Mackintosh ran out of commissions and was grossly undervalued in Britain in his own lifetime (only to become a cult figure since the Second World War), he formed a link with the inter-war years. Some of his later designs (including those for fabrics) incorporated the jagged geometrical figures sometimes known as 'jazz moderne'. Such elements appeared in Art Deco, the characteristic architectural form of the late 1920s and 1930s, so dominant in the shopfronts, cinemas and ballrooms of the period, but also making its appearance in hotels, banks and factories. Art Deco, though not oriental in any obvious overall way, owed much to oriental influences: the geometrical patterns, often brightly coloured, the strongly projecting corbels, the sunbursts, winged elements (like clocks rendered as solar discs) and other features. This was one reason why Art Deco was able to succeed and in some ways develop the more overt Orientalism of the architecture of popular entertainment reviewed above. Even in larger buildings, like factories, Egyptian and other oriental motifs could be incorporated. Both the Firestone Factory in London of 1929 and the India Tyre and Rubber Factory of 1930 at Inchinnan, west of Glasgow, had highly decorated quasi-Egyptian centrepieces.[45]

International Modernism largely squeezed out the opportunities for syncretic innovation, but the advent of postmodernism has once again elevated eclecticism into a style. The Orient has played relatively little part in recent architectural developments, which have tended to concentrate on classical pastiches, but a few isolated buildings have made stunning use of Orientalist forms. Jean Nouvel's Institute of the Arab World in Paris has recreated the pierced wooden screens or *mashrabiyyah*, so frequently seen in nineteenth-century Orientalist painting, in stainless steel with hi-tech adjustable features to respond to light changes. Inside, a ramped book stack which spirals up through six floors is said to be inspired by the minaret in Sumarra in Iraq.[46] In Doncaster, north-east England, the Dome leisure park, also opened in 1989, has a vestibule with columns and dome covered in banded tile, with a chequered floor, all intended to recreate in a highly modern idiom the feel of a Turkish baths.[47] However, oriental references are still sometimes used as terms of abuse. Terry Farrell's monstrous Century House on London's South Bank has been described as 'Babylonian',[48] although the references to Babylon are obscure. Perhaps the allusion more precisely reflects Saddam

Hussein's attempt to associate his regime with imperial Babylon through his megalomaniac reconstruction of the ancient capital, particularly as Century House is to be used by MI6.

Perhaps in the midst of all this grandiloquence we should not forget, at the other end of the architectural scale, the humble yet ubiquitous bungalow. Here we have an architectural form, square or rectangular, mainly single-storey, under an overall tented roof-space (originally suitable for thatching) and often (in the tropics invariably) boasting a verandah, which has been progressively transformed and developed from the eighteenth century to the present day. This much-maligned bungalow (from *banggolo*, the Bengali peasant's hut, or *bangla*, belonging to Bengal) was taken over, adapted and enlarged by the British to become the standard European residence in the tropics, emblematic of imperial rule itself. Close approximations of the Bengali prototype were built on the Sezincote estate in the eighteenth century, but it was not until the 1860s that it properly arrived in Britain, initially at seaside resorts as the domestic architecture of vacation and leisure. Only later did it become associated with suburbia, by which time it had spread to the United States, Australia, Africa and elsewhere.[49] Few now associate it with the East at all, except through a dim realisation of the origins of the word, for unlike the architecture examined above it carries no overtly oriental detail.

The role of Orientalism in architecture is thus enormously complex and enduring. Architecture is an art confined by structural and engineering practicalities, by function and the needs and prejudices of clients. Even more than other arts, perhaps, it is constantly confronted with the question 'Where do we go from here?', with the need to escape predictability while still conforming to basic rules. As a shackled art, it found oriental examples particularly liberating. While it is true that no major style emerged (unless 'oriental demotic' qualifies), architects repeatedly used oriental forms and inspiration (often remotely related to the real thing) to free themselves from dominant styles and arid scholarship, to express new functions and moods, even modernity.

In doing so they drew on both historic and contemporary examples. In discussing non-European architecture they often, like Fergusson, reflected some of the racial views of their day and were obsessed with the concept of cultural decline, but none the less they found in exotic forms ideas that were closer to nature. Some, like Lutyens at New Delhi, were capable of brilliant pastiche while being notoriously imperial in their attitudes and, in his case, dismissive of their Mughal forebears.[50] But many seemed to be intrigued by oriental examples even when political contexts were least propitious. Alexander Thomson was sent a drawing of an Indian temple by his brother-in-law who was serving as a soldier

in the Mutiny campaign of 1857.[51] Imperial anxieties and religious prejudice seem to have had little effect upon his interest in, and willingness
to use Indian shapes derived from such temple architecture.

Indeed, the interaction of architecture with contemporary events
is complex and problematic. As we have seen, interest in Chinese and
Egyptian forms is sometimes related to specific moments in the relationship between East and West, like Napoleon's Nile expedition or
Macartney's embassy to China, but in each case these merely provided
a fillip for an enduring fascination marked as much by continuity as by
sudden fashion. Enthusiasm for Japanese arts and crafts was clearly developed as a result of Commodore Perry's opening-up of Japan to western commerce in 1853 and the mission of Elgin that followed five years
later, but Chinese influences were not wholly eclipsed. The revival of
respect for Indian crafts and architecture in the last decades of the nineteenth century certainly had something to do with the particular interest
in the Indian princes and their courts in that period, but again it represented a revival of an enduring concern. If there is any evidence that
the New Imperialism of the late nineteenth century or continuing anxieties about the weakness of the Ottoman Empire had much effect upon
architectural fashion, it comes from the increasing ease of travel, which
may have helped to inspire the oriental language of leisure that became
so prominent in the late nineteenth and twentieth centuries. These architectural messages about recreation, however, continued well into the
twentieth century when formal imperial rule was in decline. That they
disappeared at all owes more to the rise of international Modernism than
to the demise of empire.

Finally, function tells us very little about the ideological associations of Orientalism. It might be argued that ancient architectural forms
were used for 'serious' buildings, contemporary pastiche for 'frivolous'
ones. This does not work, even if such a loaded distinction is allowed to
stand. In Glasgow alone, Arabic or Moorish elements could be found
on a theatre (the Alhambra), a working-man's lodging house (Rutland
House), a station (Botanic Gardens) and a church (Cunninghame Free
Church).[52] As we have seen, oriental styles were considered appropriate
as a vehicle for the most modern and technologically advanced forms
(exhibitions, factories, cinemas). Given that all such buildings, as well as
those associated with all forms of leisure, appeared in other styles too,
the association seems to have more to do with visibility, with a search for
a pleasing and lively mood. Any suggestion that 'progress' was being
consciously expressed within an envelope redolent of 'backwardness' seems
to fall down. Perceived oriental forms, however misinterpreted, were a
repeated source of inspiration, offering new routes out of architectural
reaction. What emerged were not copies, the constant bugbear of the

architectural commentator, but new styles infused by the design values and sometimes the spirit of another age or culture. With an architect like Thomson or a commentator like Fergusson, there is no doubt that oriental forms, albeit 'dead' ones, were being handled with sensitivity and respect, as major lessons and opportunities for modern architects. As with art, architecture offers very little evidence of a monolithic binary discourse, separating Self from Other through inimical cultural statement. This was even more true in the case of design.

Notes

1   The 'battle of the styles' is laid out in schematic form in Banister Fletcher, *A History of Architecture on the Comparative Method*, 16th edn (London, 1959), pp. 852–64, where he lists architects of the classical and Gothic schools in adjacent twin columns; it is also discussed in Robert Macleod, *Style and Society: Architectural Ideology in Britain, 1815–1914* (London, 1971) and Ian Toplis, *The Foreign Office: an Architectural History* (London, 1987).

2   Mildred Archer, *Indian Architecture and the British, 1780–1830* (London, 1968); Oliver Impey, *Chinoiserie* (London, 1977); Madeleine Jarry, *Chinoiserie* (New York, 1981); Patrick Conner, *Oriental Architecture and the West* (London, 1977); Patrick Conner (ed.), *The Inspiration of Egypt: its Influence on British Artists, Travellers and Designers, 1700–1900* (Brighton, 1983); John Sweetman, *The Oriental Obsession: Islamic Inspiration in British and American Art and Architecture, 1520–1920* (Cambridge, 1988); James Stevens Curl, *Egyptomania, the Egyptian Revival: a Recurring Theme in the History of Taste* (Manchester, 1994). See also *Rococo: Art and Design in Hogarth's England*, exhibition catalogue, Victoria and Albert Museum, 1984. Raymond Head, *The Indian Style* (London, 1986) commendably carries the story forward into the twentieth century and the architecture of popular recreation. The discussion which follows is based upon these works together with the guidebooks (too numerous to cite) gleaned from many visits to parks, country houses and other structures.

3   Sweetman, *Oriental Obsession*, p. 2.

4   Head, *Indian Style*, p. 49.

5   John M. Mackenzie, *Propaganda and Empire* (Manchester, 1984), Chapter 5 on the Imperial Institute; Toplis, *The Foreign Office*, Chapter 16.

6   Jeffrey Richards and John M. MacKenzie, *The Railway Station: a Social History* (Oxford, 1986), Chapter 3; Robert Grant Irving, *Indian Summer: Lutyens, Baker and Imperial Delhi* (New Haven, 1981); Thomas R. Metcalf, *An Imperial Vision: Indian Architecture and Britain's Raj* (London, 1989).

7   Conner (ed.), *Inspiration of Egypt*, p. 28.

8   The National Trust, *Biddulph Grange Garden* (London, 1992).

9   Thomas and William Daniell, *Oriental Scenery* (London, 1795–1808); Mildred Archer, *Early Views of India: the Picturesque Journeys of Thomas and William Daniell* (London, 1980). See also C. A. Bayly (ed.), *The Raj, India and the British, 1600–1947* (London, 1990), pp. 141–51.

10   At Glendaruel, near Dunoon, Sir Colin Campbell built replicas of the city gates of Lucknow to commemorate his role in the suppression of the Mutiny. His house has gone, but the gates remain.

11   *Sezincote* (Stow-on-the-Wold, n.d.), p. 9.

12   John Dinkel, *The Royal Pavilion, Brighton* (London, 1983).

13   Many of these soldiers sent letters home to India, copies of which were kept by the censor. A selection is to be published under the editorship of David Omissi.

14   These examples are culled from the works cited in note 2 above as well as Mark Girouard, *The Victorian Country House* (New Haven, 1979), Clive Aslet, *The Last Country Houses* (New Haven, 1982) and guidebooks.

15   See, for example, Girouard, *Victorian Country House*, p. 152: 'About the Durbar wing ... the less said the better.'

16   Head, *Indian Style*, pp. 83–4. For Chisholm, see Metcalf, *Imperial Vision* and Philip Davies, *Splendours of the Raj: British Architecture in India, 1660–1947* (London, 1985).

17   Ian Cox, 'The ornamental ironwork of Walter Macfarlane and Co.', *Scottish Art Review*, XVII (1991), pp. 3–7.

18   The Harrogate Baths were featured in *The World of Interiors*, July/August 1986, pp. 106–15.

19   For the Indian pavilions, see Head, *Indian Style*, pp. 121–33. See also Paul Greenhalgh, *Ephemeral Vistas: the Expositions Universelles, Great Exhibitions and World Fairs, 1851–1939* (Manchester, 1988).

20   Perilla and Juliet Kinchin, *Glasgow's Great Exhibitions, 1888, 1901, 1911, 1938, 1988* (Glasgow, 1988).

21   James Gilbert, *Perfect Cities: Chicago's Utopias of 1893* (Chicago, 1991).

22   John Allwood, *The Great Exhibitions* (London, 1977), p. 92.

23   MacKenzie, *Propaganda*, Chapter 4; entries in John F. Findling and Kimberly D. Pelle (eds), *Historical Dictionary of World's Fairs and Expositions, 1851–1988* (New York, 1990) and Greenhalgh, *Ephemeral Vistas*.

24   Victor Glasstone, *Victorian and Edwardian Theatres: an Architectural and Social Survey* (London, 1975); Head, *Indian Style*, pp. 134–56.

25   Asa Briggs, *The BBC: the First Fifty Years* (Oxford, 1985), illustration 4b. A larger version appears in volume II of Briggs's multi-volume history of the BBC.

26   Brian M. Walker (ed.), *Frank Matcham: Theatre Architect* (Belfast, 1980) and Head, *Indian Style*. pp. 139–41. The Belfast Grand Opera House has been bombed twice by the IRA.

27   David Atwell, *Cathedrals of the Movies* (London, 1980); Dennis Sharp, *The Picture Palace* (London, 1969); Chris Clegg and Rosemary Clegg, *The Dream Palaces of Birmingham* (Birmingham, 1983); T. Louden, *The Cinemas of Cinema City* (Glasgow, 1983); Harold Ackroyd, *The Dream Palaces of Liverpool* (Birmingham, 1987).

28   Christopher Frayling, *The Face of Tutankhamun* (London, 1992), Chapter 1; James Stevens Curl, *The Egyptian Revival* (London, 1982).

29   Illustrated in Sharp, *Picture Palace*, p. 89.

30   Quoted in Sharp, *Picture Palace*, pp. 92–4.

31   Examples are to be found in all the sources in note 25 above; see also Rudolph Kenna, *Glasgow, Art Deco* (Glasgow, 1985).

32   Susan M. Adamson, *Seaside Piers* (London, 1977) and John Walton and Richard Fischer, *British Piers* (London, 1987). So far as the Morecambe Tower building was concerned, the *Morecambe Visitor* reported on 6 July 1898 that all the shop attendants would be dressed in the costumes of the people they represented – Arabs, Egyptians, Turks, Moors, Circassians and Ethiopians.

33   Quoted in Head, *Indian Style*, p. 141.

34   James Fergusson, *On the Study of Indian Architecture*, read at a meeting of the Society of Arts on Wednesday 19 December 1866 (reprinted Varanasi, 1977) and *History of Indian and Eastern Architecture*, 2 vols. (New Delhi, 1972, first published 1876).

35   Krishna Dutta and Andrew Robinson (eds), *Purabi* (London, 1991), pp. 157–8.

36   Ronald McFadzean, *The Life and Work of Alexander Thomson* (London, 1979); Andor Gomme and David Walker, *Architecture of Glasgow* (London, 1968); Colin McWilliam (ed.), *The Buildings of Glasgow* (London, 1990).

37   Gomme and Walker, *Architecture*, p. 128.

38   Gavin Stamp, 'Bits and pieces with an elevated status', *The Herald*, 24 July 1993.

39   McFadzean, *Thomson*, p. 107.

40   McFadzean, *Thomson*, p. 263.

41   Tomoko Sato and Toshio Watanabe (eds), *Japan and Britain: an Aesthetic Dialogue, 1850–1930* (London, 1991), pp. 115–17.

42   Andrew McLaren Young (ed.), *Charles Rennie Mackintosh* (Edinburgh, 1968), p. 36.

43   Pamela Robertson (ed.), *Charles Rennie Mackintosh: the Architectural Papers* (Glasgow, 1990); Sato and Watanabe, *Japan and Britain*, p. 152; Gerald Larner and Celia Larner, *The Glasgow Style* (London, 1980) among many other sources on Mackintosh.

44   J. M. Muir, *Glasgow in 1901* (Glasgow, 1901), p. 166, quoted in Sato and Watanabe, *Japan and Britain*, p. 153.

45   Kenna, *Glasgow Art Deco*.

46   Stephen Gardiner, 'A nouvel idea', *Observer*, 27 August 1989.

47   *Guardian*, 29 September 1989, p. 20.

48   *Observer*, 1 August 1993, p. 6.

49   Anthony D. King, *The Bungalow: the Production of a Global Culture* (London, 1984).

50   *Inter alia*, Head, *Indian Style*, pp. 78–9.

51   McFadzean, *Thomson*, p. 18.

52   All of these examples are culled from Frank Worsdall, *The City that Disappeared: Glasgow's Demolished Architecture* (Glasgow, 1981), pp. 153, 125, 142.

5

Orientalism in design

IT IS a commonplace to suggest that European attitudes to oriental art made a severe distinction between the applied and the fine arts.[1] While Europeans were prepared to acknowledge the influence of 'crafts' and of the decorative arts from the earliest days of commercial contact with the East, they always maintained the outright superiority of western sculpture and painting. Pre-eminence in sculpture was hallowed by the great classical precedents, rediscovered and imitated from the Renaissance. For the art historian, particularly those nineteenth-century commentators imbued with the concept of progress, painting illustrated not only the great forward strides in realism and perspective of the late medieval and early modern periods, but also the scientific developments that were the distinguishing marks of western 'advance' – the understanding of anatomy, optics and natural phenomena.

Western painting, as in the Romantic picturesque, was prepared to depict oriental sculpture and architecture, but if architects were intrigued, European sculptors remained largely impervious to such eastern examples and painters never adopted any of the characteristics of the Persian or Mughal pictorial traditions. The influences, indeed, were almost wholly the other way, as first Chinese and Indian, and later Ottoman and Japanese painters sought to imitate European methods and styles, albeit with their own distinctive imprint, to please European clients.[2] But with the applied arts, mimicry operated in the reverse direction. From the seventeenth to the twentieth centuries, western producers of ceramics, furniture, textiles and wallpapers vied with each other, and with the originals, to orientalise their products in form, technique and decorative design. This distinction, it has often been suggested, neatly illustrates the highly normative approach to eastern art: the works of the dextrous and instinctive craftsmen could be valued and accepted on a wholly different plane from those of the true 'artist' whose genius and skills were dependent on related intellectual and scientific developments within a superior culture.

There are, however, major problems with a Saidian 'Orientalist' interpretation of these artistic distinctions. Such attitudes were not monolithic; they did not repeatedly feed off each other; and they were not necessarily related in any close or instrumental way to imperialism and racial attitudes. By the nineteenth century, the worlds of art, and particularly of design, proceeded by a sequence of revolts, or secessions, which involved the repeated revaluation of previous or other traditions. Moreover, by the second half of the nineteenth century, it was a major preoccupation of the avant-garde to break down the distinctions between the fine and applied arts, to elevate the craftsman to equal status with the artist and to assert the need for artists also to be craftsmen. This was connected with three major developments of the period. The first of these, dating from at least the 1830s, was anxiety about the extent to which industrial techniques of mass production produced artefacts which represented a serious decline in craft/art values, the reproduction of a shoddy uniformity. The second was the search for total art, the full integration of architecture and its internal environment or the theatrical union of music, words, costume, design and acting. And the third was the arrival of simplicity as the prime criterion of internal design, a simplicity which reacted against the clutter of mid-Victorian taste by using lighter colours, spare furniture sparsely distributed and pierced screens, reserving colour for bright rugs, textiles or framed prints.

These highly influential notions of progressive design, which were to continue to be significant well into the twentieth century, have their origins during the loaded pause immediately preceding the 'new imperialism' of the late nineteenth century and reached their apotheosis when the extension of imperial power was in full swing. Revaluations of eastern art and design were taking place just when pseudo-scientific racism was reaching its peak. It is true that the fresh appreciation of eastern arts was sometimes elaborately fitted into a racial hierarchy, often primarily for popular consumption, and that oriental craftsmanship and artistic values were manipulated to satisfy occidental debates about the relationship between industrial production, crafts and design, but there can be little doubt that it is in this period that there is considerable blurring between the previously well-defined fine and decorative arts.

VII   Dresser wrote that 'Persian carpets are also models of what carpets should be: they are less radiant than many of the Indian works, but are almost more mingled in colour effect'.

Turkey textiles had been entering Europe since the sixteenth century and, al- **VIII** though Christopher Dresser found them less satisfactory than Persian or Indian designs, they appeared in many paintings.

In the case of Japan, this first took place from the 1860s and led to a Japanese craze, seriously pursued by many artists, but also heavily burlesqued in the theatre. Although Partha Mitter has argued that a significant revaluation of the Indian fine arts only occurred in the twentieth century, some bridging of the gulf between the highly regarded crafts of the subcontinent and Indian art began to take place in the final years of the nineteenth century. As we shall see in the next chapter, this coincides precisely with the discovery of some aspects of oriental music, particularly that of the gamelan players of Bali who appeared at the Paris Exposition of 1889. The high noon of imperialism, far from coinciding with a downgrading of the arts of the subordinate peoples of the East (and it should be remembered that throughout this period Japan was subject to the nationally degrading unequal treaties), actually coincided with a new appreciation. Of course this fresh estimation was value-laden and sometimes culturally blinkered. It invariably involved a misinterpretation of the true provenance of examples of oriental art and of the circumstances of their production. It was used as a means of assuaging occidental apprehension about the direction of art and design, as a stick

13   Indian artists responding to European taste and a western market: *A Tiger Hunt at Jhajjar*, Rohtak district, Punjab, by Ghulam Ali Khan, Delhi, *c*.1820.

to beat reaction, and as a focus for new secessionist directions. But it also involved a closer and more respectful relationship between the artists of two cultures and the developing amalgam between the forms and techniques of the arts of different traditions became a repeated source of inspiration both to the East and to the West into the twentieth century. The increasingly syncretic arts of recent times represent not so much a break with those of an imperial past as a building upon the contacts which took place during that period.

Some of the individual artists of these late nineteenth-century movements were consciously radical in their politics, espousing socialist or quasi-socialist standpoints. Others were not. Some adopted oriental forms precisely because they served as visual representations of their radicalism; others, often accepting secondary influences, did so for what seem like purely aesthetic reasons. The latter certainly distrusted, deprecated even, the ideological bent of their associates. Among the commentators, some were fervent imperialists, precisely because they identified in imperialism a feudal and artistic atavism that was anti-industrial, anti-Modernist, anti-urban and certainly anti-socialist. Thus oriental art and crafts were used to underpin a variety of standpoints, both Modernist and quasi-medieval. To make matters yet more complex, such sources of oriental inspiration continued to be influential in the twentieth century, sometimes in craft fields – as in ceramics – sometimes as part of the reassertion of the capacity of industrial products to adhere to canons of good design – as in textiles.

It cannot be denied then that oriental arts and crafts were subjected to a repeated process of adaptation and manipulation to satisfy occidental arguments about design, transactions that often involved misinterpretations and false applications. But equally it cannot be gainsaid that out of this relationship came much mutual inspiration and growing respect. In economic terms these transactions may have been unequal, though from the standpoint of the late twentieth century, some of these inequalities were to reverse over time, but in artistic and aesthetic terms, as in the potting relationship between Hamada and Bernard Leach, the balance was very different. Indeed, in many and various ways, the crafts and design relationship between East and West had been a two-way process from the very beginnings of European contact with oriental design in the sixteenth and seventeenth centuries.

Chinese producers of ceramics and other goods had been accustomed to adapting their wares to the market from an early age. In the medieval period, their exports to the Middle East fitted the specific requirements of the market and it was some of these examples which were the first to reach Europe. By the seventeenth century, Chinese exports had more to do with European taste and fashion as they deviated increasingly from indigenous style. Thus chinoiserie, the construction of an imaginary Orient to satisfy a western vision of human elegance and refinement within a natural and architectural world of extreme delicacy, was as much a product of Chinese craftsmen as of the West.[3] If their culture was prettified, it was also idealised through such wares. As porcelain, furniture, silverware, fans and other goods became increasingly important in the 'private trade' of the employees of the East India Company, specific orders were fulfilled. The celebrated 'armorial' wares, with their curious orientalising of some of the heraldic devices and their inclusion of words that should not have been there all subscribed, of course, to the criteria in shape and size of the western dinner and tea services. If westerners preferred handles on their cups, they were supplied with handles. Beyond this, specifically western artefacts like inkwells, watch-stands, jardinières and punchbowls were produced. This adaptation of Chinese technique and style to western forms was also developed in respect of furniture, silverware and silk goods. Since by this time western craftsmen were imitating Chinese techniques, as in lacquer-work, for example, some of the pieces of furniture are often accepted as European, although they are of Chinese origin. In the case of Cantonese silver, the silversmiths reproduced the hallmarks and other markings of western makers, though they sometimes added Chinese signatures as well.[4]

This craze for chinoiserie was powerfully lampooned by Macaulay. In his *History of England*, he used the eighteenth-century Chinese fashion as a means of attacking Queen Mary and her introduction of Dutch taste to England, but he did so with all the cultural arrogance that also characterised his Indian Education minute of 1835:

> In every corner of the mansion appeared a profusion of gewgaws, not yet familiar to English eyes. Mary had acquired at the Hague a taste for the porcelain of China, and amused herself by forming at Hampton a vast collection of hideous images and of vases on which houses, trees, bridges and mandarins were depicted in outrageous defiance of all the laws of perspective. The fashion, a frivolous and inelegant one it must be owned, which was set by the amiable Queen, spread fast and wide. In a few years almost every great house in the kingdom contained a Museum of these grotesque baubles. Even statesmen and generals were not ashamed to be renowned as judges of teapots and dragons; and satirists long continued to repeat that a fine lady valued her mottled green pottery as much as she valued her monkey, and much more than she valued her husband.[5]

Macaulay was spitting into a hurricane. However much he berated the lack of perspective and 'frivolity' of Chinese wares, they had not only become standard decoration in all the great houses in the land, but they were also destined to influence fundamentally the ceramic production in Europe, both from the great potteries and eventually through industrially produced 'demotic' china with its characteristic willow pattern. Writers from John Gay to George Meredith celebrated the fascination with 'blue and white';[6] the Victorians were thoroughly intrigued by the 'willow-pattern legend' and conducted lengthy debates about it in publications such as *Notes and Queries*.[7] Charles Lamb in his essay 'Old China' described his partiality for china as 'almost feminine' and announced that in great houses he asked to see the china closet before the picture gallery. Unlike Macaulay, he had, he wrote, no repugnance for 'those little, lawless, azure-tinctured grotesques, that under the notion of men and women, float about, uncircumscribed by any element, in that world before perspective – the china tea-cup'.[8]

Within a few decades of Lamb and Macaulay, that very lack of perspective was to be one of the prime artistic attractions of oriental design. Chinese 'blue and white' and Japanese wares were to be powerfully and positively revalued in the later nineteenth century. By that time, when western factories had flooded working-class homes and the rest of the world with debased oriental designs, there was a renewed search for originals in China and Japan. At times, artists and design pundits seemed unsuspecting that these too had been adapted and produced to meet a western demand for a new and purified source.[9] The fact was that there were no originals, that, apart from the country wares of the ordinary people, oriental ceramics since time immemorial had been produced to satisfy outsiders, to meet their perception of what such pottery should look like. Even so, their compositional and design values and their very lack of perspective were going to bring fresh influences to European art. Not only generals but also the hardest-headed artists of the age were to be obsessed with oriental ceramics, wholly belying the broad hints of Gay, Lamb and Macaulay that this was a frivolously gendered craze.

European potters first imitated the unglazed red stonewares from Yixing, adding pseudo-oriental decoration, and even Chinese seal-marks, to European shapes. The polychrome decorated wares from the Arita district of Japan, both those produced by the Kakiemon family of potters and those exported through the port of Imari, soon followed in the early eighteenth century, but it was the refined and translucent 'blue and white' wares which were the real goal of the European potters. It took them some time to be able to imitate the technique and during the first decades of the century they copied oriental prototypes in the much inferior tin-glazed earthenware. British porcelain began to reach acceptable technical standards from the 1740s, somewhat later than on the Continent, such that the Bow factory actually called itself 'New Canton'. The porcelains remained expensive and largely the preserve of the upper

classes, but creamwares and pearlwares were developed to satisfy middle-
class demand. In the later eighteenth century, techniques of glazing and
printing became increasingly sophisticated and a wider range of styles
was adopted, including the more elaborate and brightly coloured Mandarin wares. Some factories, such as Chelsea and Worcester, specialised
in the Japanese techniques and decorative styles.[10]

By the nineteenth century, not only were such ceramics being
mass-produced, reaching further down the social scale as they were
cheapened in both quality and price, but they were also being exported
back to Asia. By 1800 the Chinese armorial export wares had died out;
indeed many had been produced in Europe to replace broken examples
and maintain sets. This heralded reverse export wares: by 1850 there
were at least eight companies in Scotland alone (the most important
being J. & M. P. Bell of Glasgow) exporting china to the East.[11] These
factories seemed to understand the market well and were very successful
in creating multicoloured designs for different destinations, identified
by name (in Malay characters) in the runs of pots and plates: Batavia,

14   A collection of Japanese kitchenware sent to Glasgow as part of the gift of art-
wares from Japan in 1878.

Malacca, Kalantan, Pekin, Kwantung, Siam, Johore, Singapore, Sumatra, Sunda, Borneo, Makasar, Amboina, Celebes, even Japan, to name but a few. The destinations and relative cheapness of these wares imply that they were being sold to people who would not in the past have encountered such forms and styles. They were also occasionally collected by Europeans and consequently found their way back to Europe. Oriental manufacture never ceased, despite being so seriously undercut by mass-produced items, and it continued to adapt to the desires of the West, particularly in the case of Japan after its long period of isolation was disrupted by the arrival of Commodore Perry's 'black ships' in 1853.

Other techniques, such as transfer printing, led to plates appearing with oriental scenes, hunts, Indian buildings, European settlements in the East, Chinese landscapes, and so on. Such scenes also appeared on wallpapers, initially produced in China and, although their use was unknown there, screens and fans. Chinoiserie wallpapers were particularly popular in the 1750s and 1760s, but they were used throughout the period from the early eighteenth to the nineteenth centuries. Production moved to Europe, as paper-making techniques improved and mass-produced printing became possible. Pseudo-oriental designs, involving

Bruce James Talbert, original design for 'Sunflower' wallpaper, 1878. A design   **15**
for Jeffrey and Co., boldly executed against Japanese wave and lattice patterns.

mainly stylised flowers and trees, re-emerged in the wallpapers of William Morris's Arts and Crafts movement. Oriental fans had likewise appeared from the late seventeenth century and had become a highly fashionable accessory, with their beautifully painted designs and scenes.[12] They were exported in different structural forms and a variety of media, including ivory, tortoiseshell, lacquer, silk and paper, displaying a range of painting techniques. In this case, European copies largely failed to compete with the eastern originals and China and Japan recaptured the market during the oriental vogue of the 1860s. The illustrations on such fans were to be one of several influences upon European art in the later nineteenth century.

Far Eastern fashions were stimulated by publications. One of the first of these was *A Treatise of Japanning or Varnishing* by John Stalker and George Parker of 1688, which has been described as a do-it-yourself guide of great value to furniture makers. Stalker and Parker clearly revered Japanese art, for they extolled Japan in hyperbolic terms:

> Let not the Europeans any longer flatter themselves with the empty notions of having surpassed all the world beside in stately Palaces, costly Temples, and sumptuous Fabricks; Ancient and modern Rome must now give place: the Glory of one Country, Japan alone, has exceeded in beauty and magnificence all the pride of the Vatican at this time, and the Pantheon heretofore.[13]

Due allowance must be made for Protestant pleasure at an oriental surpassing of papal Rome, but such an encomium was scarcely to be repeated until the later nineteenth century. Publications on Chinese design reached a peak in the mid-eighteenth century when a number of pattern-books purporting to illustrate Chinese design were issued. As well as Sir William Chambers's *Designs for Chinese Buildings, Furniture, Dresses etc.* of 1757, Messrs Edwards and Darly published *A New Book of Chinese Designs, Calculated to Improve the present Taste, consisting of Figures, Buildings and Furniture, Landskips, Birds, Beasts, Flowrs and Ornaments* in 1754. Paul Decker's *Chinese Architecture Civil and Ornamental* appeared in 1759, while Matthias Lock's *A New Book of Ornaments . . .* of 1752 and Thomas Chippendale's *The Gentleman and Cabinet Maker's Directory* of 1754 both contained many 'Chinese' designs.[14] Chippendale, though the most famous of the furniture makers who used Chinese motifs, was not the only one.[15] In London, Thomas Johnson and John Linnell, as well as Chippendale and Lock, turned out rococo chinoiserie. Whereas initially Chinese and Japanese techniques, like lacquer-work or japanning and gilding, were adopted by European makers, the rococo chinoiserie adopted writhing and twisting forms, often incorporating fanciful Chinese figures, which bore little or no relationship at all to Chinese techniques or design. These pattern-books, however, served to keep the exotic and imaginary Chinese decorations before the attention of designers through all the vicissitudes of fashion. Bamboo furniture and other furniture-related types, like trays, game-boards and boxes, continued to be made both in Asia and by European design plagiarists.[16]

This story of Asian exports, European imitations, often mass-produced, and a fresh interest in original techniques in the late nineteenth century can be retold in the case of textiles. The English East India Company, having failed to secure the spices of the East Indies, where the Dutch were dominant, turned its attention to India. The three centres of Company power coincided with important textile-producing regions: Cambay and Surat for cheaper cottons, chintzes, muslins and silk embroideries; the Coromandel coast in the south-east for Golconda chintzes and cotton piece-goods; and muslins, silks and silk and cotton mixtures from Bengal. The East India Company thus came to supply both ends of the market: high-quality silks and hand-painted chintzes for the rich and the aristocracy; printed chintzes (by print block) for the middling sort and cheap, plain cotton piece-goods for the lower orders, particularly slaves in the West Indies. All coloured items were fixed with dyes in which India was regarded as pre-eminent.[17]

As with ceramics, patterns were soon guided by European taste. The popular flowering tree design, seen as quintessentially Asian, was in fact a hybrid made up of Hindu, Islamic, Chinese and European elements to conform with western taste. It has been suggested that 'it was no less exotic to Asian eyes than . . . to European'.[18] From the earliest days of the trade in the 1640s the directors of the East India Company were asking for different colours and patterns to conform with English taste. By the 1660s illustrations of designs were being sent out to India for the Indian cotton painters to follow. These soon reflected the interest in chinoiserie, so that we have European versions of Chinese decoration being transmitted to India to be copied by Indian textile producers. Fantasy was, however, built upon fantasy; imaginary Orients overlaid each other. Indian craftsmen adapted and modified the model patterns in the light of their own experience; repeated copies ensured that they became unrecognisable in terms of the originals. As Irwin and Brett put it:

> English and Chinese flowers, distorted into something fanciful by Indian eyes to whom the plants were alien, were now welcomed in their new form as expressions of exotic fantasy. The wheel had turned full circle. What had earlier been sent out to help the Indian craftsmen to conform to conventions of English taste were now returning in parodied form to

feed the new appetite for exoticism. The directors [of the East India Company] wanted more and more of such goods, and the more fanciful the better![19]

Indian textiles were so superior to their European competitors that they threatened the livelihood of domestic producers. By legislation of 1700 and 1701 the English attempted to control cloth imports, but widespread smuggling led to a ban upon their use in 1720. These restrictions were relaxed later in the century, but by that time technical developments such as the copperplate process and, from 1783, roller printing ensured cheap mass production in the West. Indian textile production for export, as graphically recounted by Marx, was doomed, although Indian handloom weavers, producing for the local market, probably survived more satisfactorily than their European counterparts. The fanciful hybrid designs, exotic yet mythically oriental, continued to dominate the patterning of fabrics. By the later nineteenth century the separate streams of industrial production and Indian crafts began to converge once more.

Shawl production perfectly illustrates the relocation of weaving, the development of larger-scale industry, the ubiquity of designs of Asian origin, and the vagaries of fashion. Kashmiri shawls, made from soft goatswool, were introduced into Britain in the eighteenth century, sometimes by soldiers returning from Indian campaigns. By the last quarter of the century, inferior imitations (goatswool being unavailable) were being produced in Lyons, Edinburgh and Norwich. Around the turn of the nineteenth century an Edinburgh manufacturer put out work to the handloom weavers of Paisley. Soon the Paisley weavers, operating as a cottage industry, became dominant in shawl production and the characteristic teardrop or pine-shoot design became inseparably associated with that town. The introduction of the Jacquard loom in the 1830s led to more highly capitalised, larger-scale production, but by the 1870s changing dress fashion sent shawl production into dramatic decline. In the course of the nineteenth century, the parodying of an Indian form and design brought both prosperity and periodic distress to the weavers of western Scotland. Nevertheless, the last Paisley handloom survived in production until 1943 and the Paisley pattern, which had been developed from a number of oriental sources, had become the most familiar cliché of all textile design.[20]

Far Eastern ceramics and Indian textiles represented the development and adaptation of genuine Asian forms and patterns. Contemporary production was encouraged, extolled and undercut. Egyptian crazes were very different: design ideas derived from archaeological prototypes were developed in the West to meet European fashion. The appearance of pyramids and obelisks in garden structures, funerary devices and civic monuments was surveyed in the last chapter. There were three phases of Egyptian fashion, 1790–1830, the later Victorian period and the 1920s. Egyptian forms, motifs and scenes were applied to artefacts and *objets d'art* as diverse as furniture, plates, wine-coolers, inkstands, vases, candelabra, book-ends and clocks.[21] The most spectacular example was the Sèvres Egyptian service made for the Empress Josephine and subsequently given to the Duke of Wellington, now on display in Apsley House, London.[22] The second phase saw a particular concentration on many aspects of furniture making, including chairs, stools, benches and even pianos, ceramics, dress material and jewellery. The third, associated with the opening of the tomb of Tutankhamun, influenced all of these, as well as shopfronts and cinemas, and fed stylised motifs into Art Deco.[23]

Other syncretic furniture-making traditions developed throughout the East, European styles and originals being rendered in quasi-oriental form, including chairs, cabinets, chests, caskets, cradles and mirror surrounds elaborately carved in hardwoods with marquetry inlays, ebony, ivory, tortoiseshell and gilt decoration. Such furniture was used by European expatriates in Asia from the seventeenth to the nineteenth centuries and was sometimes brought back to the West, but it was too elaborate to have much wider influence on furniture design.[24]

Of all eastern products, however, few had a higher reputation than carpets and rugs. They were among the first Asian exports to reach Europe, initially via Venice, and were highly prized in Tudor times. Henry VIII was said to own four hundred of 'Turkey making'; Cardinal Wolsey, famously, ordered supplies from Venice; Bess of Hardwicke treasured fine examples at Hardwicke Hall in Derbyshire. Initially, they were used to cover tables, chests and walls as well as floors; only in the eighteenth century were they treated exclusively as floor coverings.[25] In the seventeenth century, some aristocratic families began to order armorial carpets from India: through the East heraldic display and self-satisfaction had moved from sculptured slabs and bosses and painted wooden panels to carpets, textiles and ceramics.[26]

From Tudor times, portraiture abounds in such carpets, each period reflecting the prime fashion in the region of production. In the sixteenth century, Star Ushak carpets were favoured as well as 'Turkey' types produced in Cairo and elsewhere in the Middle East. In the seventeenth century there was a shift towards Persian examples, which appear prominently in the portraits of Van Dyck. The floral patterns, big central medallions and naturalistic representation of humans and animals (including scenes of the hunt) appealed to Baroque taste rather more than abstract, repeated designs. The Persians, however, began to produce specifically for the European market and probably emphasised these characteristics once they knew that they were sought after. The East India Company discovered a new source in Mughal India and began to export carpets from Agra and Lahore.[27] Oriental rugs appear in the Indian portraits of Johann Zoffany, among others in the eighteenth century and, as we have seen in Chapter 4, they figure prominently in the works of the 'Orientalist' painters of the Middle East, particularly in their rendering of carpet bazaars.

Such a consistent painterly interest reflects the excitement induced in artists at the beauty of such carpets, the quality of their craftsmanship and materials, the complex and fascinating character of their designs and the technical challenge of rendering them in paint. Colour, texture, pattern, the play of light upon the pile and the contrast with the various fabrics of clothing, curtains and other hangings (themselves often displaying oriental influences in patterning) posed repeated exercises in composition, pigment, perspective and lighting effects to artists in succeeding centuries. With the Orientalists of the nineteenth century, carpets offered the opportunity to present abstract design with a Middle Eastern context of bright light, deep shade and the garments of vendors and purchasers. While attempts to imitate oriental carpets probably started in the sixteenth century, no one doubted that the quality of the eastern product could never be emulated. Designs had a considerable influence on carpets produced in the West, even, in highly debased form, upon the machine-made products of the nineteenth century.

Indeed, carpets formed a significant focus for the development of the artistic and crafts-based revolt of the later nineteenth century. Several artists and critics recognised in carpets the futility of the distinction between the fine and decorative arts. Delacroix remarked that 'the most beautiful pictures I have seen are certain Persian carpets'.[28] The painter and guru of the design revolution of late Victorian times, James McNeill Whistler, fervently admired oriental carpets, as did the leader of the Arts and Crafts movement, William Morris, the architect and designer E. W. Godwin and other commentators and designers like Charles Eastlake, Christopher Dresser and Walter Crane. In *Hints on Household Taste in Furniture, Upholstery and other Details* (London, 1868, with many subsequent editions) Eastlake noted the difference between the unique handmade qualities of eastern carpets and the numbing regularity and symmetry of mass-produced, machine-made European imitations.[29] Christopher Dresser's reverence for oriental carpets was such that he apologised that his language (in *Principles of Decorative Design* of 1873) might appear 'mystical' to the general reader: he regarded eastern rugs as pre-eminent in their softness, their richness, depth and 'fulness' of art-quality, their 'glowing neutral bloom' in radiant and bright colours, 'perfect marvels of colour-harmony'. The carpets of India, Persia, Smyrna and Morocco often had the 'effect of a garden full of flowers, or better, of the slope of a Swiss alp, where the flowers combine to form one vast harmonious "glow" of colour'. English carpets never produced these effects for 'want of skill in the ornamentist', 'want of judgment in the manufacturer', or 'want of taste on the part of the consumer', although Axminster carpets were trying the hardest.[30]

Dresser believed that 'Contact with Europeans unfortunately brings about the deterioration of Eastern art: in order that the European demand be met, quantity is produced and quality disregarded, for we cavil respecting price'.[31] William Morris thought that the degeneration of oriental arts was of longer standing. He was convinced that in recent centuries they had been debased from a golden age, and like Dresser he saw that decadence as having been induced by European influence. In a lecture delivered in 1879 he described the baleful influence of European commerce and taste upon oriental carpet and textile production from the late seventeenth century onwards.[32] Thus for Dresser and Morris, the late nineteenth-century revolution in crafts and design should have helped Asian craftsmen to rediscover the true sources and excellence of their arts as well as blend them sympathetically with the finest of European design ideas.

These efforts to break down the distinction between the fine and the decorative arts, as well as create fresh syncretic canons of taste, coincided with the revaluation of eastern pattern and ornament as well as the work of Asian craftsmen. The works of the seventeenth and eighteenth centuries that celebrated chinoiserie or japanning were merely looking for an extension in the taste and language of design, for fresh sensations stimulated by exotica. Those of the second half of the nineteenth century were seeking to achieve something much more profound, the resuscitation and purification of western arts and crafts, nothing less than a revolution in form and technique as well as design. Some sought to take that revolution further, to give it a social dimension, attempting to turn aside the repetitive work and urbanisation of industrial mass production in favour of craft guilds representing a return to the perceived artisanal formations of medieval times.[33] Thus, whereas the earlier exercises in taste had been directed at craftsmen producing for the aristocracy, the writers of the late nineteenth century were trying to reach not only architects and designers, but also the stonemasons, decorators, metalworkers and carpenters who worked in every town in the land. They also hoped to recreate guilds of potters, carpet makers, textile workers and jewellers, reproducing Asian models of both design and productive social formation, as they perceived them, in Britain. In that sense, it appears to be a reverse acculturation, an attempt to undercut the East not through mass production, but by the adoption of similar

techniques for the home market. However, the movement always acknowledged that in some crafts, Asian producers could never be excelled;
rather, by expressing fears of machine production in the East, its proponents hoped to revive and protect both western and eastern craftsmanship.

This propaganda did feed into some of the working-class auto-
didactic movements of the period and some celebrated guilds were established, but, while it may have helped to improve some aspects of
industrial design, it did little to turn aside the onward march of mass
production. Moreover, just as the schools of design established in the
early 1840s for the training of artisans had been almost completely taken
over by the middle classes, so too did these craft movements remain
firmly middle-class.

Of the many critics who commented on oriental crafts, among the
most influential were Owen Jones, Christopher Dresser (whom we have
already encountered waxing eloquently about eastern carpets) and George
Birdwood. Each wrote from different cultural and political perspectives;
each emphasised the work of a specific oriental tradition; and they directed their attention at different aspects of ornament and production
in relation to architecture, interior decoration and artefacts. All three of
them, together with Henry Cole, Matthew Digby Wyatt, Henry Dyce
and Richard Redgrave, were involved in the presentation of oriental arts
and crafts at the major London exhibitions between 1851 and 1886 and
all created arguments that were intended to enhance the western design
tradition, to improve both the values and techniques of artists and craftsmen in a wide range of fields. Oriental design was used as evidence in
the great nineteenth-century debate on whether ornament should offer
a realistic representation of natural forms or should be truthful to the
principles of nature in following its shapes in a symbolic or stylised
manner.

Owen Jones's great work, *The Grammar of Ornament* of 1856, is
a typical piece of Victorian taxonomy. He sets out not only to illustrate
and comment upon the ornamental design of sixteen cultures and periods, but also to establish laws or 'general principles' for 'the arrangement
of form and colour, in architecture and the decorative arts'. Of his
sixteen sections, no fewer than ten are oriental or oriental in inspiration
(Egyptian, Assyrian, Byzantine, Arabian, Turkish, 'Moresque', Persian
[both ancient and modern], Indian, 'Hindoo' and Chinese); one deals
with 'savage tribes'; and five are European (Greek, Pompeian, Roman,
Celtic and medieval). In adopting such a balance, Jones represented one
aspect of the Victorian reaction against the classical and Renaissance
traditions. He pronounced himself quite unmoved by Roman design,
which he regarded as merely a debased form of the Greek, and whereas
the Greeks had set out genuinely to glorify the gods, the Romans were

interested only in self-glorification. This theme of decline is much repeated in the work: each culture has a golden age, when the symbolic
representation of nature reaches its purest form, only to be lost either
through more realistic mimicry or through over-elaboration and departure from the principles of appropriate stylisation. His ideal periods were
early Egyptian, Arabian after an early imitative period and Moorish (or
Alhambraic, with which Jones became most closely associated and which
he regarded as the supreme example of delicacy and refinement combined with perfection in the distribution of the masses). Yet Jones also
extols much contemporary work from the Islamic and Indian worlds,
particularly Mughal.

The best of oriental design, Jones argued, supremely follows the
highest principles of ornament, founded in observations of nature's laws,
'grand ideas' that are 'eternal and immutable' though rendered in different forms and languages. Colour is always an aid to form and simple
elements, curvilinear or geometrical, are used to produce complicated
effects, through the free and full play of the imagination. He found all
these principles illustrated to the full in the 'gorgeous contributions' of
India, as well as Tunis, Egypt and Turkey, at the Great Exhibition of
1851. While a 'general disorder' was 'everywhere apparent in the application of Art to manufactures' in the West, the works of India and other
Muslim countries, representing 'so much unity of design, so much skill
and judgment in its application, with so much elegance and refinement
in the execution' succeeded in exciting 'a degree of attention from artists, manufacturers, and the public, which has not been without its fruits'.
He dismissed European exhibits as illustrating 'a fruitless struggle after
novelty', designs

> based upon a system of copying and misapplying the received forms of
> beauty of every bygone style of Art, without one single attempt to pro-
> duce an Art in harmony with our present wants and means of production
> – the carver in stone, the worker in metal, the weaver and the painter,
> borrowing from each other, and alternately misapplying the forms pecu-
> liarly appropriate to each.

Meanwhile, 'all the principles, all the unity, all the truth, for which we
had looked elsewhere in vain' were to be found in the transepts where
examples of Muslim design were displayed.[34]

One of the most attractive plates in Jones's *Grammar* – 'Leaves
and Flowers from Nature' – was drawn by Christopher Dresser, a distinguished botanist. He was to become, however, much more celebrated as
a critic, designer and dealer in the decorative arts, with a particular
interest in Japan. An admirer of Owen Jones, he had begun to link

botany to ornamental art as early as 1857 and published his *The Art of Decorative Design* in 1862. He was eager to link science and art and was also interested in the propagation of good design values among 'mechanics' or artisans. Hence he first published his *Principles of Decorative Design* as a series of articles in Cassell's *Technical Educator*,[35] later published as a book in 1873. Unlike the members of the Arts and Crafts movement, he was not prepared to reject industrialism, but wanted to see good design applied to industrial products. He agreed with them that there was no distinction between the artist and the craftsman: the person who could fashion a beautiful bowl, vase, chair or table was just as much an artist as the painter or sculptor. Such art should be ennobled by knowledge, judgement and beauty, rather than intrinsic value, for the best vehicles for art were the least costly materials. Whereas Jones had dealt purely in ornament, Dresser examined each of the crafts in turn: furniture, interior decorating, carpets, woven fabrics, pottery, glass and metalwork, hardware and stained glass. Like Jones, he found little worthy of praise in Roman design, while it was the East which had called forth the most

> gorgeous and beautiful developments of art which have existed, or still exist, with the Persians, Indians, Turks, Moors, Chinese, and Japanese. ... All the forms of ornament which these people have created are worthy of the most careful and exhaustive consideration, as they present art-qualities of the highest kind. I know of no ornament more intricately beautiful and mingled than the Persian – no geometric strapwork, or systems of interlacing lines, so rich as those of the Moors (the Alhambraic) – no fabrics so gorgeous as those of India – none so quaintly harmonious as those of China; and Japan can supply the world with the most beautiful domestic articles that we can anywhere procure.[36]

He surveyed all the arts of the East and thought that they generally complied with the principles of stylisation rather than imitation, concluding that even the 'commonest wares' of Japan and India 'are never utterly bad in art. Inharmonious colouring does not appear to be produced by these nations, and the same may be said of Persia and China, and, to an extent, of Morocco and Algeria.'[37] He excepted only those areas that had been in contact with Europe for too long and enjoined his working-class readers to study these arts in public collections and local museums.

Dresser's reverential view of Asian crafts and craftsmen was matched by that of Sir George Birdwood with specific reference to India. Whereas Jones and Dresser both dealt in the principles of design and ranged freely across oriental crafts (until Dresser specialised in Japan), Birdwood was interested mainly in the descriptions of Indian crafts within their social and cultural contexts. Like his counterpart Caspar Purdon Clarke in architecture, Birdwood was highly instrumental in the presentation of Indian arts at the exhibitions of the later nineteenth century and in the South Kensington Museum. His *The Industrial Arts of India* (2 volumes, 1880) comprised reprints of his handbook to the Indian Court at the Paris Exhibition of 1878 and his guide to the South Kensington collection. It has been said that Birdwood made a severe distinction between the fine arts and crafts, denigrating the former as products of a barbaric religion, and extolling the latter not only for colour, design, form and technique, but also for the social and ecological formations that went with them.[38] But he also asserted that all crafts were works of art, that the manual arts could only be fully understood through knowledge of the Hindu pantheon, and that the strength of Indians' craftsmanship lay in the seamless character of their life and their religion.[39] Birdwood's ideological stance was more pronounced than many of the other critics. He used Indian crafts to attack Victorian materialism, as stimulated by industrial production, with its associated social and environmental damage caused by urbanisation and pollution.

Birdwood provided a series of ecstatic descriptions of the whole range of Indian crafts, comparing them with the 'consistent general finish' and 'mechanical character' of European manufactures. Indeed, he deprecated the fact that the word 'manufacture' had lost its true origins and was coming to be exclusively applied to mass production. He feared the introduction of machinery to India and the sucking of hereditary craftsmen to the 'colossal mills of Bombay'.[40] This would cause irreparable damage to the natural artistry of the Indian craftsman, whose lot he compared with that of British workers:

> We cannot overlook this serenity and dignity of his life if we would rightly understand the Indian handicraftsman's work. He knows nothing of the desperate struggle for existence which oppresses the life and crushes the very soul out of the English working man. He has his assured place, inherited from father to son for a hundred generations, in the national church and state organisation; while nature supplies him with everything to his hand, but the little food and less clothing he needs, and the simple tools of his trade. . . .
>
> This at once relieves him from an incalculable dead weight of cares, and enables him to give to his work, which is also a religious function, that contentment of mind and leisure, and pride and pleasure in it for its own sake, which are essential to all artistic excellence.[41]

Birdwood connected this romantic primitivism to the relationship between village and land, aristocratic patron and crafts supplier. While such principles survived, 'the whole world has been ceaselessly pouring its bullion for 3,000 years into India', and yet all the marvellous fabrics and crafts wrought by Indian craftsmen 'have polluted no rivers, deformed no pleasing prospects, nor poisoned any air'. Moreover, these 'immemorial glories of India' expressed more fully than words 'the wisdom and beneficence of the Creator and the gladness and praise of men':

> Thus Indian Art, in every decorative detail, Aryan or Dravidian, bears witness to the universal conviction that the character of man's being and destiny is supernatural; and that human duty, and all that gives to daily intercourse the charm of art and the grace of culture, possess their reality and true meaning only in the purposes of a life beyond life.[42]

In the light of Victorian religious sensibility there could be no greater compliment.

These design commentators, together with the group around Henry Cole who were highly influential in design education and the organisation of exhibitions and museum displays, did not have a free run. Their attacks on western illusionist style and elevation of eastern symbolic representations were criticised by several anti-oriental commentators. Ralph Wornum and Sarsfield Taylor, often using the prominent *Art Journal* as their vehicle, depreciated eastern arts and expressed much hostility to the power of the Cole/Jones group.[43] They represented, however, little more than flanking skirmishes to the advance of a small army of designers who were to feed into the continuing fascination with the East that was to endure through subsequent decades. Ruskin, of course, was much more influential, but when it came to oriental arts and crafts he had to indulge in even more contorted arguments than usual to reconcile his moral disapprobation for the culture that produced them with their undoubted beauty and power.

He found the art of Indians 'delicate and refined', redolent of Turneresque power in colour, but he damned it both because 'it never represents a natural fact' and because he saw an exaggerated power of colouring as being 'half savage', a product of 'their glorious ignorance of all rules', an instinctive faculty which itself illustrated their lack of advance in moral civilisation.[44] Such a notion of the instinctual capacities of eastern craftsmen was indeed used in both a complimentary and critical fashion by commentators,[45] but in Ruskin's case it represented the fact that he found it impossible to accept the civilising power of imperialism on the one hand and yet admire the arts of subordinate peoples on the other. He was unprepared to elevate the crafts of those who had perpetrated the 1857 revolt, which had caused him such moral distress, or who produced arts which represented for him a base religion of 'vile terror', a 'barbarous grotesque of mere savageness'. In this respect, perhaps, he was consistent, but his views on environmentalism and the notion of craft guilds were much closer to those of Birdwood. The difference was that he used medieval Europe rather than contemporary India as his exemplar.

Many of Ruskin's admirers, including William Morris and M. K. Gandhi, were prepared to separate his social and moral message from his highly ethnocentric views on art. Morris did admire Indian art, though he wrote little about it, and he tended perhaps to blend all eastern art together. In a lecture in 1879, he spoke of the Cole group as drawing attention to the 'beautiful works of the East', bidding us to 'look at an art at once beautiful, orderly, living in its own day, and above all, popular'.[46] It may well be that Morris had Japan in mind as much as India, for by the 1870s it was Japanese arts that were having the most profound influence on western designers. If the rediscovery of oriental crafts and ornament between the 1840s and 1860s represented a reaction to industrial mass production and fears about the debasement of design standards, the 'cult of Japan', as it has sometimes been called, constituted a much more overt reaction to conventional values in all the arts.

Like Indian crafts, Japanese art was fed into the bloodstream of western artists through the medium of the international expositions. In 1851, Japanese material was exhibited in the Chinese section, but it was first prominent in its own right, now entirely overshadowing China, at the London Exhibition of 1862 and had a powerful effect on an extraordinary range of artists and designers. At the exhibitions in Paris (1867, 1878 and 1889), Philadelphia (1876) and Chicago (1893), the Japanese exhibits were ecstatically received.[47] The principles of Japanese art, so profoundly different from the received canons of the West, constituted a set of standards around which radical western artists could group. The handling of blank space and a line that was both sinuous and bold, the stylisation of natural forms, the absence of perspective, the clarity and restraint of decoration and the combination of refinement, elegance and simplicity in rendition enthralled western designers. The spare arrangement of interiors within a light and seemingly insubstantial frame, the use of prints, screens, pots and other artefacts and the dramatic contrasts of costume and fabric, were to influence a succession of movements, Impressionism in art, aesthetic design, art nouveau, and styles from Glasgow to the Vienna Secession.

Sir Rutherford Alcock, the British Minister in Japan, arranged the exhibits for the 1862 exhibition and its effects were to reverberate through the worlds of art and design for the next fifty years. Henry Cole hailed a 'fresh well of art', which confirmed his view, expressed after the 1851 exhibition in relation to the Indian and Islamic exhibits, that it was 'from

16 Aubrey Beardsley, *The Toilet of Salome*, pen and ink drawing, engraved for the first English edition of Wilde's play, published in 1894. It reveals the influence of Japanese prints on the work of Beardsley.

the East that the most impressive lesson' was to be learnt. William Burges, who had himself helped to organise the Medieval Court at the exhibition, considered that 'truly the Japanese court is the real medieval court at the Exhibition'.[48] It was the highest compliment he could have paid. Artists, including Whistler, Burne-Jones and Rossetti in Britain, Fantin-Latour, Manet and Tissot in France, began to collect Japanese prints, textiles and pottery (also rediscovering Chinese blue and white and other Far Eastern porcelains), and all of these began to appear as props in their paintings. More profound Japanese influences, in compositional devices, perspective and colouring can be detected in the work of artists as diverse as Albert Moore, Lawrence Alma-Tadema, Rebecca and Simeon Solomon, John Atkinson Grimshaw and at a later period James Guthrie, Aubrey Beardsley, William Orpen, Duncan Grant, Frank Brangwyn, Samuel Peploe and Gwen John.[49] Soon a stream of photographers, artists and designers travelled to Japan to experience its arts and crafts at first hand. These included Felix Beato in the 1860s, Christopher Dresser in 1876–77, Frank Dillon (who had formerly kept a studio in Cairo) in 1876, Mortimer Menpes, Whistler's assistant, in 1887 and 1896, Alfred East in 1889–90, John Varley in 1890, and the Glasgow boys, George Henry and E. A. Hornel, in 1893–94.[50]

Christopher Dresser had published his *Principles* before he visited the East, basing his descriptions upon material he had seen at the 1862 and subsequent exhibitions as well as craftwork imported by dealers. In 1877, however, he made an extensive journey in Japan in which he covered 2,000 miles, took 1,000 photographs, and visited sixty-eight potteries as well as countless manufacturers of metalwork and wood-work, lacquer, fabrics, fans, baskets, bamboo, glass, and paper materials like wallpapers, fans, umbrellas, etc. He published his account of this visit in 1882 and described the manner in which he was treated as an official visitor, was received by the Emperor and was the agent for a museum exchange between the newly founded Japanese National Museum and the South Kensington Museum in London (the V. & A.). He bought vast quantities of craftwork, all 'quite irresistible', much of it on behalf of Tiffany of New York, and became, as he put it, almost weary of so much beauty and of the need to find new words to describe it.[51]

He was, he wrote, more interested in contemporary achievements than in antiquities, and was particularly impressed by the simplicity of techniques, the absence of advanced technology and by the status of the craftsman. The skilled workman, he noted, would be respectfully received and held in lengthy conversation by a prince while the richest of merchants would be beneath his notice:

> Who shall say that the Japanese are imperfectly civilised when they thus pay homage to learning and skill, and prefer these to wealth? Is not their

civilisation rather higher than ours? . . . Here we worship wealth, while we pass unnoticed the handicraftsman, however great his knowledge or subtle his work; yet too often the merchant employing the handicraftsman has secured his gains by acts of which he ought to be ashamed. . . . I cannot help thinking that the Japanese are right in regarding the man who can make a beautiful pot, a lovely cabinet, a charming fabric, or perfect netsuki as a being superior to the mere buyer and seller of goods.[52]

By the time Christopher Dresser published his *Japan, its Architecture, Art and Art Manufacturers* in 1882, he had already become a Japanese specialist, dealing in Japanese materials. He had sold them at the London Exhibition of 1873 and in 1878 he established with Charles Holme a company for the importation of Japanese and other oriental wares into Britain. Dresser was also a designer and he began to produce Japanese-inspired textile patterns, pottery, metalwork and glass in association with a number of manufacturers. By the end of the century he was described in *The Studio* as 'perhaps the greatest of commercial designers'.

Other designers who worked in styles influenced by Japan included B. J. Talbert (furniture), Walter Crane (book illustrations, as well as textiles and ceramics), Thomas Jekyll (furniture and interior decoration) and Arthur Silver (textiles, wallpaper and other aspects of interior design). Japanese prints and woodcuts became models for book design and illustrations, including those of the celebrated and influential Kate Greenaway in children's works.[53] The architects and designers E. W. Godwin and W. E. Nesfield were caught up in the cult of Japan, although they did not travel there, and this interest in the East helped them to move towards lighter styles associated with the 'Queen Anne' phase in the 1860s. Norman Shaw and C. F. A. Voysey were also influenced by the fascination with the Far East and corresponded with its leading exponents.

What is striking about the Japanese and associated oriental crazes is that they did not remain the arcane preserve of artists and designers. Through the medium of the theatre, as we shall see in Chapter 7, they became well known throughout the country. Through extensive commercialisation, they had a wide-ranging effect upon fabrics, dress design and personal ornament. They influenced street displays for national events and became a significant aspect of interior decoration in public buildings, exhibitions and middle-class homes. Cheap imitations appeared in homes further down the social scale. Two developments mark out the period as highly unusual: first, the commercialisation of styles influenced by the East coincided with the interests of the European avant-garde for some forty years: second, British design and retailing were in the forefront of this movement and helped to disseminate it throughout Europe.

As we have seen, Christopher Dresser supplied the Japanese displays for the London Exhibition of 1873. In the same year, he founded the Alexandra Palace Company which was to stock the emporia of a Japanese village at Alexandra Park in North London. After his visit to Japan in 1876–77, when he collected goods for Tiffany & Co. of New York, he went into partnership with Charles Holme, the future founder (in 1893) of the avant-garde journal *The Studio*, to import Japanese goods. In 1879 they opened a Japanese Warehouse in London, though it did not survive long. Dresser's Art Furniture Alliance shop appeared in New Bond Street in 1880.[54] But it was unquestionably Arthur Lasenby Liberty who had the greatest effect upon the commercialisation not only of Japanese, but also of North African, Indian and Chinese materials. Liberty had learnt something about oriental textiles while working for Farmer and Rogers's Great Shawl and Cloak Emporium in Regent Street, managing their Oriental Warehouse. In 1875, he opened his own shop in the same street and grandly called it East India House. Among his first employees was a Japanese boy called Hara Kitsui.[55]

For the ensuing forty years, Liberty's became, in effect, the commercial wing of the entire Orient-influenced avant-garde. A Paris branch was opened in 1880, in the wake of the *Exposition Universelle* of 1878, and links were established with other European companies. By now the old barriers between 'high art' and 'trade' had been broken down. Liberty became a close friend of many of the artists and designers of the Aesthetic movement and they began to meet in his shop. He joined many of the Societies associated with the arts and the Orient (including the Japan Society, the Asiatic Society and the Silk Association), and his circle included leading luminaries of the theatre (including Ellen Terry), dance (Isadora Duncan), members of the Arts and Crafts movement and artists who exhibited at the Grosvenor and (later) New Galleries.[56] They were all involved in discussion of the relationships among the arts and that elusive search for a total art.[57] Arthur Liberty employed a galaxy of celebrated designers, the best known being E. W. Godwin, C. F. A. Voysey and Guy Bentley.

At its opening, Liberty's purveyed only oriental silks. But soon it had seven departments, labelled as silks, embroideries, furniture, carpets, porcelain, curios and miscellaneous. Godwin described it as an 'enchanting cave' and wrote that an artist could 'almost decorate and furnish his rooms from this one shop'.[58] Liberty himself travelled extensively, visiting Moorish Spain, North Africa, Constantinople, India and Japan (in 1889–90 with Alfred East), and made sure that textiles and other products from all of these areas were available in the shop. He was involved in bringing Indian craftsmen to an Indian village in London's Battersea Park in 1885, and had extensive displays at the Paris Exhibitions in both

1889 and 1900. Liberty's styles were much imitated and pirated and
this, together with their own mail-order catalogues, helped to spread the
fashion around the country. They furnished many hotels and other
buildings, particularly associated with the leisure and entertainment industries, and kept oriental styles in the forefront of design right up to
the First World War. Their own Arabian tearoom set a trend and they
actively disseminated the 'Moorish' smoking-rooms that became such a
feature of the period. Many a hotel winter garden and ship's promenade
deck was fitted out with their bamboo furniture. After the war and
Arthur Liberty's death, the company ceased to be at the forefront of the
avant-garde, but it maintained interest in its oriental styles, on and off,
right through to the 1970s.

For artists and designers, the successive oriental fascinations represented a curious blend of restraint and theatricality. This combination
can certainly be found in Whistler, with the second predominating in his
'peacock room' for the Liverpool shipowner Francis Leyland and his libel
action against John Ruskin, both in the 1870s. This same mixture is to
be found in the aesthetic activities of the remarkably wide-ranging and
prolific group of Glasgow artists who revered his work. Whistler's move
from Realism to a more symbolic approach, his use of ill-defined flat
backgrounds and his handling of space and colour were profoundly influenced by Japanese art.[59] Whistler also painted screens and collaborated
with E. W. Godwin in making items of furniture painted in the Japanese
manner.[60] The extraordinary school of Glasgow artists and designers who
flourished in the late nineteenth and early twentieth centuries had direct
contact with an outstanding collection of Japanese wares, some one
thousand items in all, sent to the city in 1878 as part of an exchange of
crafts and industrial information organised by Japanese emissaries and
Scottish engineers working in Japan. This collection, which included
furniture, lacquer-work, musical instruments, ceramics, metalware, textiles
and paper, became part of a large exhibition of oriental art shown in the
city in 1881–82 which had a profound effect upon students at Glasgow's
School of Art.[61]

Although Charles Rennie Mackintosh never acknowledged Japanese inspiration, in common with other exponents of the Glasgow Style
and the Glasgow Boys group of artists, he surrounded himself with
Japanese objects.[62] Enthusiasm for Japanese art, inspired by the exchange
items, was strikingly widespread in Glasgow from the 1880s and Mackintosh imbibed its influences in his handling of interior space, his use of
wood, metalwork and textiles, his pierced screens, dashes of colour against
flat and neutral surfaces, and sinuous and stylised art-nouveau decoration.[63] Moreover, it has been shown that some of the devices on the
ironwork of his masterpiece, the Glasgow School of Art, were derived

from Japanese *mon* or heraldic shields.[64] Further, Mackintosh and his associates were influenced by the 'mystic abstractions' of the Dutch Indonesian artist, Jan Toorop, which served to earn for them the sobriquet of 'the spook school'.[65] They subscribed to the aesthetic and proto-relativist notion, so important to Beardsley and others, of the autonomy of the artist, responsible only to himself and free to ignore both the morality and artistic canons of an essentially philistine society.[66] Other proponents of the Glasgow Style, such as George Walton, pursued a more pragmatic and less theoretical approach, but their textiles, carpets, stained glass and interior design took on Japanese effects often at second hand.[67]

As each wave of *japonisme* passed over artists and designers between the 1860s and the 1920s, there was never any doubt that Japanese values represented a break with tradition, a vehicle for radicalism. Whistler and his Glasgow followers abhorred the values represented by Ruskin and the academicians of the high Victorian period. The Aesthetic and subsequent movements had to find galleries in which to exhibit their work and these secessions were marked by the founding in 1861 of the Fine Art Institute (later the Royal Glasgow Institute of the Fine Arts), the Glasgow Art Club and the Glasgow Society of Lady Artists (1883), to escape the traditionalist grip of the Royal Scottish Academy. In London, the establishment of the Grosvenor Gallery in 1877 and the New English Art Club in 1886 became the settings for the exhibitions of the new artists. The Arts and Crafts Exhibition Society followed in 1888 and secessions also appeared in Munich, Berlin and, in 1897, Vienna. It was at the Vienna Secession Exhibition of 1900 and again in Turin in 1902 that exponents of the Glasgow style and members of the Arts and Crafts were to find international fame.[68] All of these movements sought to break down the division between fine art and crafts, were involved in the search for a total art, and were more or less influenced by the East, particularly Japan.

By Edwardian times, Liberty's style continued to enjoy a boom, but by then an overblown opulence and theatricality had taken over. The soft pastel shades of oriental silks that had so impressed the Aesthetic movement were being superseded by the gaudy colours and dramatic primary combinations that were to make the designs of Diaghilev's *Ballets Russes* so sensational. *Haute couture* exercised powerful effects on both design and social life, as was illustrated by Margot Asquith's notorious exhibition of the Poiret collection from Paris at 10 Downing Street (known in the popular press as Gowning Street) in 1911.[69] But at the same time, the sinuous lines, sharp contrasts and handling of space of Japanese prints, exaggerated and fed through the work of Aubrey Beardsley, became the formative influence on twentieth-century poster design.[70] From the turn of the century, images of Japan and other aspects

17   The railings of the Glasgow School of Art by Charles Rennie Mackintosh: the Japanese *mon* theme in the metalwork represents Mackintosh's adoption of Japanese heraldic forms to produce a striking pattern and contrasts with the uprights of the railings.

of the Orient circulated through the immensely popular postcards that were sold at exhibitions and other outlets, including corner stationers. Some of these were printed in Europe for the British market. Sometimes, no doubt, these images of Japan would have struck a particular resonance with those boy scouts who, from 1908, were being urged by Baden-Powell to follow the example of the Japanese, particularly their devotion to bushido law.[71]

Such images, like the work of so many artists, often purported to depict a traditional, refined and ethereal East. Ironically, of course, this cult of *japonisme* coincided with rapid westernisation and development of industrial skills in Japan, those in the heavy industries largely learned from Glasgow. Many feared the advance of mechanisation in Japan and the effects it would have on its arts and crafts. Perhaps it was for this reason that so many of the visiting artists, including Menpes, Henry and Hornel, preferred to depict a timeless, romanticised Japan. Nevertheless, Japanese crafts would survive, to be taken up in the twentieth century by Edmund Leach. Before the First World War, Leach was interested in furniture, lithographs, etchings, drawings and paintings, having been taught by Frank Brangwyn some of the artistic and crafts techniques of both West and East. But from his meeting with Shoji Hamada in 1919 and his return to England with the great Japanese potter in 1920, he became a ceramics specialist. He came to be revered by Japanese artists, who saw him as attempting to knit together western and eastern arts, not only in technique and design, but also through a particular philosophical approach to pots and to nature. Leach founded a whole school of potters, many of them working at St Ives, who carried forward his oriental syncretism into modern times.[72]

Leach represents the most celebrated instance of profound eastern influence upon a western artist in the twentieth century, but the search for syncretic forms was to be a characteristic of other artistic developments, from the graphic arts to music. These continuing attempts to seek inspiration through hybrid arts have survived, and have even been encouraged by the divisions of war and decolonisation in the twentieth century. Partha Mitter has demonstrated the ways in which twentieth-century cultural relativism and the rejection of the 'moral' and canonical approach of Ruskin led to the positive influence of Indian art upon artists and sculptors. E. B. Havell and A. K. Coomeraswamy were such successful advocates of Indian and Sri Lankan art that they influenced western critics and practitioners such as William Rothenstein, Roger Fry and Eric Gill.[73] At the same time, though it forms no part of this study, the rediscovery and reinterpretation of Indian art came to constitute an important part of the Bengali renaissance and Indian nationalism.[74]

However, Mitter's notion of a 'Victorian interlude' in design

ultimately followed by twentieth-century appreciation of the fine arts is
surely too episodic. The distinction between applied and fine arts was
already being broken down in the late nineteenth century, and the revaluation of the latter had its origins at the very least when Rodin, Degas
and Moreau became intrigued by Indian art, particularly when it was
displayed in Paris in 1900. Earlier, at the Colonial and Indian Exhibition
of 1886, when no European arts were exhibited, the Indian were placed
in the category of 'fine arts', downgrading African and others into 'ethnic' or 'savage'. Thus Indian arts edged their way up the racial hierarchy.
The high reputation of the Japanese arts had to be explained away, as
Greenhalgh has shown, by the racial regrading of the Japanese, phreno-
logy being called in as evidence.[75]

Inevitably, there was a tension between the valuation of oriental
art and design, its power to inspire western artists, and the political and
racial contexts from which it emerged. Some commentators, notably
Jones and Dresser, seemed to ignore these relationships, while for others,
like Ruskin, they were insuperable. Those who used eastern arts to renew
what they saw as the flagging or reactionary tastes of Europe sometimes
neglected the ideological dimension, as the Glasgow School seemed to
do, while others saw it as an essential constituent of a political, even anti-
imperial radicalism. Nevertheless, the record should be seen as a continuous one, in which western arts repeatedly sought a refreshing draught of
inspiration from other periods and cultures. There were of course complex social and economic forces at work which saw the products of
oriental crafts, together with the technical expertise and decorative values
which they represented, stimulated, adapted, corrupted, undercut and
exploited – though not necessarily in that order. But while some aspects
of competition (but not all) are clearly inseparable from colonial economic influence, there is no chronological coincidence between levels of
artistic valuation and imperial rule, no consistent or monolithic relationship between aesthetic movements and power. The efforts to revive western
crafts and infuse them with what were perceived to be superior levels of
design seem to have arisen out of genuine respect. And this movement,
which developed Establishment overtones, clearly differed strikingly from
the idiosyncrasies of radical artists seeking to strike out in new directions
and assert their independence from established canons partly, at least,
through the inspiration of the East. What is clear is that a full understanding of the 'oriental obsession' can only come from placing the
successive fascinations with Muslim, Indian and Japanese traditions together. When regard for eastern arts is viewed in its entirety, its relationship with imperial power becomes less a matter of Said's 'flexible positional
superiority' and more a reflection of Victorian doubt and apprehension,
suffused with a yearning for transcultural inspiration.

Notes

1   For example, in Partha Mitter, *Much Maligned Monsters: a History of European Reactions to Indian Art* (Oxford, 1977) and Paul Greenhalgh, *Ephemeral Vistas: the Expositions Universelles, Great Exhibitions and World Fairs, 1851–1939* (Manchester, 1988).

2   For examples of such European-inspired, though hybrid paintings, see Patrick Conner, *The China Trade, 1600–1860* (Brighton, 1986); Craig Clunas, *Chinese Export Watercolours* (London, 1984); Mildred Archer, *Company Paintings: Indian Paintings of the British Period* (London, 1992); C. A. Bayly (ed.), *The Raj, India and the British 1600–1947* (London, 1990); Tomoko Sato and Toshio Watanabe (eds), *Japan and Britain: an Aesthetic Dialogue, 1850–1930* (London, 1991).

3   Oliver Impey, *Chinoiserie: the Impact of Oriental Styles on Western Art and Decoration* (London, 1977); Madeleine Jarry, *Chinoiserie: Chinese Influences on European Decorative Art, Seventeenth and Eighteenth Centuries* (London, 1981); David Howard, *Chinese Armorial Porcelain* (London, 1974); David Howard and John Ayers, *China for the West* (London, 1978); John Ayers, Oliver Impey and J. V. G. Mallet, *Porcelain for Palaces: the Fashion for Japan in Europe, 1650–1750* (London, 1990).

4   Conner, *China Trade*, pp. 104–11.

5   Thomas Babington Macaulay, *The History of England from the Accession of James the Second*, Vol. III (London, 1853), pp. 56–7. Macaulay appended a footnote which read, 'Every person who is well acquainted with Pope and Addison will remember their sarcasm on this taste. Lady Mary Wortley Montagu took the other side. "Old China", she says, "is below nobody's taste, since it has been the Duke of Argyle's, whose understanding has never been doubted either by his friends or his enemies."'

6   In 1725, John Gay wrote:

>   What ecstasies her bosom fire!
>   How her eyes languish with desire!
>   How blest, how happy should I be,
>   Were that fond glance bestowed on me!
>   New doubts and fears within me war
>   What rivals near? A China Jar.
>   China's the passion of her soul;
>   A cup, a plate, a dish, a bowl
>   Can kindle wishes in her breast
>   Inflame her joy, or break her rest.

Quoted in Terence A. Lockett, *Oriental Expressions: the Influence of the Orient on British Ceramics* (Stoke-on-Trent, 1989); George Meredith, *The Egoist* (London, 1879), p. 413.

7   A question about the origins of the willow pattern appeared in the first series of *Notes and Queries*, vi, 27 November 1852, p. 509.

8   Charles Lamb, 'Old China' in *Essays of Elia* (London, 1889).

9   Sato and Watanabe (eds), *Japan and Britain*, p. 80; Antonia Lovelace, *Art for Industry: the Glasgow–Japan Exchange of 1878* (Glasgow, 1991), p. 42.

10 Lockett, *Oriental Expressions*; B. Watney, *Eighteenth-Century English Blue and White Porcelain* (London, 1979).

11 A collection of such 'reverse export wares' is to be found in the Royal Scottish Museum, Edinburgh.

12   I am grateful to Alison Grant for information about oriental fans; see Nancy J. Armstrong, *Fans* (London, 1984) and *Fans from the Fitzwilliam* (Cambridge, 1985); also Susan Mayor, *Collecting Fans* (London, 1980).

13   Sato and Watanabe (eds), *Japan and Britain*, pp. 16–17.

14   Susan Lambert (ed.), *Pattern and Design: Designs for the Decorative Arts 1480–1980* (London, 1983), p. 101.

15   Christopher Gilbert, *The Life and Work of Thomas Chippendale* (Bristol, 1978), especially pp. 86–7, 112–16.

16   Lambert (ed.), *Pattern and Design* and Conner, *The China Trade*.

17   John Irwin and Katharine Brett, *The Origins of Chintz, with a Catalogue of Indo-European Cotton-paintings in the Victoria and Albert Museum, London and the Royal Ontario Museum, Toronto* (London, 1970); John Guy and Deborah Swallow (eds), *Arts of India, 1550–1900* (London, 1990), pp. 156–71.

18   Irwin and Brett, *Origins of Chintz*, p. 16.

19   Irwin and Brett, *Origins of Chintz*, p. 5.

20   John Irwin, *Shawls: a Study in Indo-European Taste* (London, 1955) and *The Kashmir Shawl* (London, 1973); David R. Shearer, *Why Paisley?* (Paisley, 1985); *Paisley Shawls* (Paisley, n.d.); Valerie Riley, *Paisley Pattern* (Glasgow, 1985).

21   Patrick Conner (ed.), *The Inspiration of Egypt: its Influence on British Artists, Travellers and Designers, 1700–1900* (Brighton, 1983), pp. 37–55; see also Richard Carrott, *The Egyptian Revival: its Sources, Monuments and Meaning, 1808–1858* (Berkeley, 1978) and James Stevens Curl, *Egyptomania, the Egyptian Revival: a Recurring Theme in the History of Taste* (Manchester, 1994).

22   Charles Truman, *The Sèvres Egyptian Service 1810–12* (London, 1982).

23   For a popular account, see Christopher Frayling, *The Face of Tutankhamun* (London, 1992); see also B. Hillier, *Art Deco* (London, 1985).

24   For examples of such furniture, see Victoria and Albert Museum, *Art and the East India Trade* (London, 1970), illustrations 10 to 23 and Mildred Archer, Christopher Rowell and Robert Skelton, *Treasures from India: the Clive Collection at Powis Castle* (London, 1987), pp. 79–86.

25   A good account of the artistic and design influence of oriental carpets can be found in John Sweetman, *The Oriental Obsession: Islamic Inspiration in British and American Art and Architecture, 1500–1920* (Cambridge, 1988); see also Donald King and David Sylvester, *The Eastern Carpet in the Western World from the Fifteenth to the Seventeenth Century* (London, 1983) and David Sylvester, *Islamic Carpets from the Collection of Joseph V. McMullan* (London, 1972).

26   Archer, Rowell and Skelton, *Treasures from India*, p. 9.

27   Guy and Swallow, *Arts of India*, pp. 75–6, 97.

28   Quoted in Sweetman, *Oriental Obsession*, p. 288, footnote 30.

29   Charles Locke Eastlake, *Hints on Household Taste in Furniture, Upholstery and other Details* (Dover, 1969, first published in book form in 1868), p. 108.

30   Christopher Dresser, *Principles of Decorative Design* (London, 1973, first published 1873), pp. 94–106, particularly p. 99.

31   Dresser, *Principles*, p. 161.

32   Quoted in Sweetman, *Oriental Obsession*, p. 288, footnote 29.

33   E. P. Thompson, *William Morris* (London, 1977); Sato and Watanabe (eds), *Japan and Britain*, pp. 115–17, 125–30.

34   Owen Jones, *The Grammar of Ornament* (London, 1986, first published 1856), pp. 77–8.

35   Foreword by Marina Henderson to the 1973 republication of Dresser's *Principles*.

36   Dresser, *Principles*, p. 11. See also his characterisations of eastern and other favoured arts on p. 13: 'the power and vigour of Egyptian ornament, the refinement of the Greek, the gorgeousness of the Alhambraic, the richness of the

Persian and Indian, the quaintness of Chinese and Japanese, the simple honesty and boldness of the Gothic', whereas he had no sympathy with 'the coarse Assyrian, the haughty Roman, and the cold Renaissance'.

37 Dresser, *Principles*, p. 161.

38 Mitter, *Much Maligned Monsters*, p. 237.

39 George C. M. Birdwood, *The Industrial Arts of India* (London, 1880), Vol. 1, pp. vi, 1.

40 Birdwood, *Industrial Arts*, Vol. II, pp. 9–10, Vol. 1, p. 136.

41 Birdwood, *Industrial Arts*, Vol. II, p. 146.

42 Birdwood, *Industrial Arts*, Vol. II, p. 176.

43 Mitter, *Much Maligned Monsters*, p. 225.

44 Ruskin quoted in Mitter, *Much Maligned Monsters*, pp. 239–47.

45 Greenhalgh, *Ephemeral Vistas*, p. 148.

46 Quoted in Mitter, *Much Maligned Monsters*, p. 250.

47 Sato and Watanabe (eds), *Japan and Britain*, pp. 17–22 and *passim*; Greenhalgh, *Ephemeral Vistas*, pp. 146–9.

48 Quoted in Sato and Watanabe (eds), *Japan and Britain*, pp. 77, 27. For Alcock's continuing interest in Japanese crafts, see Sir Rutherford Alcock, *Art and Art Industry in Japan* (London, 1878).

49 Sato and Watanabe (eds), *Japan and Britain*, pp. 102–17 and 142–9.

50 William Buchanan, *Mr Henry and Mr Hornel Visit Japan* (Glasgow, 1978); E. A. Hornel, *Japan* (Castle Douglas, 1895); Roger Billcliffe, *Edward Atkinson Hornel* (Glasgow, 1982); Roger Billcliffe, *The Glasgow Boys: the Glasgow School of Painting, 1875–1895* (London, 1985); Mortimer Menpes, *Japan: a Record in Colour* (London, 1903). Menpes travelled and painted extensively in the East. He also attended and illustrated Curzon's Delhi Durbar and published *The Durbar* also in 1903.

51 Christopher Dresser, *Japan: its Architecture, Art and Art Manufactures* (London, 1882), pp. vi–vii, 9, 50–1, 209 and *passim*.

52 Dresser, *Japan*, pp. 179–80.

53 Sato and Watanabe (eds), *Japan and Britain*, pp. 117, 127–32.

54 Dresser, *Japan*. Dresser's partner, Charles Holme, published *The Influence of Japanese Art on English Design* (Warrington, 1890). See Widar Halén, *Christopher Dresser* (Oxford, 1990).

55 Alison Adburgham: *Liberty's: a Biography of a Shop* (London, 1975). See also Mervyn Levy, *Liberty Style: the Classic Years, 1898–1910* (London, 1986), Barbara Morris, *Liberty Design, 1874–1914* (London, 1989), and the Victoria and Albert Museum, *Liberty's 1875–1975* (London, 1975).

56 In 1890, Arthur Liberty won the Silver Medal of the Society of Arts, of which he was also a member, for a paper on 'The industrial arts and manufactures of Japan'.

57 See Adburgham, *Liberty's, passim*, for an account of the artists, writers and theatrical people who gathered around Liberty's and for efforts to link the arts, pp. 48–9. It is an interesting fact that Liberty's also attempted to popularise Celtic designs, but found that they were much less popular than their oriental wares. For Liberty's work in the theatre, see Chapter 7.

58 Quoted in Adburgham, *Liberty's*, pp. 21–2.

59 Among many works on Whistler, see particularly, Denys Sutton, *The Art of James McNeill Whistler* (London, 1963); Hilary Taylor, *James McNeill Whistler* (London, 1978); Frances Spalding, *Whistler* (Oxford, 1979). See also Peter Ferriday, 'The peacock room', *Architectural Review*, CXXV (1959), pp. 407–14 and The Fine Art Society, *The Aesthetic Movement and the Cult of Japan* (London, 1972). See also Michael Sullivan, *The Meeting of Eastern and Western Art* (London, 1973).

60   The Hunterian Art Gallery of the University of Glasgow contains the Whistler/
      Godwin 'Harmony in Yellow and Gold: the Butterfly Cabinet', a painted screen
      by Whistler, some of Whistler's blue and white porcelain collection, as well as
      many of his paintings. See *James McNeill Whistler at the Hunterian Art Gallery:
      an Illustrated Guide* (Glasgow, 1990).

61   Lovelace, *Art for Industry*. See also Félix Régamey, *Japan in Art and Industry*
      (London, 1893) and Olive Checkland, *Britain's Encounter with Meiji Japan,
      1868–1912* (Edinburgh, 1989).

62   Gerald and Celia Larner, *The Glasgow Style* (London, 1980); Andrew McLaren
      Young (ed.), *Charles Rennie Mackintosh: Architecture, Design, Painting* (Edin-
      burgh, 1968) and the various Mackintosh catalogues of the Hunterian Art Gal-
      lery of the University of Glasgow.

63   William Buchanan in the *Charles Rennie Mackintosh Newsletter*, 25 (spring 1980)
      quoted in Robert Macleod, *Charles Rennie Mackintosh: Architect and Artist*
      (London, 1983), p. 25. See also F. Yamada Chisaburo, *Japanisme in Art: an
      International Symposium* (Tokyo, 1980).

64   Macleod, *Mackintosh*, p. 57. This has been confirmed by an unpublished thesis
      on Mackintosh by Hiroaki Kimura.

65   McLaren Young, *Mackintosh*, p. 6; Macleod, *Mackintosh*, pp. 36–7.

66   Brian Reade, *Aubrey Beardsley* (London, 1987); Linda Gertler Zatlin, *Aubrey
      Beardsley and Victorian Sexual Politics* (Oxford, 1990).

67   Karen Moon, *George Walton: Designer and Architect* (Oxford, 1993).

68   Peter Vergo, *Vienna 1900: Vienna, Scotland and the European Avant-Garde*
      (Edinburgh, 1983); Elizabeth Cumming, *Glasgow 1900: Art and Design* (Am-
      sterdam, 1992).

69   Adburgham, *Liberty's*, p. 91.

70   Sato and Watanabe (eds), *Japan and Britain*, pp. 147–59 for postcards, posters
      and theatre designs.

71   R. S. S. Baden-Powell, *Scouting for Boys* (London, 1908), p. 34.

72   Tony Birks and Cornelia Wingfield Digby, *Bernard Leach, Hamada and their
      Circle* (Oxford, 1990).

73   Mitter, *Much Maligned Monsters*, pp. 270–286.

74   T. Guha-Thakurta, *The Making of a New 'Indian' Art: Artists, Aesthetics and
      Nationalism in Bengal, c.1850–1920* (Cambridge, 1992).

75   Greenhalgh, *Ephemeral Vistas*, pp. 96–7, 209.

6

Orientalism
in music[1]

WRITING IN the *Radio Times* in 1932, Alex Cohen suggested
that 'superior people' had sniffed at Elgar's concern with the 'spirit of
England'. Such detractors thought that he should have equipped himself
by 'the study of oriental mysticism followed by a few years as a Hindu
ascetic'. Instead, Elgar had mixed 'the faith of St Francis the Visionary
and an admiration for Cecil Rhodes, the Empire-builder'.[2] Thus Cohen
was juxtaposing as polar opposites Elgar's imperialism with the Orientalism
of the radical, cosmopolitan school of twentieth-century composers. Elgar
did make some nods towards the East ('In Smyrna', 'Arabian Serenade'
and the 'Crown of India' Suite), but his Orientalist gestures were en-
compassed within an uncompromisingly western style. Thus, twentieth-
century Orientalism in music could be seen by some as a revolt against
Elgar's nationalistic and imperial world-view.

In a recent important, if wayward work, Robert Stradling and
Meirion Hughes have examined the political context of the English
musical renaissance, 1860–1940.[3] Their book is dedicated to the destruction of the notion that music is an autonomous, hermetic art, somehow immune from its political, social and intellectual contexts (an unlikely,
if durable proposition which Edward Said also takes issue with in his
Musical Elaborations).[4] Thus the supposed distinction between 'absolute'
and 'programmatic' music becomes unreal: all music is socially constructed

and 'reflect(s) the dynamics of existing power relationships'.[5] They seek to demonstrate that the accepted canon of the English renaissance reflected a specific 'gentlemanly' social milieu, particular power-centres (like the Royal College of Music in South Kensington)[6] and fashionable concerns with a 'national' style, rooted in folk music, the Celtic revival and English pastoralism. Those who did not conform with this nationalist mix, but sought 'alternative conjunctures', for example in cosmopolitan and Modernist ideas, were written out of the record. By not conforming to the dominant – and bourgeois – musical ideology, they failed to secure the imprimatur of the senior musical academics, influential performers and conductors, or powerful media like the BBC.

No doubt many objections may be raised to the Stradling and Hughes thesis on the grounds of the technical and aesthetic relativities of the music they discuss. Concepts of 'quality' are of course also socially constructed and time-specific, but the curators of the canon are disturbed when they are blithely left out of account.[7] Nevertheless, this stimulating work, though disfigured by a perpetual prose sneer in relation to the 'cow-pat' music of the pastoral revival, has much relevance to the discussion of the role of Orientalism in music over at least two centuries. They themselves, however, are dismissive of the Orientalist concerns of composers, categorising them as passing fads. But the statistics and the sheer durability of the Orientalist obsession in music are against them. So numerous are western music's excursions into the Orient that it is almost impossible to compile a complete list.

Since the seventeenth century composers in every generation have explored the East for musical and dramatic inspiration. They have sought to extend the language of music by utilising eastern instruments, tunes, or perceived melodic, harmonic and rhythmic conventions. They have mined oriental history and fable for programmatic ideas, operas or ballets; they have attempted to create eastern colour by evoking places visited on journeys; they have taken poems (particularly Chinese or Persian and invariably in translation) and set them as songs. Occasionally, they have set out to reflect contemporary events and people. And, in more modern times, they have attempted to adopt approaches to eastern philosophies and religions, creating new moods and a wholly fresh sound world through an advanced syncretism. By the late twentieth century, Asian composers have themselves begun to mix reinterpreted eastern conventions with western instrumental forms.

The emphases have changed from period to period and there has been an undoubted climax of Orientalist activity in the twentieth century, when the number of works produced by composers from widely different backgrounds has constituted something of a tidal wave. In the earlier period, composers often responded either to intriguing contemporary

influences or to fashion. From the late nineteenth century, some composers have viewed eastern influences and philosophy as one of the principal wellsprings of their music. Between those two extremes, some have
contributed major works to an Orientalist canon; others have appeared
merely to dabble, while in fact they have been exploring new sound
systems which then influencd their subsequent music even though it had
moved out of its Orientalist phase. Some, like painters, have travelled in
North Africa, the Middle East and India or have made the pilgrimage to
international exhibitions or to Bali itself to hear gamelan music. This
chapter is devoted to examining these changing emphases within a major
musical canon and to considering the extent to which such concerns
represented a musical complicity within western imperial dominance of
the East or a repeated search for a radical new voice.

Thus the analysis encounters problems at a whole variety of levels.
First it faces one of the fundamental difficulties of musical discussion,
that it is a hugely popular medium for which full technical understanding
is restricted to a relatively small inner circle. Yet its esoteric character is
contrasted with its function as an international artistic language and its
capacity, through opera and song, to convey the variety of language itself
to a wider audience. Thus in this chapter it is necessary to expand well
beyond the principal focus of Britain, while recognising that the European tradition was fully expressed in the United Kingdom through performance (as art was through national and private collections and
reproductions). In more modern times, a very considerable school of
British Orientalist composers emerged and these will be discussed later
in the chapter.

There are additional complications. As in other areas of this analysis of Orientalism in the arts, we are dealing with a variety of Easts.
Hence, a central aspect of the analysis must be the extent to which these
Orients are collapsed or specifically demarcated in different periods and
contrasting national traditions. Moreover, the interpretation must embrace at least five levels of the musical contribution to Orientalism:
musical effects, the 'programmes' of descriptive instrumental works, the
plots and characters of operas and ballets, the words and mood of songs,
and the modern relationship between music and philosophy. To add to
the complexity, this multi-layered approach must be conducted through
both chronological and thematic strands. Music has to be set not only
within its political/historical context, but also in relation to adjacent arts
and the intellectual world in which they are embedded. This raises the
question as to how quickly music reacts. Is it, as Simon Rattle has suggested,[8] a laggard art which tends to respond several decades after other
aspects of the intellectual/cultural complex, or is it capable of responses
as rapid as any other?

Orientalism in music before the nineteenth century

There is an oft-repeated, but seldom proven notion that Morris dancing and other aspects of English folk song and folk festivals have their origins in Moorish southern Spain and North Africa.[9] Certainly the gypsy tradition has been seen as a means of conveying musical styles from the East across Europe. It has also been asserted that the medieval Crusades helped to feed oriental instruments and musical ideas into the music of western Europe. But we are on surer ground from the sixteenth and seventeenth centuries. There are two main sources of influence: the Ottoman Empire, both its Turkish heartland and the Levant, and the 'Moorish' lands of the West. We know that there were Ottoman musicians in Venice (they appear in contemporary paintings) and that their street performances influenced Venetian composers. The classic instance is Monteverdi's Vespers of 1610, where certain aspects of the fioritura (or embellishments) and trills are akin to Islamic music. The Spanish musical tradition likewise acted as a conduit for Islamic influence. The music of Domenico Scarlatti offers many echoes of the dance rhythms and musical ideas surviving through the guitar music he encountered when court composer in both Portugal and Spain between 1721 and 1757. Flamenco retains some of its Moorish connections.

But the major Orientalist passion of the eighteenth century centred on the court intrigue and military prowess of the Ottoman Empire, the standard seraglio stories which were repeated, with many variants, almost endlessly, and the janissary bands which became hugely popular throughout Europe. The astonishingly prolific operatic treatment of the Ottoman court and the seraglio will be considered later, but it is worth noting in passing that Davenant's *The Siege of Rhodes* (1656), which features Suleiman the Magnificent as a more or less noble Turk, is sometimes considered to be the first English opera, while Purcell wrote incidental music for Aphra Behn's play *Abdelazar*.

All of this music has to be placed in the context of the threat posed to Europe by the Ottoman Empire until the later eighteenth century. While the Siege of Vienna of 1683 was unsuccessful and Turkish assaults seemed to be resolved by the Treaty of Carlowitz of 1699, in fact the threat from an admittedly much weakened Turkey continued to be perceived as a real one. Until the Treaty of Jassy of 1792, wars between the Ottomans and either Austria or Russia were endemic, covering some forty-two years of the century. The Russo-Turkish war of 1768–74 coincided with many of the seraglio productions in Europe and also produced a diplomatic revolution, when Austria considered that a pact with the Turks was preferable to Russian success and the overrunning of Ottoman lands. This eighteenth-century decline of the empire into the status of the 'Sick Man of Europe' not only produced an extraordinary upsurge in cultural expressions of 'Turkomania' (in dress, textiles, plays, operas, spectacles, etc.), but also a re-thinking of Europe's relationship with the Near East.

The janissary band neatly reflects this combination of fear and respect, shifting as the cultural landscape responded to the geological changes of political and military relations.[10] The role of the band not only in sustaining troop morale and maintaining marching rhythm, but also encouraging soldiers in the heat of battle, was much noted by Europeans. From the end of the seventeenth century, European rulers began to adopt the instruments and techniques of the janissary band into their own military music. Europeans were fascinated by the powerful and consistent rhythmic beat, together with the often cacophonous noise of the combination of shawms, fifes (military flutes), brass and percussion. This percussion battery (soon known as the 'batterie turque') included bass drums, kettledrums, cymbals, triangles, large tambourines and the crescent, or jingling johnnie. This sound world, duly assimilated and converted to western musical techniques, not only had a striking influence upon military music,[11] but also upon the development of the modern symphony orchestra and eighteenth-century music written for it.

Although C major was regarded as the standard Ottoman key, 'Turkish' music was often represented through rapid shifts between major and minor, rapidly descending minor scales, and repeatedly reiterated patterns, both rhythmic and melodic. Thus accentuated and near-hypnotic rhythms were combined with repeated leaping thirds, plangent appoggiatura (grace-notes), and a startling chromaticism. Some of these instruments and musical techniques were used, for example, by Haydn in his 'Military' Symphony, no. 100, by Mozart in his Turkish rondos to the Piano Sonata K. 331 and Violin Concerto K. 219, and by Beethoven in his Turkish March and Chorus of Dervishes in his incidental music to *The Ruins of Athens* and even in the finale of his Ninth Symphony. At first sight, these examples (though they are but the most famous of a very large corpus of works) seem only to make obeisance to a passing fad, but in these as in all borrowings from eastern music, we have to note a process of incorporation.

When exotic instruments and rhythmic and melodic figures are first introduced into a native tradition, they stand out as dramatically and intriguingly alien. If, however, they are fully assimilated – as was the case with these 'Turkish' elements – they cease to operate as an exotic intrusion. Nevertheless, the language of music has been extended and enriched. Of course, the borrowing was highly modified in the process and those aspects of the loan tradition which were regarded as unacceptable were rejected. Thus the complex and sometimes indeterminate rhythmic patterns, the wavering pitches and fractional tones, the single unharmonised lines of eastern music were largely ignored (at least until modern times). Although the process of assimilation was highly selective, although it often made unwarranted assumptions to fit the perceptions of the borrower, although it converted instrumental sounds to its own use, flattening out their exotic potential in doing so, still the contact had created a new syncretic language. The embrace of the dominant tradition certainly involved reduction and ultimate near-disappearance within the new canon, but the change and development built into the process was essentially dependent on these new catalytic elements. A major cultural form has been mildly destabilised and restabilises itself into a fresh period in its history. All that differs in succeeding encounters between West and East is that the destabilising process varies in intensity.

Opera and ballet went through similar destabilising processes. Not for nothing did Dr Johnson describe opera as an exotic and irrational entertainment. From the late seventeenth century, 'Turkish' interludes appeared in ballets and in the newly invented opera-ballet form. One of the most celebrated of the latter was Rameau's *Les Indes Galantes* of 1735 which featured scenes in Turkey, Peru, Persia and North America. One part of the 'batterie turque' gave its name to the exotic dance, the tambourin, whose energetic measures were accompanied by a drum and a tambourine. The power of *Turquerie* was such that supposedly Turkish scenes appeared in dramatic performances set wholly in Europe.[12]

Many operas featured some of the great figures of the Ottoman Empire and their protagonists, Bayazid I, Mohammed I, Suleiman I, Suleiman II and Mohammed IV, Tamerlane and the Albanian resister, Sanderbeg. The Bayazid/Tamerlane confrontation in the early fifteenth century was set by some thirty-three composers, most famously by Handel in 1724. Although the setting of contemporary events was relatively unusual, the Siege of Vienna in 1683 by Mohammed II's grand vizier, Kara Mustafa, was on the operatic stage within three years. These 'janissary operas' penetrated to the furthest corners of Europe. The German composer, Joseph Martin Kraus, wrote *Soliman II* for the court theatre of Gustav III of Sweden, a work which incorporated a classic march of the janissaries. In the late seventeenth and early eighteenth centuries these performances often made little visible concession to their eastern contexts, with little in the way of 'Turkish' music and with performers in the grandest of western dress. Nevertheless, they were sufficiently well known to be parodied on the popular stage.

By the second half of the eighteenth century, the prime obsessions of both opera and more popular musical forms were seraglio stories and eastern fables loosely associated with the Arabian Nights. These included Grétry's music for *Zemir et Azor* and settings by many lesser composers.

But the most intriguing treatments are those which mixed European and Turkish characters. The competition among three European harem slaves, Spanish, Circassian and French, for the attentions and love of the sultan was the theme of the immensely popular *Soliman II* by Favart, with musical numbers by Paul Gilbert, which received countless performances in France and throughout Europe in the late eighteenth century. Only occasionally are the sexes reversed. Grétry's popular *La Caravane du Caire*, which received no fewer than 500 performances in Paris between 1783 and 1829, as well as others throughout Europe, was unusual in that it featured a European male competing for an eastern woman. By this time, these productions had become an excuse for grand sets, elaborate staging, exotic costumes and novel effects which rendered Orientalist performances ideal for the growing rage for spectacular theatre.

By far the most common story, however, was the seraglio abduction, in which a European woman is seized for the sultan's harem, becomes the object of his hopeless love, but remains true to her lover at home, who eventually rescues her, often after a magnanimous gesture from the sultan himself. The story is spiced by the coarse and incorrigibly lewd pursuit of the woman's servant by the harem guard, who is finally confounded when all join in the praise of the nobility of the sultan. This basic story, with many embellishments and variants, has a long dramatic history. From the mid-seventeenth century, there was a tendency to contrast western romantic love and constancy with the lasciviousness and cruelty of the 'lustful Turk'. By the eighteenth century, however, the crudely binary characteristics of the story were changing. Just as seventeenth- and eighteenth-century scholarship produced a major revaluation of Islam, dispensing with many of the myths of the Middle Ages, so did the theatre respond with a greater ambivalence.[13]

As W. Daniel Wilson has put it, 'turkomania vacillated between cosmopolitanism and xenophobia'.[14] Certainly the treatment of the abduction story in opera in the 1760s and 1770s, culminating in Mozart's masterpiece *Die Entführung aus dem Serail* of 1782, reflected much ambivalence. Wilson has identified at least fourteen operatic treatments of the seraglio tale in this period and they tend to blend notions of the cruel and lewd Turk with the idea that he is redeemable by western concepts of love (of which, by implication, he is capable) and, even more significantly, he displays noble gestures unlikely in the West itself. The relationship between the constant lover come to rescue his betrothed from the harem and the sultan has many variants, but often, as in Mozart's version, the sultan has every reason to repay old and bitter scores. By not doing so, he offers a lesson to the West and provides the opportunity for criticism of western policy through the display of elevated behaviour on the part of the 'Other', thereby confirming a convention of Enlightenment literature in which other societies were seen to display the Utopian ideals for which Europe should be striving.[15]

It is true that in Mozart's *Die Entführung*, the situation is complicated by the fact that the pasha is a European who has converted to Islam. But it is noticeable that his main cultural interests, architecture and gardening, are precisely those that were attributed to eastern potentates. Moreover, in the *Singspiel* the pasha Selim is a speaking part only, so that Mozart sidesteps the problem of how to represent him in music. No such problem arises in the case of the comic harem guard, Osmin. Mozart utilises 'Turkish' music for all of Osmin's key moments in the drama: when he proclaims that the intruders should be 'first beheaded, then hanged, then impaled on red-hot spikes' both at the beginning and the end of the drama; and when in 'Vivat Bacchus' he is seduced by Cyprus wine, a drink 'fit for the gods', thus suggesting that Muslims can easily be converted from their unaccountable prohibition. But Turkish music is also most strikingly used for the chorus of janissaries who proclaim the nobility and honour of the pasha Selim.

The character of this 'Turkish' music has been closely analysed: it embraces repeated thirds in the melody, sometimes alternating with fifths; escaped notes or upper thirds decorating a descending scale; repeated notes in both melody and accompaniment, often decorated by short grace-notes; long initial notes succeeded by shorter ones; 2/4 metre; the interplay of A minor and C major, emphasising the harmonic concentration on thirds; and inflections characterised by a raised fourth. As Thomas Bauman has put it, all these musical devices tend to challenge notions of stylistic consistency and introduce 'contrast, disruption, tonal irregularity'.[16] But this irregularity is decidedly not associated with Manichaean opposites. In the characterisation, race, gender and class are constantly interleaving each other. Osmin may be, in Mozart's own words, 'foolish, coarse and spiteful', but he is a classic comic character of low life: his hyperboles of cruelty and lust have a satirical edge. Selim, on the other hand, threatens Konstanze with violence to force his will upon her, but never actually uses it and in the end recognises that love can never be secured through force.

Mozart after all was supplying his Austro-Hungarian audience not with a simple presentation of alterity, a contrast between Europeans and orientals, but with three separate 'Others': the Spanish Konstanze, the English maid Blonde, two Spanish males, Belmonte and Pedrillo, plus Osmin and the ambiguous Selim. The Spanish origin of the abducted female was, it is true, a convention of the seraglio tales, but the English maid was a satirical invention, intended to demonstrate the alleged freedoms of the English even through their independently minded servants. Thus, various national characteristics are overlaid upon each other.

In other operas by Mozart with an Orientalist element, there is a tendency to contrast good and bad characters, but the moral dividing-line never coincides with the national one. In the unfinished opera *Zaide*, the overseer of the slaves, Allazim, is a noble baritone figure who appeals to the Sultan Soliman to have pity upon the lower orders. In *Thamos, König in Egypten*, good and bad characters are compared within the Egyptian context. More famously, *Die Zauberflöte* contrasts the lustful Moor, Monostatos, with the noble high-priest figure (by implication, Egyptian) of Sarastro. It might be argued that here an ancient culture is being contrasted with a modern threatening, Islamic one.[17] But in *Così fan tutte*, when the two men return dressed as Albanians (and therefore as Muslims) to test their lovers' fidelity, the women are immediately fascinated and intrigued.[18] (What's more, the Albanians appear to music in the key of C major and with clarinets, trumpets and kettledrums.) Eastern men have a charming allure to go with their music. They represent an exciting edge, a release from conformity and from entrapment in a conventional relationship.

In all of this eighteenth-century Orientalism, the imperial boot is on the other foot. It is the Ottoman Empire which is feared and then accommodated. Yet it is impossible to find a monolithic discourse of alterity. Even the late seventeenth- and early eighteenth-century works sometimes portray the noble Turkish ruler, no doubt as a form of wish-fulfilment in danger. Later, the repeated social, moral and sexual destabilisations which match the introduction of new musical elements cut across the simple dividing-line of contrasting cultures. It is a dramatic landscape cut not by a single river, but a whole sequence of clefts and streams involving a variety of different nationalities, class-conflicts and gender battles. The introduction of oriental elements is designed not so much to stimulate ethnic hatred but to increase the range of visual and musical invention. The most stereotyped characters (Osmin and Monostatos, for example) are themselves destabilised by their interleaving with similar characters from European low life.

The Romantic period

Mozart is the acknowledged genius of classical Vienna, whose music brilliantly conveys the ambiguities of his librettists' creations. But other composers, like Grétry in his several Orientalist works, and Boieldieu in the popular *Le Calife de Bagdad* of 1800, used their oriental settings to help them increase the range and colour of their orchestrations. Certainly, the fascination with the East continued unabated into the nineteenth century. Rossini, matching the move of the Orientalist fable into the popular theatre, turned it into one significant setting for both his operatic satire and more serious treatments. Of his thirty-seven or so operas composed between 1812 and 1829, some thirteen are set in the eastern world of the Mediterranean, though it should be remembered that the demand for 'lenten operas'[19] meant that several of these used biblical themes. What's more, in his cosmopolitan search for locations he also used Switzerland, France, England, Scotland and Spain. (As a statistical comparison, that other highly prolific opera composer, Handel, placed about a dozen of his forty creations in the East, although in his case it is invariably the Orient of the classical world.)

The interest continued to be Europe-wide. Cherubini's Orientalist output spanned his *L'Alessandro nell'Indie* of 1784 and *Ali Baba* of 1834. Both Weber and Meyerbeer set *Abu Hassan* in 1810, a notably Orientalist period in the theatre (see the next chapter). Meyerbeer wrote some four Orientalist operas in his long career, one of them (*L'Africaine*) with highly indeterminate geography.[20] It was performed after his death in 1864. Halévy used the Mediterranean Orient twice, in *La Juive* of 1835 and *La Reine de Chypre* of 1841. But in his search for the exotic setting he also turned to the United States: the events of *L'Eclair* take place near Boston. In this context, it should be noted that Rossini's famous *Italian Girl in Algiers* and its counterpart, *The Turk in Italy*, were themselves echoing Cimarosa's *The Italian Girl in London* (1778), which treats Britain as a highly exotic location and makes many jokes at the expense of the English. This extreme variability of the exotic location will be considered further below.

None of these composers, however, actually travelled outside Europe. The organist, pianist and priest, George Joseph Vogler (1749–1814), is an intriguing exception. He travelled in North Africa and the Middle East and incorporated indigenous tunes in his keyboard works. Interestingly, he taught both Weber and Meyerbeer, the latter working with him for some two years. Vogler led the way where others soon followed. In the nineteenth century, this search for a fresh idiom led composers to explore the possibilities of other oriental settings, progressing further east as they did so. And as the century wore on, they increasingly travelled in search of fresh inspiration.

Two projects fused in this musical journey: one was the search for new orchestral colour, as the modern orchestra developed towards its full size and range of instruments; the other was a proto-ethnomusicological search for the intriguing melodic and rhythmic invention through which it could be exploited. But the East was not of course the single object of this exploration. Indeed, one of the major problems with the discussion of Orientalism in the arts is that it tends to be given a privileged alterity: it is viewed as the single Other against which Europe was constantly setting itself. In fact, musical eclecticism reveals the manner in which the Romantic movement sought out a variety of internal as well as external Others in this search for fresh sounds and moods. To detail but one fashion, Haydn and Beethoven arranged Scottish airs for an Edinburgh publisher; poetry of the mythical Celtic bard Ossian was set by Schubert and Brahms; the verse of Robert Burns stimulated *lieder* by Schumann, Franz and Jensen; Mendelssohn and, notably, Bruch composed music containing Scottish elements. Sir Walter Scott inspired an extraordinary number of European operas, many of which (like Donizetti's *Lucia di Lammermoor*) became Scottish spectacles. Dances derived from Scottish models – the écossaise, the schottische and the schotse – became immensely popular throughout Europe.[21]

Exotic spectacle and fresh melodic and rhythmic patterns were also to be found in Spain, Russia (and her quasi-oriental and oriental hinterland so fascinating to the Russian national school of composers) and in the dances and folk music of Poland, Hungary and Czechoslovakia, exploited so successfully by Chopin, Liszt, Dvořák and Smetana. Whereas eighteenth-century composers saw the Orient as a source of opera libretti which extended their normal concentration on classical history and myth, those of the Romantic period sought to create spectacle and innovative musical ideas out of a whole range of geographical settings as well as the Gothic past, both legendary and more or less historical. These folk, Gothic and chivalric sources were later to be important in the English musical renaissance and were to fuse with the Celtic revival.

It is perhaps easier to illustrate this point by jumping out of chronological sequence. The short-lived Bizet presents an interesting case of an opera composer who attempted to exploit each of these exotic and historical sources in turn: *Ivan IV* (1862, Russia and the Caucasus), *The Pearl Fishers* (1863, Ceylon), *The Fair Maid of Perth* (1866, Scotland), *Djamileh* (1871, Egypt), *Carmen* (Spain, 1873–75). Each seeks to create a new musical language out of a strikingly different location and of these the most convincingly exotic is *Carmen*. Bizet never visited Spain, but he assiduously sought out Spanish music in Paris. To leap forward in time, the contemporary composer Judith Weir (born 1954) has set operas in similar cosmopolitan milieux. It has been said of her that her music is capable of assimilating 'all sorts of ethnic flavouring, Scottish, Chinese, Spanish or Serbian, without resorting to parody and pastiche'.[22] Similarly, Philip Glass moved out of his minimalist phase with *Satyagraha*, first performed in 1981, on the life of Gandhi, and the Egyptian *Akhnaten* (1984).[23] Thus, as modern composers have continued to acknowledge, Dr Johnson in effect got it right. The conventions of opera, demanding such a total suspension of disbelief, often do demand the dramatic distancing of time and place.

The examples in the previous paragraph reveal the extent to which composers succeeded in moving on from their focus on the Mediterranean and Middle Eastern Orient. The French, however, remained obsessed with it and embraced it even more comprehensively through travel. Apart from Vogler, the first notable Middle Eastern traveller/composer was Félicien David (1810–76). Interestingly, it was radical politics that took him there. David, who studied at the Conservatoire under Cherubini, joined Enfantin's Saint-Simonian community at Ménilmontant and composed music for its rituals. When the French government suppressed the cult in 1832, Enfantin, David and a few other followers left for Egypt to preach their doctrines and, as they thought, restore that country to its ancient prosperity. Thus a radical movement, finding itself unwelcome in Europe, turned to a hopefully receptive East as the saviour of its socialist ideas. David visited Constantinople, Smyrna, Jaffa, Jerusalem and Cairo, where he lived for two years, supporting himself by giving piano lessons. In 1835 he visited Beirut and travelled home. By this time, his politics had been entirely superseded by a fascination with the East and a determination to act as its ambassador in music.

On his return he wrote a sequence of *Mélodies orientales*, in the preface of which he announced that the melodies were genuinely oriental, but had been fleshed out with European harmonies. These were subsequently republished as *Les Brises d'Orient* and *Les Minarets*. But his greatest success was *Le Désert*, a three-movement symphonic ode for spoken voice, choir and orchestra which was very popular in the nineteenth century. Its various sections were entitled 'desert storm', 'prayer to Allah', 'caravan', '*rêverie du soir*', and 'the muezzin's call'. The desert landscape was evoked by a long repeated pedal C, an effect which Berlioz greatly admired along with the rest of the work. David later wrote works on Moses and the Sinai, Christopher Columbus, Eden, and Lalla Rookh of 1862, which the writer in the *New Grove* describes as a masterpiece evoking a dreamy atmosphere through an aromatic orchestration (a highly Orientalist phrase, but indicating a drift towards a new orchestral language to be taken further by Debussy and the Impressionists, who also turned to the East).

Auber expressed the wish that David would get off his camel (which he occasionally did – he set an opera in Brazil!), but though he had many shortcomings as a composer, he thoroughly instituted the nineteenth-century Orientalist style. He influenced Bizet, Delibes, Saint-Saëns, and passed on orchestral ideas to Thomas, Gounod and Massenet. He may even have fed some elements of his sound world into Verdi's *Aida*. He never abandoned his Saint-Simonianism, but his music has generally been analysed as ideologically free. Whether that is true or not, it is certainly written from the standpoint of respect and affection. He undoubtedly saw himself as unveiling the East to the West in a sympathetic light.

His much greater contemporary, Berlioz (1803–69), who offered him extravagant praise, also explored the East in music, although he never went there, contenting himself with a passion for reading travel books. In the 1820s and 1830s he wrote cantatas, *Le Cheval arabe*, *La Mort de Cléopatre* and *La Mort de Sardanapoule*, which are clearly intended to be the musical counterparts of the Orientalist paintings of the period. (*La Mort de Sardanapoule* was given an additional conflagration scene after he had won the Prix de Rome prize.) Venturing further afield, he made settings of Thomas Moore, notably *Lelio* and his *Irlande* collection, as well as exploring many of the literary and geographical passions of the Romantic period (including his music for *Rob Roy*). His monumental masterpiece is of course *The Trojans at Carthage*, which has been seen by Said as reflecting the French imperial interest in North Africa of the period.[24] However, the prime dramatic force of that work comes from the Romantic notion of individual figures trying to work out their personal destinies while caught up in heroic events. Berlioz combined radical political views (as did Bizet later) with the most innovative musical technique of his day, so little understood in his own time that his apocalyptic visions have only been fully appreciated in the twentieth century. It is true that direct oriental influences play very little part in his music, but it is clear that his exotic subjects were often necessary to the liberation of the powerful and nervy rhythmic and harmonic devices which permeate his works.

Orientalism, whether in subject-matter, melodic and rhythmic invention or ethnomusicological borrowings, became one significant stream in French music for the rest of the nineteenth and much of the twentieth centuries. It may be possible to see this as the cultural analogue of developing French political power in North Africa; it may even be possible to regard Berlioz's staggering sound depiction of developing derangement, disintegration and suicide in *La Mort de Cléopatre* as somehow reflecting the inevitable political destruction of the eastern world; but there is no evidence to suggest that Berlioz had such ideas in his head when he wrote it in 1829, a year before the French invasion of Algeria. More importantly, little of this music can be seen as somehow representing a cultural wing of a conservative imperialism, holding up the onset of more radical techniques. This notion has been promoted in respect of Orientalist painting and was challenged in Chapter 3, but musically the Orient seemed to offer the prospect of repeated radical renewal.

If any French composer can be directly linked to service in the North African Empire it is Ernest Reyer (1823–1909). In 1839 he was sent to work in a government department in Algiers, but his main desire was to escape into music. In 1848 he settled in Paris and during the second half of the century he produced a succession of Orientalist works: *Le Selam*, a symphony in four parts to a text by Gautier, *Saccountala*, a ballet by Gautier, *La Statue*, based on the Arabian Nights, and his opera, *Salammbô*, after the novel by his friend Flaubert and produced at the Opéra in 1890. The latter, a succession of sumptuous settings, stayed in the repertoire for forty years, but his music was much too akin to that of David and Delibes to mark any kind of fresh departure. It is this kind of Orientalist music which serves to highlight the genuinely innovatory genius of a figure like Bizet.

Bizet's *Djamileh* was subjected to accusations of Wagnerism; critics viewed it as offering all atmosphere and no action, its novel harmonic and orchestral effects as a bizarre and disagreeable approach to atonality. As Winton Dean has put it, exoticism for Bizet was not an external thing, a simple searching for novelty, but a need rooted in his deeply felt desire for new effects, a truly innovative language.[25] His dramatic song, 'Adieux de l'hôtesse arabe' combined exotic elements into a harmonic experiment of ever-varying colour. In *The Pearl Fishers*, a work which he subsequently rejected, Dean considers that 'most of the genuinely original music is concerned with the exotic element',[26] the opening choral dance, for example, revealing 'incisive rhythms, sharp modulations and touches of chromaticism'. Again, perhaps, it might be possible to see the central plot conceit of a sacred virgin yielding to love as somehow parallel to the seductions of European imperialism, but it was a favourite Romantic theme and in the opera it takes place purely within a Ceylonese context.

In the hands of a lesser composer like Delibes, these effects become more mannered. He followed the precedent of Louis Spohr's popular *Jessonda* (1823) and Massenet's *Le Roi de Lahore* (1877) in setting an opera in India, although *Lakmé* (1883) differs from the other two in dealing with Indo-British relations (*Jessonda* is set in the Portuguese period, while the plot of *Le Roi* is purely Indian). In *Lakmé*, there are certain moments when striking new colours are created, particularly in the 'Bell Song' in the second act. Here a British officer loves an Indian woman who sacrifices herself in order to save him. The imperial interpretation is obvious: the indigenous woman as sacrificial victim for the greater good of the civilising mission, though the theme of cross-racial love is movingly portrayed in the music. The prolific Massenet set other operas in the East and in Spain, but it is Massenet's rival, Saint-Saëns, who can be seen as the most conservative of the Orientalist composers of the French school.

Saint-Saëns's conservatism was perhaps rooted in the fact that his talent so far outran his genius. Interestingly, he was closely connected with some of the Orientalist painters: he knew Ingres, who had originally been trained as a musician, and he travelled in the Middle East with the painter Georges Clairin.[27] In 1873 he made the first of many trips to Algeria and worked on some of his music there, including sections of *Samson and Dalila*. He also visited the Canaries, Russia, Egypt and travelled further east into the Indian Ocean. Among his Orientalist *oeuvre* were his suite 'Algérienne', his piano fantasy 'Africa', with its wildly tempestuous changes of mood, a one-act Japanese opera, *La Princesse jaune*, whose exotic harmonies allegedly influenced Messager in his setting of Pierre Loti's novel, *Madame Chrysanthème*, brass-band music, 'Sur les bords du Nil', dedicated to the Khedive Abbas Hilmi, and his Fifth Piano Concerto, the 'Egyptian'. The latter is a highly programmatic work, with evocations of an Egyptian morning, the croaking of frogs in the Nile valley, and the thud of his steamer's propeller in the last movement. Most strikingly, the G-major passage in the same movement is a Nubian tune which he collected, presumably near Aswan, where Nubian songs and wedding music are a major feature of the river to this day.

But there is no doubt that his Orientalist masterpiece was *Samson and Dalila*. Saint-Saëns originally intended to write an oratorio in the Mendelssohn tradition which he greatly admired, but was persuaded to turn it into an opera.[28] Although much of it was written by 1870, it was not performed until Liszt took it up and provided a production at Weimar in 1877. Despite being rapturously received, it was not produced in France until 1890, mainly because of hostility to biblical subjects. When it finally broke through at the Opéra in 1891, it became an immense success and received 500 performances by 1922 (950 by 1976, the Opéra's third most popular after *Faust* and *Rigoletto*). Edward VII was instrumental in securing the lifting of the Lord Chamberlain's ban on such a biblical theme and it became equally popular in Britain. (Saint-Saëns was indeed greatly admired in Britain, where he was given an honorary degree at Cambridge and played 'Africa' to considerable acclaim; he also wrote an opera, *Henry VIII*, an 'Idylle écossaise' and a piece entitled 'Le Parc à Richmond'!)

Once more, it might be possible to wring some contemporary political significance from the confrontation between Samson's Hebrews and the Philistines, his seduction by Dalila and the loss of his powers before summoning them back for the final apocalypse, and indeed Ralph Locke has done just that.[29] Greatly influenced by Said and Nochlin, he has interpreted the Hebrews as standing in for the West, Judaism for Christianity, and the Philistines as emblematic of a failed and conquerable East. Dalila becomes in this interpretation an eastern seductress who can destroy if not opposed. But there are far too many ambiguities in the opera to support such a simple binary analysis. Dalila seems to be torn between love, at least genuine sexual passion, and patriotism. Moreover, it is hard to imagine that a Parisian audience would wholly identify with what Locke calls 'the principled, almost puritanical Hebrews'. The Philistine women sing in Act I of springtime, rosebuds and love. Even the *bacchanale*, with its apparent throwing off of all restraint, must have left its *fin-de-siècle* and twentieth-century audience in a certain emotional turmoil in terms of identity.

In any case, the main impact of the work is the melodic invention and the orchestration, Saint-Saëns's finest: the strung tension and febrile atmosphere of the second act, the remarkable three arias for Dalila, the perfect integration of the ballet scenes, and the extraordinarily alluring power of the *bacchanale*. The key structure is intensely dramatic, marking the swing from the public to the private domain in a most striking way. If the French Orientalist movement produced a figure akin to the painters, it was certainly Saint-Saëns. Yet Liszt knew innovative writing when he heard it and there is no question that Saint-Saëns, limited as he was, summoned up remarkable music to match the challenge of the story. Interestingly, his music was used in the early days of films and has been much parodied in later Orientalist film scores. Edward Said has seen this as indicating the risible aspects of Orientalist music,[30] but he fails to recognise that in the choruses of the Philistines Saint-Saëns was himself probably parodying the laboured choral entries for the Prix de Rome. Subsequent skits fit a long tradition of parody which goes back to the eighteenth-century theatre and has been highly effective even with the greatest of music.

Saint-Saëns's work was seen as one battery in the resistance to the onward march of Wagnerism, particularly after the Franco-Prussian war of 1870–71 when there was a renewed effort to maintain a distinctive French tradition in the face of Wagnerian passions in all the arts, particularly literature. He was, however, totally overtaken in his long life by new and much more radical musical developments, themselves also reactions to Wagner and some of which again turned to the East for inspiration, but before moving on to discuss late Romanticism, Impressionism, Modernism and the English revival later in this chapter, it is necessary to backtrack to consider the Orientalist canon elsewhere in Europe. Early in his career, Saint-Saëns had been told by Gounod that the resources of sonority of the orchestra were still largely unexplored.[31] This could stand as a motto for some of the developments that took place in Germany, Russia and Italy during the period. As more exotic tunes became available, they served to inspire composers to extend just such sonorities.

Carl Maria von Weber wrote an overture to Schiller's *Turandot* based upon a genuine Chinese folk-tune which had come his way.[32] It was presented on the whole orchestra in a number of different shapes, figurations and keys and, though its first audience found it bizarre, it was considered sufficiently interesting to be taken up by Hindemith at a much later date for a series of variations ('Turandot scherzo, symphonic metamorphosis of themes by Weber'). Some Indian melodies had begun to arrive in Europe by this time and, although there is little evidence of direct influence, composers responded to the fascination with India of Romantic writers.[33] Schumann wrote his *Das Paradies und die Peri*, based on Moore's *Lalla Rookh*, in the early 1840s. Schumann himself may indeed have had a hand in the translation of the Moore original. Unlike the French school, however, these were marginal works.

For the Russian nationalists, however, the search for oriental inspiration was much more central and was also partly bound up with finding a patriotic alternative to Wagner. For this reason, the French discovery of Russian music in the 1880s marked an important step in the creation of a cultural bond between the two states. Glinka (1804–57) is generally regarded as the first composer to attempt a truly Russian style. Yet he travelled widely and was immensely eclectic: he incorporated melodies from the Ukraine, Poland, Finland, Georgia, Central Asia, the Middle East and above all Spain into his work. Like so many other composers, he wrote several pieces with Spanish titles. In his opera, *Ruslan and Liudmila*, he introduced much novel material, particularly the Persian Chorus in Act III. He also encouraged Balakirev to pursue an interest in exotica. At first Balakirev paid the ritual obeisances to Spain: he wrote a fandango, étude and serenade on Spanish themes, an overture on a Spanish march, and later intended to create a drama on the expulsion of the Moors from Spain. The turning-point for him came, however, when he spent two or three months in the Caucasus collecting Georgian and Persian melodies. He then wrote songs with a quasi-oriental vein and published a collection of Russian folk-songs in 1866. His Symphony in C Major made use of both Russian and oriental material, but his grandest piece in the idiom was his oriental fantasy, 'Islamey' for piano, a work of notorious technical difficulty. 'Islamey' was based on one of the tunes he had collected himself, together with another one which he heard at Tchaikovsky's house.

Rimsky-Korsakov was also fascinated by this melodic material and tunes surface in his *Oriental Fantasy, Antar* and *Schéhérazade*, with its massively rich orchestration, based on greatly enlarged woodwind, brass and percussion sections, overlaid by the languid solo violin. (He also wrote, of course, a Spanish Caprice.) Rimsky-Korsakov's adherence to the 'Eurasian' school of Russian composers is well borne out in his operas, such as *The Legend of the Invisible City of Kitezh and the Maiden*

Fevroniya and above all *Sadko*, with its songs of Viking, Venetian and Indian merchants mingling on the quayside. The 'Indian Song' became a popular concert piece in the twentieth century, particularly as a vehicle for Jüssi Bjorling.

Borodin's *In the Steppes of Central Asia* and his theatrically stunning 'Polovtsian Dances' from *Prince Igor*;[34] Mussorgsky's *Khovanshchina* (particularly Act IV, with its dance of the Persian slave girls) and his unfinished *Salammbô* after the novel by Flaubert;[35] and much of Glazunov's music also reflect this assimilation of eastern elements in order to create a distinctively Russian national tradition. Anton Rubinstein's music was similarly touched by this eastern interest[36] while Glier wrote works based on Azerbaijani, Tadzhik and Uzbekistani folktunes. His ballet, *The Red Poppy*, which depicts the Russian revolutionary relationship with China, also contains distinctly Orientalist elements. Arensky wrote a ballet, *Egyptian Nights*, and Alexander Tcherepnin, who married a Chinese woman, continued the reliance upon the East which for Scriabin became a total obsession. This fascination acknowledged the cultural blend of West and East which had long been characteristic of the Russian arts and of the musical traditions of the Orthodox Church. Thus it can be found informing even distinctively Russian historical works like Mussorgsky's *Boris Godunov*. Its repeated connection with an interest in Spain (with its matching syncretic culture) is yet another example of exotic parallelism.

In a quite different mood, Verdi's *Aida* has been much discussed as his sole major excursion into Orientalism (he was to treat *Nabucco* and *Otello* very differently, although the latter's ballet music contains a muezzin's call derived from David's *Le Désert*). Edward Said professes to find *Aida* a cold opera, emblematic of the composer's distaste for Egypt, and one highly implicated in European imperial expansion in the region in the second half of the nineteenth century.[37] Said offers a major critique of the opera in *Culture and Imperialism*, a bizarre analysis which I have criticised at length elsewhere.[38] Here it need only be said that Verdi's approach to Orientalism is at one and the same time circumspect and wholehearted. Although he went to Florence to examine a genuine Egyptian flute, he resolved not to use it in any way, nor did he adopt any oriental tunes. Yet his music sounds highly novel, as a result of its intense chromaticism, its striking combination of keys and dramatic modulations, and its orchestral colouring derived from his emphasis on flutes, harp and trumpets.

What emerges strikingly from the opera is that the savage grandeur of the public scenes has a satirical edge to it, Verdi the nationalist guying imperial triumphalism and consciously offering a rebarbative rodomontade. The real focus is on the private drama and on Ethiopian nationalism. While he succeeds in creating an extraordinary oriental atmosphere, he makes it clear that he is really interested in private lives and hopes frustrated against the backdrop of public events. Far from being cold, it is filled with passion, the nationalist and patriotic fervour of Amonasro and Aida ('O Patria Mia'), the unrequited love of Amneris, the jingoistic rage of the priests, indicative of Verdi's anti-clericalism, and the final consummation of the lovers in the tomb, where nationalistic divisions cease to matter. In so far as the opera can be seen as classically Orientalist in the Saidian sense, it is not through the music at all, but through the production values which have ever created a fantasy land of Egypt, influenced by the French Egyptologist Mariette. In fact, its plot and its musical loyalties are a very backhanded compliment to the Khedive who commissioned it.[39]

Musical radicalism in the late nineteenth and early twentieth centuries

Music moved into a period of extraordinary ferment in the late nineteenth and early twentieth centuries. The dominance of Wagner and the struggles of the French and Russian schools to escape from his shadow were overtaken by the emergence of Impressionism, late Romanticism, *verismo* opera, serialism and other forms of Modernism. It might be reasonable to expect that this radical turmoil would reject the repeated appeal to exotic inspiration which had characterised so much of what had gone before. But this was very far from being the case. In some respects the exotic became even more important than it had been, taking on a wholly new significance as it did so. As before there were many exotic sources: Spain continued to be an inspiration, particularly as it was now producing its own school of composers; folk music became even more important; cosmopolitanism was encouraged by extraordinary performances at the international exhibitions and by new ethnomusicological publications and projects; the black music of the United States became a fresh fascination, particularly when jazz and its various derivatives began to enter the world stage. But, despite this fanning-out of interests, the Orient maintained its prominent position.

The Holy Grail of musicians and opera composers of the nineteenth century had been the search for the total art. Weber had professed himself intent upon this quest. Wagner, of course, became its high priest. This concept of the fully integrated art form concerned itself with the combination of text and poetry, music, drama, sets and staging, design, textiles and effects. Wagner turned to mythical and medieval worlds for the contexts in which his cosmic art could flourish. In the era of the musical revolution, composers were no less obsessed with total art, but its bases now shifted considerably. Some still sought it in opera; but others saw music as capable of achieving some forms of totality without drama. The new complete art was to be based on an escape from national forms, a search for an embracing cosmopolitanism, and the union not so much of text and music (although text often survived) as of philosophy or spirituality and musical invention. The most radical even began to think in terms of music and senses other than the aural: colour, sight and even smell, what might in more modern times be described as a psychedelic experience. Some composers continued on much more conventional tracks than these, but created whole new late Romantic sound worlds, incorporating both the decadence and the sense of inflated psychological drama of the turn of the century.

Claude Debussy's formative decade in Paris was the turbulent 1880s when the French Symbolist poets appeared to have fallen under the sensual sway of Wagner and yet French art and music were struggling into new national forms. In 1889, the Paris Exposition Universelle brought together innovative ideas in art, design, crafts, architecture, textiles, and also music. It was one of the first great cosmopolitan musical jamborees in which singers, dancers and musicians from Africa, the Middle East and Asia contributed to the traditional ethnic spectacle. European folk music was also celebrated, with performances by, among others, singers and instrumentalists from Hungary, Romania, Spain, Finland and Norway.

Of all of these, however, there is no doubt that the greatest musical impact among professional musicians was the Javanese dancing to the accompaniment of performers upon the gamelan. Debussy was captivated. The gamelan helped to form the kaleidoscopic harmonies and shifting tone colours which his elusive Impressionist style was struggling towards. He became preoccupied with chimes, bells, echoes and moments of silence. His quartet of 1893, his *Pagodes* and many other works bore the mark of this oriental influence.[40] (Interestingly, he also wrote a *Marche écossaise* in 1891!) His most complete attempts at an oriental style were to be for the theatre, in his ballets *Khamma* and *No-ja-li*, both completed around the time of the First World War.[41]

Khamma, with an ancient Egyptian setting, was commissioned by the dancer Maud Allen, who had made a sensation with her *Vision of Salome* (to a score by Florent Schmitt – see below) and was considered to be the main rival of Isadora Duncan. The commission became a penance to Debussy and his reactions to it alternated between irritation and send-up, but none the less he composed it with some seriousness and searched for novel effects, in the use of piano, celesta and muted trumpets, its gamelan-like sonorities, its Stravinskian rhythms and its near-bitonality. The work was orchestrated by Charles Koechlin, who was also fascinated by the East. *No-ja-li*, set in Formosa, carried the influence of the gamelan yet further. These ballets not only symbolised Debussy's debt to the East, but also his rejection of Wagner: famously he found the music-hall in London more appealing than the Ring cycle which he forced himself to sit through at Covent Garden.[42]

Although Debussy's contact with the East was solely through the *Exposition*, other French composers had direct experience of North Africa and Asia. Albert Roussel was a marine officer in Indo-China from 1887 to 1894 and paid a visit to India, Ceylon and Indo-China in 1909. A sequence of Orientalist works followed, through which Roussel succeeded in escaping from the influence of Debussy and Impressionism. In his *Evocations*, he conjured up Ellora, Jaipur and Benares, which had particularly impressed him. But in his remarkable opera *Padmavati* he arrived at his own mature style, much admired by the great scholar and performer Nadia Boulanger. Although he declared himself to be eschewing openly exotic music, he did use some eastern melodies, but through bold and harsh harmonic sequences and striking, though restrained, orchestration, he created a whole new sound world. He made a further musical excursion into the Orient with his *Deux Poèmes chinois* for soprano with piano accompaniment.

Maurice Delage, a pupil of Ravel, also paid a visit to India, as a result of which he wrote his *Quatres Poèmes hindous*, evocations of Madras, Lahore, Benares and Jaipur. In *Benares*, a cello is played pizzicato in order to sound like a sitar and there is some highly evocative woodwind writing. Like Charles Koechlin he wrote a number of vocal works and a ballet, based on Kipling's *Jungle Book* and other writings. Moving further east, he composed seven *hai-kai*, based on Japanese tunes. Delage was a highly refined and fastidious composer, but his master, Ravel, who was several years his junior, was much more unbuttoned in his originality. Ravel proclaimed himself to be enthralled by the East and by Spain and a number of works testify to this classic combination, including *Rhapsodie espagnole*, *La Valse*, *Schéhérazade* and *Deux Mélodies hebraïques*, through which he created highly atmospheric and stunningly rhythmic music that succeeded in being both distinctively twentieth-century and highly popular. But perhaps the most original of Ravel's exotica are his *Madagascan Songs*, written to an American commission in 1925 and based upon Madagascan folk-songs which warn of the cruelties of the white man. Piano, cello and flute accompany the singer through a succession of melancholic minor keys.

Ravel insisted that his profound fascination with the Orient had influenced him since childhood. This was also true of Koechlin, a pantheistic communist sympathiser, who wrote a succession of works based on Kipling's *Jungle Book* over a period of forty years. As the *New Grove* puts it, his music ranges from a state of demonic energy to a diaphonous luminosity, deriving from chords using superimposed fourths and fifths. Koechlin's was a highly original talent and, similarly, Jacques Ibert's musical life was devoted to the avoidance of fashions and dominant influences: he wanted to free himself by pursuing a music that related outwards to other arts and to all aspects of imaginative experience. It comes as no surprise to find him travelling in Spain and Tunisia and writing a programmatic piece, *Escales*, which evokes the atmospheres of three different Mediterranean ports, including Tunis. Poulenc had no need to travel: he joined the gamelan admirers when he heard them played at the Paris Exhibition of 1931 and his concerto for two pianos is heavily influenced by the experience. The next generation of composers turned to the East yet once more. Messiaen (1908–93) visited Japan and, like Delage, wrote *hai-kai* using Japanese musical motifs. He made an intensive study of the complexities of Indian rhythms based upon a thirteenth-century Indian source and tried to relate them to their religious and philosophical symbolism. His *Turangalila* symphony (written between 1946 and 1948, the name itself being a compound Sanskrit word meaning vitality and life) uses radical rhythmic and harmonic techniques within a lush orchestration.

It might be thought, following Said, that this French obsession with the East must be rooted in its imperial experience of North Africa and Indo-China, but the French were far from alone. The same interests swept Austria, Germany, Russia, Eastern Europe and Britain: whenever and apparently wherever composers searched for a new voice, they always turned to the East as a major source of innovatory experiment. At the melodic level a considerable fillip was given to this activity by the publication of compendia of world tunes, as in A. W. Ambros, *Geschichte der Musik*, which reached its second edition in 1880 and contained musical examples from India, China, Nubia, Byzantium and Ancient Greece, among many others. Ambros was himself often dismissive of some of this material, but none the less it was plundered by composers. He was in any case very far from being the only source: musical travellers in the East were by now collecting melodic ideas.

Mahler turned to the East in ways that confirmed rather than transformed his style. He turned the supposedly eastern pentatonic scale into one of his own trade marks and underpinned it by an exotic-sounding orchestration and a destabilised counterpoint which Donald Mitchell has called 'heterophony'.[43] In *Das Lied von der Erde*, Mahler set Chinese poems from an anthology, *The Chinese Flute*, published in 1907 by Hans Bethge and purporting to be by the Chinese poet Li Be Bai. In fact Bethge had derived them from translations made by Judith Gautier, daughter of Théophile, in the 1870s and a collection by Hans Hermann published in 1905. By the time they had passed through this progression, many of the poems bore a relatively remote relationship to the originals. What's more, Mahler cheerfully changed the words himself in order to fit his musical invention. In other words, it all sounds like a classic Orientalist progression: a western-reconstructed set of oriental poems is used to inspire music which, in its pentatonal, rhythmic and percussive effects also sounds vaguely eastern. Moreover, its bitter-sweet melancholy, its evocations of what Mitchell has seen as its central duality, spring and autumn, dream and reality, hope and despair, life and death, are much more indicative of Mahler's psyche than of Chinese literature. Yet ultimately it is not the western construction of the Orient which matters: this is far from being an oppressive vision, rooted in the culture of imperialism. What does matter is that Mahler's vision of the poetry and of the appropriate music to accompany it, however distorted through a western prism, produced a unique work of distinctive genius, a work which may not have happened if Mahler had not encountered what he thought were Chinese poems and attempted to set them in atmospherically eastern ways.[44]

The setting of Indian, Persian, Chinese and Japanese poems became a major project of western music in the twentieth century. Poetry of the great Bengali philosopher and polymath, Rabindranath Tagore, was set by Zemlinsky in his Lyric Symphony and in other works.[45] Zemlinksy, like Schoenberg, toyed with Theosophy and eastern mysticism, but Zemlinsky chose to reject Schoenberg's atonality and, influenced by Mahler, moved into oriental interests as a means of maintaining his resistance to Viennese tonal radicalism. Even that most outrageously powerful, yet infinitely adaptable prophet of the twentieth century, Stravinsky, found an excursion into eastern poetry irresistible. He was just completing *The Rite of Spring* when he encountered a little anthology of Japanese lyrics. He wrote that 'the impression which they made on me was exactly like that made by Japanese paintings and engravings'. These brief, angular and spare settings, though sometimes highly energetic, must have helped purge Stravinsky of some of the violence and dissonant power of *The Rite*. Stravinsky's Japanese lyrics and Delage's four Hindu poems were premiered at the same concert in Paris in 1914 and Delage may indeed have influenced Stravinsky in turning to the East.[46]

Richard Strauss, Fauré and Szymanowski all wrote songs based on Persian poems and Strauss made one Indian setting. Frank Bridge composed songs after Tagore and, in more modern times, David Blake wrote songs 'In Praise of Krishna'. (He also composed 'The Bones of Chuang Tzu' for the Aldeburgh festival, having been greatly influenced by

Messiaen's Far Eastern interests.) Yet it was Chinese poetry which was to be most frequently set. A collection of Chinese poetry in English was published by H. A. Giles in 1896, but it was Arthur Waley's translations, published at the end of the First World War, which were to influence an entire generation of British composers. Granville Bantock wrote some sixty Chinese songs, while Bernard van Dieren, who settled in England, used German translations of Chinese poems in his Chinese Symphony for five soloists, chorus and orchestra (1914), which was much admired and played in his own day. York Bowen composed four Chinese songs in 1920; Constant Lambert set eight songs by Li Po in the 1920s; the American Charles Griffes produced five poems of China and Japan during the First World War, using five- and six-tone scales and melodies collected for him in Japan;[47] Benjamin Britten wrote his 'Songs from the Chinese' for Peter Pears and Julian Bream, while Martin Dalby wrote eight Chinese songs based on Waley in the 1960s; Steptoe set six Chinese lyrics; and Cornelius Cardew (politically, a very radical figure) composed settings of Confucius. The composer and conductor Antal Dorati has also set Chinese poems in his *Herbst*. This is by no means a complete list.

Songs based on Orientalist poetry were generally concerned with mood, a melancholic atmosphere expressed in spare musical settings. But other aspects of Orientalism maintained the tradition of dealing in rich, rhythmic and, in the twentieth century, increasingly erotic music. Oscar Wilde's play *Salome* of 1893 struck a dramatically decadent *fin-de-siècle* chord and the musical settings by Richard Strauss and Florent Schmitt (a ballet sequence for the dancer Loïe Fuller) transferred that decadence and psychological intensity into music, heightening it in the process. Strauss's *Salome* created immense controversy, though its libretto, largely by Strauss himself, significantly altered aspects of Wilde's play. Some have questioned whether *Salome* is genuinely an Orientalist work, even going so far as to see its most overtly Orientalist moment, the notorious 'dance of the seven veils', as its weakest music.[48] Strauss himself, however, had no doubts. He saw existing operas based on oriental and Jewish subjects as lacking 'true Eastern colour and blazing sun'. He was also sure that the dance adequately fitted the rest, with its strong colours and rhythms, its inexorable crescendo, and its striking use of xylophone, tambourine and woodwind. As in his tone-poems, he was concerned with a sense of time and place as well as with the portrayal of extreme personality.

The opera represents a supreme example of Expressionism in music. Musically as well as dramatically, it has a startling originality and imaginative flair, veering from sarcasm to barbaric frenzy, from melancholic unsatisfied power to the intense longing of voyeurism, from multiple

cross-rhythms of impossible love to cruel voluptuousness, erotic demen-
tia and extremes of sexual repression. The music has a nightmarish quality,
with all the inbuilt terror and potential for catharsis of the nightmare
itself. The tempestuous orchestral sound is full of dissonances, non-
functioning harmonies, blazing colouring, and a vertiginous tendency to
the atonal. Mahler described it as one of the greatest masterpieces of
the time. But is it portraying the East? There can be no doubt that for
Strauss the biblical and Middle Eastern subject, as mediated by the
imagination of Wilde, was a remarkable source of inspiration. Through
this combination, he produced a major artistic masterpiece which reflects
the cultural, intellectual and psychiatric state of Europe of the period.
The highly orientalised dance of the seven veils is a dramatic vehicle for
this contemporary analysis of psychological exposure and repression.

To underline the point, Florent Schmitt's erotic and highly-
coloured setting, effective despite using a smaller orchestra than Strauss,
was specifically designed for a dance representing physical liberation from
the constraints of the Victorian period. Szymanowski's oriental music
was also infused with eroticism, derived from his own visits to North
Africa.[49] But the composer who turned his vision of eastern eroticism
into a major philosophical and spiritual approach to music was Scriabin.

Scriabin has been both worshipped and vilified. An extreme personality, he produced music which took the notion of the union of life,
thought and the arts to its ultimate point. If the Strauss of *Salome*
marked the apotheosis of worldly decadence, Scriabin reflected the tran-
scendental ambitions of an age intrigued by the possibility of syncretic
religion, mystical, erotic and other-worldly. He was enthralled by the
Theosophy of Madame Blavatsky and by a range of contemporary philo-
sophers. He spent his life in search of the major masterpiece, a work
which by uniting art, thought and spirituality could transform the world.
Throughout he blurred the line between physical and spiritual ecstasy.
His Fourth Piano Sonata was intended to express both the French concept of the 'little death' of the orgasm and the hope of nirvana and
dematerialisation, as did his Fourth Symphony, the 'Poem of Ecstasy'.
His Fifth Symphony, 'Prometheus, Poem of Fire', used his strange synthetic chord of a thirteenth, minor seventh and augmented ninth, dis-
posed in fourths to help convey its sense of diabolic intensity and range
of moods from the ecstatic to the contemplative. Robert Craft has called
him the 'prophet of multi-media expression' and attempts have been
made in modern times to perform 'Prometheus' with lighting effects and
clouds of scents.[50]

Scriabin worked on an opera which was so impractical as to be
all philosophy and no action. Towards the end of his life, he was still
searching for his ultimate work designed to blend text and music and

proposed to set it either in England (not the least of his eccentricities was to become Anglophile towards the end of his rather peripatetic life) or Tibet. He planned to visit India, but died before he was able to make the journey. It is perhaps not surprising that his reputation has swung from voguish celebrity to almost total neglect, but he has been rediscovered in modern times – particularly his piano music – when his mystical and syncretic elements have been matched in rock music, alternative theatrical experiences and cult movements of various sorts. For Scriabin, the East really was a career and all the radical elements of his music were rooted in his search for a philosophical and religious accommodation between East and West.

Ferruccio Busoni shared a certain rootless cosmopolitanism with Scriabin.[51] Born, like Puccini, near Lucca, Busoni abandoned Italy for – as he saw it – the more radical Germany. Whereas Puccini remained the highly Italian composer of *verismo*, Busoni searched for a universal music which would know no geographical or ethnic distinctions. He tried to create a theory in which nature, form, means and a theory of progress could be combined into musical expression; he hoped that through mystic experience it would be possible to escape the concept of western linearity. He was fascinated by bells and the complex haze of overtones they could create and almost inevitably turned to eastern sources for musical inspiration and dramatic opportunity. He started, but did not finish, incidental music for Oehlenschlaeger's *Aladdin* (including the homophonic 'Hymn to Allah'), and he set Gozzi's *Turandot* before Puccini, using Arab and Chinese tunes. Like many contemporaries he was intrigued by occultism and spiritualism; he embraced a mystical pantheism and dreamed of creating a dramatic composite of music and magic. As well as his eastern interests, he wrote music on Red Indian, Jewish and Spanish themes (the latter a piano fantasy on Bizet's *Carmen*).

Puccini was a more down-to-earth figure, though no less complex psychologically, complexities which are well conveyed in his two great Orientalist operas, *Madame Butterfly* (composed 1901–03) and *Turandot* (composed, final scene unfinished, 1920–24).[52] Puccini's biographer, Mosco Carner, in a sequence of penetrating works, has analysed these operas in terms of the composer's own psychology, his working methods, his responsiveness to popular culture, and his capacity to create his finest and most innovative music out of his accommodation of exotica.[53] Carner has interpreted Puccini's operas as repeatedly exploring the unattainable love which itself passed the composer by in his difficult and loveless marriage. Although at various times Puccini proclaimed himself as not attracted by eastern themes, in fact the first opera he ever saw was *Aida*, which he revered, and it is not surprising that he was also a great admirer of *Carmen*. At one stage in his career he considered writing an opera about the Buddha and another based on Kipling's *The Light that Failed*.

He acquired the Madame Butterfly story from the melodrama of the American playwright David Belasco, which was itself based upon a novella by John Luther Long. The Turandot theme, already set by Busoni, was based upon Gozzi's eighteenth-century play (which Schiller had adapted into a German version). Its atmosphere was probably partly influenced by *Chu Chin Chow* and *Mr Wu*, which Puccini saw in London. As he was later to do with *Turandot*, he devoted himself to an intense period of researching appropriate music and effects. For *Butterfly*, he used seven Japanese tunes, including several which were sent to him by the wife of the Japanese ambassador to Italy, Madame Ohyama. By that time a number of publications contained Japanese melodies and Messager had used some for his setting of Loti's *Madame Chrysanthème*.[54] If *Butterfly* (composed 1901–03) reflects a certain amount of *fin-de-siècle Angst*, some of the sense of moral disintegration and sexual neuroses which accompanied the high point of imperialism, it unquestionably arouses sympathy for its abused heroine and antipathy for her casual rejection by the American naval officer. Moreover, it utilises some genuine Japanese musical conventions, whole-tone scales, tritones, pedals (sustained notes persisting through changes of harmony) and ostinato (a repeated bass figure).

With *Turandot*, Puccini's final work, he went even further in the search for authenticity. He used eight genuine Chinese tunes (three of which turn up in Chinese songs published by Bantock as early as 1898), and the music is strongly pentatonic, with much dissonance, bitonality, heterophony and advanced polyrhythmic patterns. While it remains essentially western, particularly in its lyrical passages, nevertheless it emerges as a remarkably syncretic essay in instrumental exoticism with complex sonorities and rhythms. As Carner has rightly argued, exotic milieux seemed to inspire Puccini's most free and innovative music.[55] It is intriguing to discover that Alfano, who completed *Turandot* after the composer's death, himself wrote an opera entitled *La Leggenda di Sakuntala* (first performed 1921) on the great Hindu epic.

Puccini certainly indulged in a certain amount of ethnomusicological activity in order to secure a hybrid authenticity for his operas, and by the inter-war years, ethnomusicology was beginning to be a full-blown discipline. Béla Bartók not only collected thousands of Hungarian, Romanian, Slovakian and other folk-songs, but also visited Biskra in North Africa. In his ballet *The Miraculous Mandarin* he used quarter-tones, slow string glissandi and approached atonal music to create an exotic effect. After the First World War, Paul Hindemith wrote music on a Burmese marionette play, *Nusch Nuschli*. There are many more examples of composers seeking oriental effects or eastern locations as a means of liberating their most innovative ideas.

British composers and Orientalism in the twentieth century

One of the themes of this chapter has been the extent to which composers have journeyed through folk music and exotica in the search for a national style. This is equally true of some of the leading figures of the English musical renaissance. Some looked to folk-song collecting and the Celtic revival, which, as Sir Thomas Beecham wittily remarked, had a tendency to wax as the British Empire waned; others to the East where British rule still seemed to predominate; some to a combination of these; while Vaughan Williams led the march back to the rural idyll of the English countryside. 'March' is the right word, for many of these composers were great walkers, holidaying in male groups and savouring the English landscape and village life just before its tranquillity vanished for ever.

Granville Bantock is the supreme case of a dual fascination with the exotic and the Celtic. As his daughter has described, his home was a 'veritable storehouse of eastern treasures', including Japanese prints, boxes and cabinets, statues, shrines and plates.[56] He and his wife furnished their houses from Liberty's orientalia and he sometimes dressed in eastern costume. (Busoni, incidentally, surrounded himself with images of the Buddha, while Scriabin had a favourite Chinese figurine.) He also collected Persian manuscripts, illustrated versions of *The Rubáiyát* and other Orientalist works like the translations of Persian and other poetry by Edwin Arnold. He learned Arabic and Persian and his son became an authority on oriental languages. Later in his life he travelled extensively in the Far East.

But Bantock was also fascinated by his Scottish ancestry and went on walking-tours of the Highlands. As well as his Hebridean and Celtic symphonies and many other 'Celtic' works, he wrote an enormous corpus of Orientalist music, including *Four Chinese Landscapes*, *In the Far East*, *The Fire Worshippers* (after Moore's *Lalla Rookh*, to which he later returned when he wrote *Oriental Rhapsody* for brass band and *Lalla Rookh* for piano), *The Pearl of Iran*, a one-act opera, *Omar Khayyám*, a vast work for soloists, chorus and orchestra which was very popular before the First World War, *Five Ghazals of Hafiz*, *Kubla Khan* and many Chinese songs to translations by his friend L. Cranmer Byng. Bantock's interest was not only related to his other artistic passions, but also to his left-wing political sympathies (he wrote a Labour March) and his sense of the inadequacy of the individualist, man-centred western universe. It is perhaps not surprising that Bantock found Vaughan Williams and his nostalgic pastoralism thoroughly 'stuffy'.[57] Distinctly 'unstuffy' was the extraordinary composer Lord Berners, a diplomat, socialite and wit, who also wrote large quantities of Orientalist music, some effectively parodying the taste.

The interest of Gustav Holst in the Orient has been described by Stradling and Hughes as no more than a passing fad,[58] thus reflecting the approach many musicologists take to the entire Orientalist canon, simply because they cannot understand it. In truth, Holst's interest in the East was not only central to his philosophy of life, but also influenced his musical language even after he had moved on in the period after the First World War.[59] Holst's stepmother was a Theosophist. He joined the Hammersmith Socialist Society at Kemscott House where he met William Morris and George Bernard Shaw, conducted the Hammersmith Social-ist Choir, and joined their healthy outdoor pursuits like cycling. He believed in the Hindu doctrine of Dharma and proclaimed himself as still adhering to it in a letter to Vaughan Williams at the time of the general strike in 1926. V. W. recognised that 'it is the blend of visionary with the realist that gives Holst's music its distinctive character'.

Captivated by a work of Friedrich Max Müller, he resolved to study Sanskrit. His three-act opera *Sita* was a large-scale work, full of what Holst himself called 'good old Wagnerian bawling'. It was based upon the *Ramayana*, the Hindu epic which is replete with spirits and demons, gods and mortals, and has never been produced. In his 'Hymns from the Rig Veda' he searched for the sound values which he thought would suit the mood and philosophy of the originals, which he trans-lated himself. In his second opera *Savitri* he abandoned the influence of Wagner and turned to the other extreme. It has been described as an astonishing achievement: it is a spare, dark-hued work, hauntingly beau-tiful, yet highly intense in its bitonal counterpoint, contrasting strikingly with some of the more overblown music being written at the same time. This time he set an episode from the *Mahabharata*, representing the triumph of love over death, with only three singing parts, of which the mezzo role of *Savitri* is pivotal, and the most economical of stagings. It has remained within the repertoire and was a perfect vehicle for the voice of Janet Baker.

After *Savitri*, Holst returned to a further set of Choral Hymns from the Rig Veda which, like *Omar Khayyám*, became extremely popu-lar with amateur choirs of the time and were championed by some of his conductor friends.[60] A holiday in Algeria in 1908 encouraged him to write *Beni Mora*, an oriental suite comprising two dances and a highly original finale, 'The Street of the Ouled Naïls', featuring a four-note motif he had heard played repeatedly by local musicians in a street procession. This fragment is reiterated some 163 times and creates an extraordinarily hypnotic effect, though it is mixed with an amazing variety of other music, producing a kaleidoscopic effect of melodies, keys and rhythms.

While it is true that Holst seldom returned to oriental sources after the war, there can be little doubt that his interest in the East and North Africa helped him to produce a distinctive musical voice that was to infuse the rest of his output. Sanskrit literature initially led him to imitate the world of Wagner, then inspired him to escape from it totally. His search for a new sound world through these works and his Rig Veda hymns was to influence the whole of the rest of his output. A close listening to *The Planets*, his most famous work, reveals the continuing effects of his Orientalist experimentation with rhythms and orchestration, particularly in his use of woodwind, brass and percussion. His oriental interests were no passing fad; they were a liberating source.

In the inter-war years, the musical interest in Orientalism begins to move further in the direction of ethnomusicology. Delius's *Hassan* perhaps represents the older search for a westernised version of atmospheric exotic colouring. It originated as incidental music for the play by James Elroy Flecker to be produced in London in 1921 (in the event, the first performance took place in Germany in 1923), and it has been said that the strikingly original choruses and interludes contain some of his best work.[61] With John Foulds, however, we move into a wholly new era of syncretism. Foulds (1880–1939) is a remarkable figure, only now being rediscovered more than fifty years after his death. He combined an interest in the Celtic with a willingness to write incidental music for the theatre and, above all, a search for a new musical language through the exploration of either the distant past or the exotic present. This range is represented by his *Keltic Lament*, his music for Shaw's *Saint Joan*, his *Hellas*, a suite of Ancient Greece, utilising classical Greek modes, and his Indian *Three Mantras*.[62]

Foulds moved towards an interest in Theosophy, mysticism, and Indian music through the influence of his second wife, Maud McCarthy, who had known the leading Theosophist, Annie Besant, and was moreover an expert on Indian music. Foulds had experimented with microtones early in his career and was working on Indian-inspired music in the 1920s, but his syncretic ambitions were furthered when he became director of Indian music at All-India Radio in Calcutta in 1935. He not only sought to transfer Indian ideas into western music, but also attempted to introduce western notation and synthetic concepts to groups of traditional Indian instrumentalists. His *Three Mantras* are the surviving preludes of his Sanskrit opera, *Avatara*, which is lost. In 1928, the distinguished oriental art historian, E. B. Havell, wrote in a letter that Foulds was 'at work on a grand opera on the subject of Sri Krishna'.

Foulds's biographer, Malcolm MacDonald, has written that the *Three Mantras* seek to represent in music the

> endlessly repeated verbal formulae . . . used to induce spiritual or mystical states, each state being conceived as having its own particular rate of vibration. Foulds's orchestral *Mantras*, in different ways exploit the idea of perpetual (but perpetually *varied*) repetition, building up complex and corruscating processes of variation upon tiny basic cells, which carry the larger structures expressed through contrasted themes. As all three movements share a preoccupation with chains of perfect or augmented fourths, and also certain melodic materials (presented, however, in radically different guises in each movement), they attain an impressively organic, quasi-symphonic unity. . . . This 'inexorable' music generates a gigantic kinetic energy, over which Foulds constructs some hair-raising poly-rhythmic complexities.[63]

Foulds also wrote an *Indian Suite*, and other works were lost when he died of cholera in Calcutta in 1939.

In the same year as Foulds's death, Benjamin Britten was introduced to the music of the gamelan by the American composer, Colin McPhee, who lived in Bali, studying its remarkable musicians, at various times between 1931 and 1939.[64] McPhee and Britten later recorded transcriptions for two pianos of Balinese ceremonial music. In 1955, Britten and Pears went on a world tour which took them to the Middle East, South Asia and the Far East. Thailand and Bali were included on the itinerary and Britten wrote excitedly to Imogen Holst, Gustav's daughter, that 'at last I'm beginning to catch on to the technique, but it's about as complicated as Schoenberg'.[65] Just as the gamelan, usually heard at European exhibitions, had influenced Debussy, Ravel in his *Mother Goose* suite, Poulenc and others, Britten's musical language was at the very least developed by this and other oriental musical experiences (such as those accompanying the Japanese *Noh* plays).

The colours and rhythms of the gamelan infuse Britten's full-length ballet, *The Prince of the Pagodas* (particularly the second act). In this he produced highly-coloured, exciting music, a rich diet, as Peter Evans has called it, full of brilliant and brash display.[66] There is some dispute among Britten commentators about the greatness of *Prince*, but there can be no doubt at all that the experience continued to reverberate through Britten's music, not only in *Curlew River* but also in the later operas. As with Holst, although the music moved on from its directly Orientalist sources, it never quite escaped that exciting contact. Intriguingly, Britten also used the gamelan in his *War Requiem*, where he created a musical heaven through an exotic instrumentation, including the xylophone, antique cymbals and musical bells.

Although Michael Tippett's music was not so fundamentally influenced, he too found it imposible to escape the lure of the gamelan, particularly in the slow movement of his Triple Concerto. The gamelan has, indeed, become something of a cliché. The American John Cage produced the effect of a gamelan orchestra by means of the prepared piano in his *Interludes*. There is now a group called the Strathclyde Gamelan Players and Elaine Agnew has written *Over the Sea to Java*. The instrument, in all its variety, is sometimes used in schools' music and the training of teachers.[67]

Indeed, as with the Orientalist songs listed above, the number of twentieth-century western composers who passed through this often transforming effect of the different musical traditions of the East is almost endless, from the American Henry Cowell, who made a serious study of oriental music in the Germany of the 1920s (but was instructed by musicians and musicologists from India and Indonesia) to Philip Glass, who worked with Ravi Shankar; from the Australian Percy Grainger, who heard Chinese music in the Chinatown of Melbourne and introduced these ideas in his *Eastern Intermezzo* and other works, to Ronald Stevenson who opens his Violin Concerto with an Indian raga. Now there are many Asian composers who are similarly working in syncretic forms, including the most celebrated in the West, Takemitsu, and lesser known figures like Naresh Sohal who brings Indian subject-matter and musical ideas into western music.

However, none of the results of this work constitutes a pure form of ethnomusicology. In his April 1994 BBC radio interview, Edward Said suggested that composers, like writers, had created a monolithic discourse of the East until the inter-war years of the twentieth century. Then musicians like Bartók began to treat the East as a true partner and thereafter musical traditions could grapple with each other on a basis of equality. This Whiggish approach is surely unconvincing. In all of these instances, including the modern ones, what emerges is more or less a hybrid form, a graft in which different stocks achieve a varied balance. Of course it is true that there may be more highly developed forms of syncretism in the twentieth century, but this need not overturn the notion that oriental influences in the past have been any less radical in their day. Now that 'world music' has become such a major force in the whole area of popular music, we have never been more alert to the variety of musical traditions. But that is not to say that what is achieved is any more radical for our time than the influence of exotic elements on composers in the 'long nineteenth century' up to 1914. It is significant, to take but two examples, that major commentators on both Bizet and Puccini see these composers as achieving their most innovative voices through incorporating exotica in their music.

Above all, it is important to recognise that the oriental obsession in music has been a continuing one, invariably representing a new wave of radicalism, a fresh search for melodic invention, instrumental colour and rhythmic complexity. At no time has this repeated appeal to the East been monolithic and seldom has it been reactionary: its phases do not march apace with the rise of western imperialism. Indeed, it achieves its most radical phase – as in the case of art and design – at the high point of imperial power in the late nineteenth and early twentieth centuries. Its practitioners were just as likely to be artistic revolutionaries as imperial fellow-travellers, Holst rather than Elgar, Foulds rather than Vaughan Williams. Orientalism offered one repeated appeal (along with other forms of folk or exotic music) for those who pursued 'alternative conjunctures'. From the beginning of the twentieth century, the search for syncretic forms moves into a more comprehensive mode, attempting to incorporate not just mood and colour, but also something of the philosophy and spirituality of the East. These are filtered through western perceptions just as much as any previous response had been, but this does not invalidate the artistic experience of the new language that emerges.

Thus a variety of Easts, successively Turkey, the Arab lands, the Caucasus, Russian Central Asia, India, China and Japan, served to offer one opportunity for discovering the necessary destabilising elements which broke up whatever served as convention in each period. Out of each phase of destabilisation there emerged a developed form, still western of course, but more or less transformed by its new melodic or rhythmic experience. If the East represented imagination to the West's rationality, in music it offered new melodic lines, different tonal systems, fresh rhythms of great complexity, and striking instrumental colour. Deeper into the twentieth century, the powerful rhythms and improvisatory forms of jazz and other black music were to perform the same function.

Meanwhile the relationship with other arts is complex. Where music was intended to accompany plot or text, clearly there was a tendency to draw on literary developments already well entrenched. If, however, the text represented a delayed reponse, the music through which that text was set was likely to be responding to newly discovered forms from the East. If plot and text often did exhibit elements of the essentialism of literary approaches to the East, invariably the radical character of the music (particularly in the greatest of works) by underpinning and extending characterisation often blunted the stereotypes by satire or transformed them by its universalising power. We can see this kind of effect running through the work of Mozart, Verdi, Bizet, Puccini and many others. Sometimes, the new conjunction could stimulate theatrical innovation too. What's more, in a France struggling to escape German influence, in a Russia seeking to create a distinctive voice – Eurasian, resistant to western Europe and appropriate to its independent artistic traditions – and a Britain attempting to find a national form, the appeal to folk and exotic elements represented a key route out of conformity. Even the most conservative of composers – Saint-Saëns comes most readily to mind – could participate in this search and discover their own approach to innovatory forms as a result.

Thus, eclecticism becomes a virtue rather than a vice. Nor should it be dismissed as marginal, always a response to passing fashion, additional decorations without structural significance. Many composers only touched on Orientalist themes; others took a deeper interest but still moved on; and only a few turned it into a lifetime's specialism; but in almost every case it was a significant moment in the development of their art. Some of course seemed barely touched by it and found other ways of developing novel ideas, but it has been a central argument of this chapter that Orientalism should be seen as one element within a wider search for folk and exotic sources of inspiration (in which Spain and Scotland both figure prominently), which could help to contribute to a national style. Thus Russian, French and British composers were all promiscuous in their plunderings. If the Germans seemed less eager (though still active) in this field, then it is because of their established dominance and greater cultural self-confidence. But with many composers it is possible to identify Orientalist influences, the coloured stream of silt derived from contacts with the East, flowing on through their music. From the Turkish contribution to the sound of the orchestra and its rhythmic potential in the eighteenth century to the explorations of Holst, Britten and Messiaen in the twentieth, the influence of the East has been a far from negligible contribution to the development of western music.

Notes

1   This chapter arises from a lifetime's love of music. While many books on music and composer biographies have been used in its compilation, much of its information and interpretations are based upon performances heard and seen, concert and opera programmes, radio talks, BBC continuity announcements, record sleeves and CD booklets, and standard reference works such as *Grove's Dictionary of Music and Musicians* (London, both the 1966 and 1980 editions), the magnificent *Viking Opera Guide*, edited by Amanda Holden (London, 1993), the *Concise Oxford Dictionary of Opera*, edited by Harold Rosenthal and John Warrack (London, 1979) and several others. I am grateful to those BBC producers and compilers of talks who helpfully sent me transcripts. It should be apparent that it is not always possible to reference this eclectic range of sources.

2   Alex Cohen, 'Elgar: Poetic visions and patriotic vigour', *Radio Times*, 2 December 1932.

3   Robert Stradling and Meirion Hughes, *The English Musical Renaissance, 1860–1940* (London, 1993).

4   Edward W. Said, *Musical Elaborations* (London, 1991), p. xii.

5   Stradling and Hughes, *English Musical Renaissance*, p. 8.

6   Interestingly, the first building of the Royal College was Orientalist in form, with 'Indian bays' (projecting windows with oriental detail), *chujjas* (heavy overhanging eaves) and a ventilator cover in the shape of a howdah. It was designed by Lt Henry Cole of the Royal Engineers, the son of the celebrated Henry Cole who had been instrumental in setting up the college. Raymond Head, *The Indian Style* (London, 1986), p. 84.

7   See for example the review of Stradling and Hughes by John Bentley in the *Guardian*, 20 July 1993.

8   In a series of television programmes on the influence of the East on western music broadcast in 1992.

9   For example, in Stradling and Hughes, *English Musical Renaissance*, p. 176.

10   W. Daniel Wilson, 'Turks on the eighteenth-century operatic stage and European political, military, and cultural history', *Eighteenth-Century Life*, 2 (1985), pp. 79–92. Eve R. Meyer, '*Turquerie* and eighteenth-century music', *Eighteenth-Century Studies*, 7 (1973–74), pp. 474–88.

11   Henry George Farmer, 'Oriental influences on occidental military music', *Islamic Culture*, 15 (April 1941), pp. 239–40.

12   Wilson, 'Turks on the eighteenth-century operatic stage', pp. 82–4.

13   Ian Richard Netton, 'The mysteries of Islam' in G. S. Rousseau and Roy Porter, *Exoticism in the Enlightenment* (Manchester, 1990), pp. 23–45.

14   Wilson, 'Turks on the eighteenth-century operatic stage', p. 83.

15   Rousseau and Porter, *Exoticism*, introduction.

16   Thomas Bauman, *Die Entführung aus dem Serail* (Cambridge, 1987), p. 94; see also pp. 62–74 and *passim* for a discussion of janissary bands, the Viennese love of Turkish music and the destabilised and innovative character of Mozart's music.

17   Nicholas John (series editor), *The Magic Flute* (Opera Guide Series, London, 1980).

18   Nicholas John (series editor), *Così fan tutte* (Opera Guide Series, London, 1983).

19   During the period of Lent, biblical themes were considered to be particularly suitable, when the stage was constrained in its approach to more everyday subjects.

20   Other Orientalist operas (at least in terms of plot) from the same period which were once popular but are now seldom performed include Daniel Auber's *Le Cheval de bronze*, which involves a party of Chinese visiting the planet Venus, Peter Cornelius's *Der Barbier von Bagdad* (though a flop at its first performance) and Karl Goldmark's *Die Königin von Saba* (the Queen of Sheba).

21   Roger Fiske, *Scotland in Music* (Cambridge, 1983).

22   Holden (ed.), *Viking Opera Guide*, p. 1232.

23   Philip Glass, *Opera on the Beach: Philip Glass on his New World of Music Theatre* (London, 1988); John Rockwell, 'The Orient, the visual arts and the evolution of minimalism: Philip Glass' in *All-American Music: Composition in the Late Twentieth Century* (New York, 1983).

24   Said, *Musical Elaborations*, p. 65.

25   Winton Dean, *Bizet* (London, 1975), Chapters IX, X.

26   Dean, *Bizet*, p. 172.

27   James Harding, *Saint-Saëns and his Circle* (London, 1965), pp. 17, 76.

28   Camille Saint-Saëns, *Outspoken Essays on Music* (Westport, Conn., 1970, first published 1922), p. 171.

29   In the programme for the 1991 Covent Garden production of *Samson*, unpaginated.

30   In an interview on BBC Radio 3 'Music matters', 2 April 1994.

31   Harding, *Saint-Saëns*, p. 51.

32   John Warrack (ed.), *Carl Maria von Weber: Writings on Music*, trans. Martin Cooper (Cambridge, 1981), pp. 170–1; John Warrack, *Carl Maria von Weber* (Cambridge, 1976), pp. 74–5.

33   P. J. Marshall, 'Taming the exotic: the British and India in the seventeenth and eighteenth centuries' in Rousseau and Porter (eds), *Exoticism*, p. 61.

34   Borodin spent many hours during the last years of his life in the St Petersburg public library studying Arabic music. He was particularly interested in the examples of forty tunes from Arab music which had been collected by Nicolai Christianovich.

35   Slave girls were something of a cliché in nineteenth-century Orientalist opera and produced a disclaimer by Weber on behalf of Meyerbeer's *Wirth und Gast*, where a slaves' chorus had been viewed as 'a gross libel on Turkish society'. They were, said Weber, introduced to the Vienna production with a view to filling the theatre and in order to obtain some women's voices for the chorus. This reveals an interesting sensitivity in 1815: Warrack, *Weber, Writings on Music*, p. 139. *Salammbô* was given a concert performance by the Kirov Opera at the Edinburgh Festival in 1991.

36   Rubinstein, like so many other composers, wrote music on Moore's *Lalla Rookh*. Other examples of Russian Orientalist music include Humperdinck's *Moorish Rhapsody*, Ippolitov Ivanov's *Caucasian Sketches* and Prokofiev's juvenilia piece, *Hindu Galop*.

37   In the BBC Radio 3 interview, note 30, above. See also *Musical Elaborations*, p. 65.

38   Edward Said discusses *Aida* at some length in *Culture and Imperialism* (London, 1993), pp. 134–57. My critique can be found in a review article, 'Occidentalism: counterpoint and counter-polemic', *Journal of Historical Geography*, 19 (1993), pp. 339–44. See also Nicholas John (series editor), *Aida* (Opera Guide Series, London, 1980) and Julian Budden, *Verdi* (London, 1985) particularly pp. 272–9. Verdi himself rated *Aida* very highly.

39   It must be said, however, that Verdi was prepared to pander to his Parisian audience in offering Orientalism when required: he added Orientalist music to his *Jérusalem* for its Paris production, and also provided Orientalist ballet music for *Otello*.

40   Edward Lockspeiser, *Debussy* (London, 1963), pp. 40, 50 and *passim*.

41   Robert Orledge, *Debussy and the Theatre* (Cambridge, 1982), pp. 128–48, 186–94.

42   Orledge, *Debussy*, p. 187.

43   In radio talks as well as his many publications on Mahler.

44   Mahler played parts of *Das Lied* almost every day for the last two years of his life. Alma Mahler, *Gustav Mahler: Memories and Letters*, translated by Donald Mitchell (London, 1973), p. 187.

45   The conductor and composer Hans von Bülow wrote a work entitled *Nirwana*.

46   Stravinsky was also fascinated by oriental instruments which he heard in St Petersburg and that had reached Russia via the Caucasus. He tried to represent their sound by piano, harp and cymbalon.

47   Griffes, who has been called America's only genuine Impressionist composer, also wrote a Japanese pantomime entitled *Sho-jo* and his best known work, *The Pleasure Dome of Kubla Khan*.

48   Nicholas John (series editor), *Salome/Elektra* (Opera Guide Series, London, 1988), particularly p. 15. The counter-view has been expressed by Michael Kennedy, for example in the booklet accompanying the Decca recording of the opera conducted by Solti. Some of the production history of *Salome* can be found in Alan Jefferson, *The Operas of Richard Strauss in Britain, 1910–63* (London, 1963).

49   Szymanowski reflects the complexities in the Orientalism argument. He visited North Africa in the years before the First World War, returning to Poland in 1914. He steeped himself in Arabic and Persian culture, composed settings of Persian poems, and was a fervent admirer of Islamic art. Yet he almost certainly indulged in sexual tourism and he wrote a work entitled 'The Song of the Infatuated Muezzin', using the intonations of the muezzin's call, which some have seen as blasphemous.

50   Fabian Bowers, *Scriabin: a Biography of the Russian Composer, 1871–1914*, 2 vols. (Tokyo, 1969). For the Craft quotation, see Vol. 1, p. 8. See also Boris de Schloezer, *Scriabin, Artist and Mystic*, trans. N. Slonimsky (New York, 1990).

51   Antony Beaumont, *Busoni, the Composer* (London, 1985).

52   Puccini's works are strikingly Orientalist when compared with what had gone before. Offenbach's Chinese operetta, *Ba Ta Clan* (1855) has nothing Orientalist about its music at all. Gilbert and Sullivan's *The Mikado* (1885) included fragments of authentic Japanese tunes and some pentatonic flavouring. In Lehar's later *Land of Smiles* (1929), '*chinoiserie* gives way to melancholy lyricism', as the writer in the *Viking Opera Guide* (p. 561) puts it. See also Sullivan's *The Rose of Persia or the Story-teller and the Slave* (not with Gilbert), which has a highly Orientalist plot. Indeed, operetta can, perhaps, be accused of Orientalism in the Saidian sense more than most forms, but the stereotyping is blunted by the satire which is so obviously intended to apply to the home society.

53   Mosco Carner, *Puccini: a Critical Biography* (London, 1958); Mosco Carner (ed.), new edition of Guiseppe Adami (ed.), *Letters of Puccini* (London, 1974); Nicholas John (series editor), *Turandot* (Opera Guide Series, London, 1984), which contains an article by Carner, pp. 19–34; *Madam Butterfly* (Opera Guide Series, London, 1980).

54   Another 'Japanese' opera of the period is Mascagni's *Iris*, of 1898, which contains an uncomfortable blend of *verismo* and exotica without any of the inspiration of Puccini.

55   Carner, *Puccini*, pp. 368–9.

56   Myrrha Bantock, *Granville Bantock: a Personal Portrait* (London, 1972), p. 81 and *passim*.

57   Bantock, *Bantock*, pp. 125–6. Eugene Goossens considered that Bantock had helped to create a national school through exploiting orchestral colour to the full, p. 99. Oriental interests and concern with colour very much went together.

58   Stradling and Hughes, *Musical Renaissance*, p. 115.

59   On Holst, see Imogen Holst, *Gustav Holst* (London, 1938), Michael Short, *Gustav Holst: the Man and His Music* (Oxford, 1990), Michael Short (ed.), *Gustav Holst: Letters to W. G. Whittaker* (Glasgow, 1974) and the excellent entry on Holst in the *New Grove*.

60   Holst's letters to the Newcastle choir conductor, W. G. Whittaker, reveal the popularity of his choral *Hymns from the Rig Veda*. His *Two Eastern Pictures*, based on Sanskrit poems, with their atmospheric harp music and ethereal sounds for female voices, are still sometimes performed. The manner in which these pieces, together with Bantock's *Khayyám*, were taken up within the amateur choral tradition says something about the search for a national style through an oriental medium. Holst himself said that if something is worth doing, it is worth doing badly, reflecting an English amateur tradition which gives the lie to Said's notion of music performance as an 'extreme occasion' in *Musical Elaborations*. It is one of the characteristics of that book that it generalises unacceptably from the American experience and pays too much attention to – often eccentric – American or Canadian performers, like the ineffable Glenn Gould.

61   In the entry on Delius in the *New Grove*.

62   Malcolm MacDonald, *John Foulds* (Rickmansworth, 1975). See also the *New Grove* entry on the composer.

63   This is quoted from a note by Malcolm MacDonald in the Lyrita recording of Foulds's *Three Mantras* (London Philharmonic Orchestra, conducted by Barry Wordsworth).

64   Colin McPhee (1900–64) wrote a number of works based upon the gamelan, including *Tabuh-tabuhan* (1936) and *Balinese Ceremonial Music for two pianos* (1940). In the former he combined western instruments with Balinese gongs. His *A House in Bali* (first published 1944) contains a moving account of his study of the gamelan 'clubs' of Bali and their relationship with the artistic and social life of the island. His major work is *Music in Bali* (New York, 1966).

65   Michael Kennedy, *Britten* (London, 1981), p. 71. This discussion of Britten's oriental interests is derived from Kennedy and from the musicologically more detailed Peter Evans, *The Music of Benjamin Britten* (London, 1979).

66   For Evans's discussion of *Prince of the Pagodas*, see *Music of Britten*, pp. 223–35.

67   The teacher-training department of Lancaster University has a set of gamelans for use in the training of music teachers.

7
Orientalism in the theatre

THE THEATRE had the potential to combine all the arts surveyed so far. It brought together the art of stage scenery, the design of sets, costumes and props, the music of song and the instrumental pit, the architecture of both the building in which the performance took place and the fantasy world portrayed beyond the proscenium arch, and the text and characterisation of the play. Not all performances, of course, had fully worked texts, but ideas, ideologies and images of other cultures were projected through performers, their appearance and their stage 'business'. This chapter is concerned with the theatre's rationalisation of the arts and exploitation of the oriental 'Other' in a popular context. Like the rest of the volume, it will pay less attention to text than to the artistic vehicles through which a conceptualisation of the East was conveyed.

The world of orientalised opera and its search for a music pushing beyond the conventional frontiers, the Orientalism of much theatre architecture and of the grand exhibitions which were the setting for dramatic activity have been covered in previous chapters. Here we turn from the more intellectualised arts to a popular medium, a form which is much influenced by fashion in the other arts, which often parodies them and, whether through burlesque, satire or other more admiring imitative approaches, carries such artistic notions to a much wider audience. This is not to say that the popular theatre is wholly parasitic. It does of course develop its own unique forms, pursues its own independent course, and responds to audience desires as dictated through the box-office. It is, however, a potent vehicle for the conveyance of dominant ideologies, as I was concerned to point out when I surveyed the dissemination of imperial ideas in my book *Propaganda and Empire* of 1984.[1] These themes have been developed extensively – and more rigorously – in a variety of works both within and without the Manchester University Press 'Studies in Imperialism' series.[2]

The primarily visual approach of this treatment will be confirmed by including within it the essentially theatrical panoramas, dioramas and cosmoramas which became so popular from the beginning of the nineteenth century. Throughout, it will be the relationship between the theatre and the other visual arts which will be stressed, including the use of the theatre as a showcase for fabrics, textile design and crafts, which reaches a great climax in the early twentieth century. In the same period, as has been frequently pointed out, many of the techniques and attitudes of the nineteenth-century theatre were transferred into the early cinema and continued to hold sway there for a number of decades.[3] There have been some attempts to analyse Orientalism in the cinema, but a great deal of work remains to be done in this area.[4] Apart from passing references, and the architecture considered in Chapter 5, the world of the silver screen lies beyond the scope of this chapter.

Throughout its modern history (that is from Tudor times), the theatre has been much concerned with empire, the extension of European power, and with the discovery of and relationships with other cultures. From Shakespeare's classic treatments in *The Tempest* and *Othello*, through the widespread genre of abduction plays (including those of Aphra Behn) of the late seventeenth and eighteenth centuries (already encountered as the sources of operas) to the major fascination with India, South America, American Indians and the Pacific in the Enlightenment period, the theatre grappled with issues of race and power. By the late eighteenth and nineteenth centuries, these interests had become almost dominant. The fantasy world of the Arabian Nights had taken up residence in pantomime. Military and naval events, shipwrecks and the settings of conflicts between good and evil moved out of European contexts into the wider world.

A number of theatrical, as well as intellectual and political conditions influenced this progressive relocation of performances. The character of the conspiracy of pretence in which actors and audiences indulge is ultimately rooted in a sense of shared community. The community may be local, regional or national; it may be based on class, religion and urban or rural economic interest-groups. But ultimately sections of the audience (and they may of course identify with different communities of interest) react to a moral or religious message, shared ideals which mark them out as distinctive, a fantasy world which introduces 'Others' through which they can more clearly know themselves, and the widening horizons of a newly explored world. Even the most local of rural theatrical experiences could make references to much wider geographical contexts, but as the theatre became more formalised, more accessible and more subject to nation-wide tours, it was a newly formed national identity which became the prime focus of the sense of shared community. As the nineteenth century wore on, some of the class content of the early melodramas, for example, was eliminated in favour of a cross-class sense of communal purpose.[5]

Moreover, the patent system of restricted theatre licensing in London, which survived until 1843, encouraged a variety of evasions to avoid the dialogue which constituted the prime definition of the drama which could only be performed in the licensed houses. Pantomime was one such immensely popular form. The topical theatre, with its concentration on military events, was another. When the patent system was finally abolished, the power of the Lord Chamberlain grew and censorship of the West End stage was more rigorous. Domestic, political and class conflict, depictions of the royal family or of politicians, references to the Irish problem or to biblical scenes and religious controversy were all banned and continued to be so until the twentieth century. Although the Lord Chamberlain's writ only ran in the West End of London, these norms communicated themselves to the licensing authorities elsewhere in the capital and the country. The result was that subjects involving discovery, empire and war, the depiction of 'Others' and the creation of a fantasy world through scene-painting, costumes and exotic props were particularly acceptable.

All of these considerations were re-emphasised by the development of a highly topical theatre, a theatre through which audiences were introduced to the main events and ideas of the age. Such topicality led to the portrayal of battles (including naval encounters in the extraordinary aquatic theatre pioneered at Sadler's Wells during the Napoleonic wars), rebellions, journeys, historical events and even archaeological discoveries.[6] The other distinctive theatrical forms of the age, melodrama and spectacle, were also bent to these purposes, if in more generalised contexts. Thus, audiences were sometimes confronted with the 'facts' of actual happenings; at other times with fictional drama set within contexts with which they were largely familiar.

A number of developments have been identified as taking place between the late eighteenth and early twentieth centuries. It has been suggested that the theatre at first was genuinely informative or educative, introducing audiences to material invariably new to them.[7] In the course of the nineteenth century, however, many other media came to present

18 Léon Bakst, costume design for an odalisque, *Schéhérazade*, 1910. Choreography by Fokine to music by Rimsky-Korsakov. A continuation of fin-de-siècle decadence with billowing oriental shapes and motifs representing a revolution in costume design for the ballet.

similar matter: panoramas and related visual forms, illustrated and popular journals, paintings and prints, publications for the young, school
texts, music with topical 'programmes' and street spectacle, pageantry
and exhibitions. By the later years of the century, the theatre was rubbing up perceptions, confirming ideas and prejudices, retelling events
and notions already well known to the audience. The separation of the
classes in the layered tiers of the conventional theatre form may have
helped to produce different responses in the various parts of the audience, but by the last decades of the century this variety of reaction may
well have been smoothed out by shared patriotic sentiment and sense of
imperial purpose.

As we have already seen, melodrama became much less class-
specific, often using racial difference as a substitute for domestic conflict.
At the same time, the theatre became progressively more respectable, not
only in terms of social acceptability, but also through its seating arrange-
ments, its careful control of liquor, elimination of soliciting by prosti-
tutes, and – especially in the case of the music-hall – self-censorship in
order to concentrate on the material which was deemed politically and
socially unexceptionable.[8] Moreover, the spectacular theatre strove increasingly for realistic effects, vying to produce fresh gasps of wonder
from an audience looking for fresh sensation beyond the proscenium
arch.[9] These developments were encouraged by new technology in lighting and staging. Spectacular drama and pageantry could even escape the
confines of the theatre altogether and re-emerge in the vast auditoriums
of exhibitions and the new sports stadiums of the twentieth century.

In all these forms, it has long been argued that eighteenth- and
nineteenth-century drama had a tendency to deal in morally clear situations, conflicts between heroes and villains, between justice and legal
perversion, despotism and constitutionalism, 'true' religion and supersti-
tion, debauchery and elevating romantic love, excess and restraint.
Heroic stereotypes were created for the patriotic programme of both de-
fence of the motherland and conquest of the outer regions of the globe,
stereotypes which embraced the working-class Jack Tar and (later) Tommy
Atkins as well as the aristocratic or bourgeois officer.[10] The major heroes
of the century, like Nelson or Havelock (as in Dion Boucicault's *Jessie
Brown or the Relief of Lucknow* of 1862) or Gordon (in, for example,
Muskerry and Jourdain's *Khartoum!* of 1885, one of several plays about
the fall of Khartoum), appeared repeatedly on the stage, the embodiment of heroic attributes and key examplars for an imperial people.[11]

It is, perhaps, not surprising that in all these developments the
imaginary Orient and its associated Orientalism should have figured
prominently. The East offered opportunities for stunning set design by

artists (like David Roberts) who sometimes travelled in the Mediterranean and Levantine worlds, a development encouraged further by the appearance of the panorama. Exotic architecture, plants and animals were all used to convey the sensation of spectacular novelty through which the audience could identify difference and potentially confirm their own supposed uniqueness in appearance, moral values and power. Above all, costumes, fabrics and accessories were used to create a sense of an opulent fantasy world which could itself be appropriated through spectacle, imperial power and unequal commercial transaction.

The main question which faces the historian of Orientalism in the theatre is the extent to which plays and performances dealt in binary moral absolutes. How far were Self and Other portrayed in simple, clear-cut conflicts of good and evil? To what extent, indeed, did Asian peoples, whether in fantastic or 'realistic' guises, constitute the primary Other in such dramatic renderings of moral dilemmas? How far can the Orientalist discourse be found in popular culture, translating high art and the work of intellectuals for the masses? And how far, and in what ways did these portrayals change and develop with the unfolding of the imperial enterprise in the eighteenth and nineteenth centuries?

The sixteenth- and seventeenth-century stage tended to treat India with respect and awe, as did European travellers of the time. Sometimes this respect was expressed through the spurious image of riches and plenty. In Marlowe's *Tamburlaine*, the opulent East – later associated with the devil in Milton's *Paradise Lost* – was depicted as an ideal, contrasting strikingly with a disadvantaged West: 'for goodnesse of scituation, temperature, health and fertility' India was 'far better than any other country'. It 'never feeleth famine, nor scarcity'.[12] Dryden's image of the East also embraced riches and beauty, a suitable bride, as in *Alexander's Feast*, for the West.

The eighteenth century abounded with dramatic material associated with exploration, the discoveries of the Enlightenment and imperial wars in India. The relationship between painting and theatrical settings and presentations is neatly illustrated by the massive history paintings which were provided by Francis Hayman for the Saloon at Vauxhall Gardens in the early 1760s.[13] One and perhaps two of these featured events in India: a heroic Robert Clive meeting Mir Jafar after the Battle of Plassey and the other possibly Sir Eyre Coote receiving the surrender of Pondicherry. Captain Cook appeared on the stage, particularly in John O'Keefe's pantomime *Omai, or a Trip Round the World*, which ran in London and the provinces to capacity audiences between 1785 and 1788.[14] Omai was the Tahitian who was brought to Britain by Cook, lionised in London society and frequently painted as a classically noble figure. Tipu Sultan of Mysore, an adversary through several Mysore wars until defeated and killed after the battle of Seringapatam in 1799, was treated differently, as an evil enemy overwhelmed by the virtues of British military might, his family treated with the magnanimity of heroic imperial generalship. Tipu was portrayed upon the stage throughout this sequence of wars, even although the British were inevitably preoccupied with the Napoleonic campaigns during that period. A play, 'a story told in action', entitled 'Tippoo Saib or British Valour in India' appeared on the London stage in June 1791. It included 'a battle dance and a representation of an English and Indian Grand Martial Procession'.[15] It was the first of several, for other dramatic portrayals of Tipu appeared in 1792, 1799 and 1838 (*Arajoon or the Conquest of Mysore*). They clearly offered opportunities for spectacle and martial display at a time when the theatre was also devoting much attention to the military encounters of the French wars.

As we have seen in earlier chapters, the Napoleonic period was a time of prominent Orientalism and this was indeed reflected in the theatre. As David Mayer has shown, the pantomime, which constituted an ideal means of avoiding dialogue (though far from completely) not only adopted features of the *Thousand and One Nights* and the *commedia dell' arte*, but also developed its own conventions and used them to make sharp social and cultural comment. Pantomimes used all forms of distancing to create their effects: some set scenes in the ancient world, using the Roman Empire and Druids, while many turned to Gothic, Chinese, Indian, Persian, Egyptian and Japanese architecture or settings to produce their sensational and satirical extravaganzas.[16] The East not only enlarged the imaginative world of the pantomime, but also provided vehicles for satire on industrialism, dandyism, the Corn Law controversy, early tunnelling and new technology, particularly steam vessels and railways.

The East was certainly portrayed within the conventions of Indian wealth and Egyptian opulence, the locus of the nabobs' fortune-making, attracting social dissent and fascinated wishful-thinking in equal measure. But the range and scale of 'Othering' in pantomimes was exceptionally diverse. Welsh, Irish, Scots and Yorkshiremen regularly appeared as 'Others', while the tradition of parody, often used for operas and better known plays, also produced a parallel alterity for maximum comic effect. A good example is John Home's tragedy, *Douglas*, immensely popular in the later eighteenth and early nineteenth centuries. (At an early performance in Edinburgh, a member of the audience is said to have shouted 'Whaur's your Wullie Shakespeare noo'!) Joseph Grimaldi, the greatest exponent of early nineteenth-century pantomime, parodied Home's lines:

My name is Norval; on the Grampian Hills
My father tends his flocks, a frugal swain.

as

My name is Munichow; on China's plain
My father feeds his pigs, a stingy swain.[17]

Here the audience is invited to laugh at the Scots by seeing them transformed into Chinese, Norval into Munichow (equally funny names),
their sheep into pigs. This would certainly have been more difficult later
in the century, but here the process of identifying an Asian Other is
totally destabilised by viewing the Scots as equally remote and corres-
pondingly risible.

There were many other parodies in pantomime, ranging from
operas like Weber's *Der Freischütz* and Mozart's *Don Giovanni*, the
contemporary Gothic fashion, hunt scenes, aquatic events, and celebrities
in high art like Paganini. In all of this it is hard to see the oriental Other
as uniquely singled out for racial treatment in respect of patterns of
imperial dominance. Indeed, the pantomime established a tradition of
retributive comedy to deflate the high and mighty, both in social and (as
the opera and Shakespearian parodies indicate) cultural terms. Oriental
potentates were used to point up the satire of the first; crazes for chinoiserie and Egyptiana the second. The use of exotic settings also gave
rise to an extension of the notion of animal drama. The use of dogs in
theatrical display was common, but pantos also introduced elephants,
apes and other creatures.

It is an interesting fact that at the height of the Napoleonic wars,
the theatre season of 1811–12 was notably Orientalist in tone, with *Blue
Beard*, *Timour the Tartar* and *Harlequin and Padmanaba* all being
performed in London.[18] When Napoleon was first defeated in 1814,
before his escape from his exile on Elba, the celebrations in London
included the erection of a 'temple' and a Chinese bridge and pagoda in
St James's Park. This may have reflected the chinoiserie interests of the
Prince Regent. It may be, though this is pure speculation, that victory
in Europe was seen as in some way paralleling the great clash of eastern
empires or the imposition of European commercialism in the Far East.
Or, as seems more likely, the Orientalist tone may have associated celebrations with Asian festivity, garden architecture and fireworks.

Certainly, these notions were debated at the time. In 1813 *The
Times*, in a review of the pantomime *Harlequin and the Red Dwarf*,
extolled the advantages of Orientalist scenery and Asian history. So
powerful were the effects of the décor of this particular performance that
the reviewer was surprised that

our painters have not turned more fully to the treasures of the Eastern Tale. Our landscape is pale to the hues of Eastern vegetation. Our historic figures are harsh and cold, to the stateliness are majesty, the gloomy stateliness and sweeping majesty, of the Leaders of Asia: their story, full of sudden and appalling change – Monarchs hurried from the dungeon to the throne and from the throne to the dungeon – invasions that rush over a continent like a deluge, and return as swiftly back to their recesses – revolutions that burst in a moment round secure dynasties, and seat the slave in the palaces of his Lord! But the 'fable' of the East is the very wantoning of an imagination, overwhelmed by its own incongruable fertility. Its forms of fantastic loveliness and supernatural power, its winged Spirits, its haughty and malignant Genii, its Enchanters in the midst of forest and cavern, lighting the fires of incantation, and calling round them shapes of other worlds – its magic hosts, its tents and standards, blazoned with gems and gold – its towers of imprisoned beauty fenced strong with many a spell, pour upon the mind and memory in dazzling and splendid confusion.[19]

This is a fascinating statement, full of allusions to the sublime and the Gothic, viewing the East not as the Other to be despised and conquered, but as illustrating all the characteristics most highly valued in the cultural fashions of the age. It is of course a generalised and stereotypical East, an East to be appropriated, but not because of its derogatory connotations; an East not only dazzling in its imaginative power, but also in its vegetation, its characters and (by implication) its fabrics. There is, moreover, more than a hint of boredom with the Hanoverians, a desire for a grander dynasty and an easier political escape than that afforded by western conventions. It also suggests a certain amount of escapism from the grinding and bitter warfare of Europe, the campaigns which Ruskin was later to describe as 'chemical and mechanic', which 'build nothing but tombs'.[20] The naval and military encounters of the Napoleonic wars certainly received ample stage treatment, but the East offered a more melodramatic, a more personal, medieval and even chivalrous approach to the sweep of history and turnover of dynasties.

Just such themes, together with the fundamental and unwelcome alternative approaches to kingship, appeared in Byron's *Sardanapalus* of 1821. This play, which has been described as the apex of Byron's dramatic achievement, poses questions about the character of monarchy and leadership which, through the spectacular context of ancient Assyria, reflected on contemporary dynastic discontents.[21] Sardanapalus attempts to break with the old repressive and warlike order of his predecessors, such as his hunting and campaigning father, Nimrod, seeking to create instead an idealistic, sybaritic and artistically sophisticated court, building cities instead of making war, striving for an earthly paradise of cultured indolence. Faced with rebellion, however, he is forced to abandon his role as a kindly and negligent ruler and egged on by his heroic Greek concubine, Myrrha, courageously takes up arms, is wounded and ultimately dies with her on a vast funeral pyre. Thus the play not only posed the central dilemma of monarchy and pessimistically proposed that the cultured earthly paradise was unattainable, whether in the East or the West, but also offered opportunities for striking oriental costumes, spectacular settings and the pyrodramatic climax of the final conflagration.

There were a number of spectacular productions of this play in Britain, France and the United States. Macready performed it in London, Liverpool and Manchester in 1834, when the characters adopted Turkish dress and the backdrops were based on the apocalyptic paintings of John Martin. In 1853 it was revived by Charles Kean with particularly spectacular scenery, utilising the advice of Sir Henry Layard, whose excavations at Nineveh, published in 1849, had created something of a public sensation.[22] One reviewer described this production as 'altogether unparalleled for stage display'.[23] The advice of *The Times* in 1813 had indeed been followed. Charles Alexander Calvert revived the play with even greater attention to archaeological detail in 1875 and it enjoyed a long run in both London and Liverpool. It was still being produced in the English provinces in the 1890s. Its serious message became progressively obscured (perhaps because it was seen to be so much less relevant in Victoria's reign than in those of George IV and William IV) and became an excuse for oriental spectacle on a grand scale. Moreover, it seems to have lost the kind of sentiments expressed in Kipling's poem *Recessional* of 1897. Macready had included in the final soliloquy lines which Kean subsequently cut:

> Time shall quench full many
> A people's records, and a hero's acts;
> Sweep empire after empire, like this first
> Of empires, into nothing; but even then
> Shall spare this deed of mine, and hold it up
> A problem few dare imitate, and none
> Despise.[24]

Thus, the play originally conflated East and West, ancient and modern times, in exploring the character of the kingly state and its political and social order. As these became less problematic through Victoria's identification with Britannia's purpose, it became a vehicle for the public display of archaeological triumphs and of stage technology. As it moved further from Byron's intention, it certainly became more Orientalist, yet also a showcase for western scholarship and technology. What is clear, however, is that it expressed a shifting and far from monolithic discourse.

In the same decades, India became an important location for melodramas which also responded to the needs of the age. Heidi Holder has analysed a number of these and has identified a sequence of interesting developments in the course of the nineteenth century. She confirms Gilman's view that stereotypes are 'inherently protean rather than rigid', highly mutable, shifting in character to fit the circumstances of the time. Holder has identified three periods of melodramatic activity. In the early colonial melodramas set in India or the Middle East and dating from the 1820s to the 1850s, there is a very considerable fantasy element, involving for example fantastic transformations across the race line. In plays such as William Barrymore's *El Hyder or the Chief of the Ghaut Mountains*, J. H. Amherst's *The Burmese War*, W. T. Moncrieff's *The Cataract of the Ganges or The Rajah's Daughter* (1823) and J. T. Haines's *The French Spy or the Siege of Constantina*, Self and Other are alternately fused and separated, destabilised and re-formed.[25] Interracial couples (normally, it is true, a white male and Asian female) feature prominently and audiences seem to have been fascinated by the crossing of racial lines. Moreover, the conflict between good and evil is normally worked out among indigenous factions with Europeans interacting with them to promote the victory of truth and justice. However, British law is often contrasted with Indian, for example the issue of 'suttee' or widow-burning, which was such a live issue to evangelicals and Utilitarians during these decades. Convinced by the rectitude of western enlightened law, native princes are capable, however, of acts of magnanimity.

In the later melodramas, which Holder dubs 'imperial', such as *Khartoum!*, Courtenay Thorpe's *The Light that Failed* (after Kipling, 1898) and Gilbert Murray's *Carlyon Sahib* (1899), there is a much greater emphasis on uplift, edification, conviction in the rightness of the imperial enterprise. The fantastic element recedes and the plays attempt to portray the 'facts' of the imperial situation in a more realistic form. The moral conflict is now worked out between white and indigenous forces. With the final phase, or 'autumn' melodramas (the period of which overlaps with the 'imperial' in the late Victorian and Edwardian eras), a new development takes place. Plays such as Paul Merritt and Augustus Harris's *Youth* (1881), George Rowe and Harris's *Freedom* (1883), George Sims and Arthur Shirley's *The Star of India* (1896) and Shirley and Benjamin Landeck's *Tommy Atkins* (1895), are, in Holder's view, historically ungrounded, representing the proving of white character and the working-out of domestic difficulties in an exotic locale. Now European encounters European: India and Indians (or some other Orientalist context) merely become a backdrop to the exploration of a moralised European conflict. Thus, they are 'politically significant, but dramatically moribund'. Indigenous peoples have virtually disappeared, rendered invisible by the pseudo-scientific racism and social Darwinism of the time.

In fact, of course, this development can be readily explained by the character of imperial history in the period. Holder fails to note that in the early decades of her study, the British lacked rivals in India. The eighteenth-century conflict with the French had passed. The fear of the Russians and the 'great game' of the North-West Frontier was yet to develop with the tsarist conquest of Central Asia. Only indigenous resisters posed a threat to the British, and the popular theatre seems to have been expressing a combination of earlier social relations with the fantastical elements of the Romantic approach. By the later decades of the century, the British had passed through the complex moral shriving of the 'Mutiny' and had developed, as the Murray's *Handbooks* to India so clearly demonstrate, a concept of historically didactic tourism, remembering heroic sacrifice by visiting Lucknow, Kanpur and other scenes of martyrdom.[26] With the 'autumn' melodramas, the British have become obsessed not only with the new aggressive imperialisms of European rivals, but also with invasion scares and a terror of renewed conflict in Europe, warfare which threatened not only the motherland but also the transformation of the imperial map of the world.

However, this morally reductivist view and progressive elimination of indigenous instrumentality has been implicitly challenged by others. Holder has herself noted that the concept of, and respect for so-called 'martial races' appears in these plays.[27] As in Kipling, Tommy Atkins and his superior officers express regard not only for the fighting capacity of their foes, but also for their supposedly simpler social structures and notions of legal retribution – in other words the yearning for a de-industrialised social, economic and legal order represented in different ways in the thinking of both Right and Left in the period, and neatly encapsulated in the heterogeneous politics of John Ruskin, so attractive to Liberals, early Socialists and even some elements of Conservatism.[28] Similarly, J. S. Bratton has analysed the complexities of the dramatic presentation of the working-class hero in the period, particularly in the figure of Jack Tar. She has seen Tar as an ambivalent figure, morally destabilising at home, but heroic and ethically clear-sighted when translated into the imperial locale.[29]

The Tar character appears in many imperial settings, including anti-slavery plays such as *Ashore and Afloat* (1864) and others earlier in the century, where he is sometimes depicted as resisting racial attitudes and attacks and even encounters the noble Arab figure familiar in the early abduction plays and operas. In the later period, the Tar plays became more 'realistic' in their stage presentation, more concerned with the technology which marked out Europe from the subordinate peoples of empire, more chauvinistic and violent, but in some ways also more complex. In the central plot device of these melodramas, 'the false accusation of crime, and the expiation of a supposed guilt', opportunities arose for a highly complex treatment of the moral dilemmas of empire. In some of the melodramas of the 1880s and 1890s, particularly those at the Adelphi, in which the lead was generally played by William Terriss, Bratton has identified a 'concentration upon the expiation of imperial guilt by the sacrifice and return to life of the hero'. Bratton forcefully concludes that 'the Jack Tar melodrama in the last quarter of the century negotiated at a profound as well as at a more obvious level the acceptability of British imperialism to the people'. While there were many highly bellicose and jingoistic plays, deplored by both contemporaries and historians,

> the formal structures of melodramatic writing could give the plays further and more important ideological dimensions. Plots involving the Terriss development of the Tar hero were concerned, in an inexplicit, antithetical and emblematic mode, with meeting the moral and ethical problems that jingoism presented. In this they carried on the process begun in the 1820s, whereby this particularly charged image of the British hero was used to engage with central issues in the negotiation of imperialist and domestic ideology. Such performances were, I would argue, very powerful elements in nineteenth-century British culture, not only because they offered the ordinary individual a stirring and satisfying sense of national identity but because they implicated him [*sic*] inescapably in British imperialism, while at the same time accommodating doubts and tensions created by that role.[30]

David Mayer has identified similar complexities and attempts at negotiating the dilemmas of power in the 'toga plays' or melodramas set in the Roman Empire which were immensely popular between 1880 and 1920.[31]

Mayer has suggested that, far from being purely escapist, these plays grappled with real issues of the day, including the problems of imperial power. These plays generally pitted a Roman hero, imprinted with the decadent grandeur of the late Roman Empire, against a Christian female, who heroically stands out against the mores of the age and either ultimately prevails or takes the hero with her to a martyr's death in the circus ring. Historic figures were often mixed with fictional characters – as in the popular juvenile stories of the day by G. A. Henty and other writers. These plays invariably received the approval of the church authorities of all denominations and, as Mayer has put it, appealed to audiences for whom theatre-going was previously viewed as either frivolous or immoral. But the moral lines were far from clear. It was after all an age of classical learning, when the Roman Empire and the British were often compared. The Romans were viewed as a parallel culture, appealing in its majesty yet supposedly contradictory in its cruelty, a civilising influence on Britain's remote and savage past, yet paradoxically requiring to be overthrown to permit England's national culture ultimately to flourish. Rome was both 'desirable and frightening. It simultaneously attracted and repelled'.[32]

These plays, which sometimes had Middle Eastern settings and could therefore be presented in Orientalist ways, presented a wide range of moral complexities. It may be that church-goers viewed them as a pure conflict between good (in female Christian form) and evil (in male 'pagan' guise). But others may have seen an analogy with the British potential for both moral and political decline. The heroine could be read as both heroic martyr and adventuress weaning the male from his imperial duty. The hero could be viewed as capable of Christian redemption or as losing his martial fibre through romantic feminine involvement. Thus it was possible for the audience to identify with both sides. The plays can be seen as representing the late Victorian crisis of confidence, the conflict between rationalism and religious faith, masculine military duty and a soft feminine irrationality. They also used music to indicate the contrasting moods of the drama and, like *Sardanapalus* – though in more familiar contexts – drew on spectacular and pyrotechnic stage displays. Thus the toga tradition fitted with the shifting and unclear stereotypes, the complex and often paradoxical moralities, the efforts to grapple with the fundamental contradictions of empire, to be found in the other melodramas of the period.

Orientalist spectacle

The Orientalist aspects of the spectacular theatre have never been analysed for their relationships with the other arts or for the expectations of their audiences in terms of their curious blend of excitement, escapism and education. In this section of the chapter, I propose backtracking across the nineteenth century to analyse these aspects of oriental spectacle. To do so, it is necessary to connect the spectacular theatre to other visual forms, notably the panorama, the diorama and the cosmorama, all of which used the Orient as a major feature of their offerings.[33] The panorama originally presented a 360-degree image to be viewed from a central gallery, while its more sophisticated successors offered vast continuous tableaux either on canvas which was gradually unfurled or on enormous painted boards which were slid into place by an elaborate system of rollers. By these means, visual performances lasting several hours could be mounted.

The panorama had its origins at the end of the 1780s and was originally used to present circular images of major cities. The earliest and

best known example was Edinburgh. Soon, however, it was being used
to depict major battles. The Battle of the Nile appeared on a panorama
in 1799; the fall of Seringapatam soon followed; and in the course of the
nineteenth century all major military actions were displayed, including
the events of the Indian Mutiny of 1857, the bombardment of Alexan-
dria and the battle of Tel-el-Kebir in the Egyptian invasion of 1882 and
Omdurman in the reconquest of the Sudan in 1898. Other major interests included archaeological discoveries and the most celebrated eastern
ruins, as well as apocalyptic events of the past. Baalbek, Jerusalem, Thebes,
the Pyramids at Giza and the excavations at the caves of Ellora in India
all appeared in this guise. Distinguished painters and set designers like
David Roberts and John Martin contributed many panoramas, including
such subjects as the Flight of the Israelites from Egypt and Belshazzar's
Feast. A number of artists, such as Frederick Catherwood and Augustus
Earle, also became celebrated for their panoramas. Many of the latter
assumed an exploratory and didactic purpose: trips around the world, the
Overland Mail to India, which was presented with the assistance of the
P. & O. company, journeys to Hong Kong and, later, across the Trans-
Siberian Railway, emigration views, surveys and information on Austra-
lian colonies and New Zealand and images of eastern cities like Benares,
Delhi and Hong Kong. A Delhi artist even produced spectacular images
of the Mughal Emperor's Durbar Procession in Delhi in 1815.

Panoramas were tremendously popular throughout Europe in the
nineteenth century. In Britain, they were distributed widely and were
just as successful in the provinces as in London. A celebrated panorama
operated in Leicester Square between 1793 and 1863 and there were
several other major sites in London. There was a famous Rotunda on the
Mound in Edinburgh, the attractions of which were advertised for some
years by an elephant which paraded around the city, and most provincial
cities had some means of displaying these visual treats, whether in a
dedicated building or a converted theatre or hall. They continued to be
shown well into the Edwardian era of the twentieth century, although
the rapidly booming popularity of the cinema inevitably extinguished
them by the First World War. Panoramas have been seen as a highly
successful bridge between high art and mass entertainment. They also
represented major technical advances in perspective, the science of optics
and efforts at a fresh representation of the world. Certainly Sir Joshua
Reynolds and the history painter Benjamin West greatly approved of
them, as did the art critic and social commentator, John Ruskin. Ruskin
described the Leicester Square Panorama as an 'educational institution of
the highest and purest value' which should have been supported by the
government as a beneficial 'school instrument'.[34]

The panoramas were clearly a major cultural presence, a means whereby images of the world, of other cultures, of technological and military advances, of geographical and archaeological discovery could be transmitted to the public. Few of them survive, though we have a good idea of their character through engravings and miniature versions for home use. It is clear from all of these that the Orient was indeed a significant source of subject-matter, an eastern world which embraced all the interests of the time, ancient, biblical, Islamic, imperial. Like the paintings surveyed in Chapter 3, these images did of course comply with the canons of the picturesque. They set out from the known, the images of Edinburgh, London and Glasgow which were initially so popular, and proceeded to investigate the lesser known, exploring time, space, cultural and chronological distance, and incidentally the botany, geology and zoology of their chosen subjects. Many were painted by artists who had visited the regions depicted or were developed from images brought back by surveyors and amateur artists. They were often designed for sensation, despite the sober judgement of Ruskin, and depicted an over-blown and opulent East, a powerful and sometimes riotous architecture, masses of humanity decked out in curious and sometimes exciting garb and ornament, and a violent clash of arms. As the century wore on, imperial subjects, embracing colonial warfare (like the Zulu War of 1879), emigration, commerce and travel, became increasingly popular.

Yet these panoramas have also to be analysed in ways that connect them to surrounding cultural forms. Their technical achievements were considerable, as was their search for a fresh vision of the world, their extension of the language of colour and design, and their relationship to costume, fashion, furniture, crafts and the architecture of leisure. Above all, they contributed to the taste for spectacular theatre in which plot and dramatic device became less important than visual sensation – the costumes, jewels, weapons, props, architecture, plants and animals which made the theatre a centre of documentary presentation, now so readily satisfied by television.

The Theatre Museum Archive in Covent Garden, London, offers a ready route into this display.[35] This repository concentrates not on play texts, but on all the accessories of performances, production plans, designs, images, programmes, playbills and reviews. The archive's resources were surveyed in relation to a number of the key, and highly popular Orientalist theatrical presentations of the nineteenth and early twentieth centuries. These included the 'burletta opera spectacle' *The Earthquake or the Spectre of the Nile* at the Adelphi in 1828 and 1829, the presentation of Hindu dancers and music, *The Bayadères*, also at the Adelphi in 1847, the Grand Oriental Spectacle, *The Desert or the Imaum's Daughter* at Drury Lane in 1847, *The Grand Mogul* at the Comedy Theatre in 1884, Gilbert and Sullivan's *The Mikado* of 1885 (and one of its revivals in 1901), *The Nautch Girl* (The Savoy, 1891), *The Geisha* (Daly's, 1896), *Carnac Sahib* at His Majesty's, *San Toy* at Daly's (both 1899), *A Chinese Honeymoon* (The Strand, 1901), *The Cingalee* (Daly's, 1904), *Amasis or an Egyptian Princess* (New Theatre, 1906), *The Chinese Lantern* (The Strand, 1908) and *Chu Chin Chow* (His Majesty's, 1916). While the London theatres are identified in this list, it ought to be remembered that most of these went on provincial (and later in the century, imperial) tours. In some cases, their music reached a wider audience, while images of the sets and display often appeared in *The Illustrated London News* or other illustrated journals.

The Earthquake or the Spectre of the Nile created a whole range of theatrical spectacle which brought together Egyptian archaeology and the fashion for Egyptian design in the period, the 'sublime' effects of a major natural event (described in the programme as 'That Terrific Convulsion of Nature') like an earthquake, ancient religious rites and necromancy. (The latter did of course become bound up with illusionism, which was invariably depicted in oriental settings.[36]) In several scenes the entire stage was filled with Egyptian ruins, including those of Dendera, pyramids, a temple of Isis, a passage up the Nile and views of Egypt painted by Tomkins. It is perfectly clear from the descriptions of the 'superb scenery', the machinery, dresses ('the costumes from the most correct authorities'), music, properties and decorations that plot and text were incidental to spectacle, that it was the presentation of the visual effects of Egypt, achieving didactic purpose through entertainment, that was most important. In effect, this was a living panorama.

The Desert of 1847 constituted a theatrical presentation of Félicien David's programmatic music considered in Chapter 7. Again the emphasis was on the spectacle of Islamic buildings, the thousands of lamps, the vast cast (including a chorus of a hundred voices), the cavalcades, including twelve camels, fifty horses and two elephants and the colours, effects and winds of the desert. On the face of it, we have a classic Orientalist performance, a European vision of vast geographical and meteorological effects, architectural grandeur, impressive ceremony and human and animal processions. It is essentially a circus vision. Yet its relation to the supposed monolithic discourse of Orientalism is surely much more complex. Audience and reviewers went to be impressed not only by the power of stage illusion and the theatre technology that it represented, but also by those geographical and cultural characteristics so extolled by *The Times* in 1813. The audience was clearly meant to be attracted rather than repelled. This was certainly a form of sedentary tourism, but it unveiled the East as revealing many of the characteristics wished for in western art and ceremony.

By contrast, *The Bayadères or Priestesses of Pondicherry* of the same year was intended to be virtually an act of anthropological display. In 1838 a production at the Adelphi entitled *Hassan Pacha or the Arab's Leap* had included a performance by a visiting troupe of 'Bedouin Arabs', who were described as having 'remarkable power and matchless ease' in their dance routines. Now five female dancers and three male musicians had been brought to Europe by a French agent, M. Tardivel, who had negotiated with the Indian temple authorities and pledged that they would never be 'required to infringe the laws of their religion'.[37] In fact, of course, the very journey to Europe, which the senior dancer herself seems to have resisted – she 'discountenanced the whole proceeding' – would have done just that. Nevertheless, dancers and musicians performed a whole sequence of dances and semi-rites against a backdrop of a temple, a shrine, an unexplained 'attack by native troops' and the inevitable scene of suttee or widow-burning. They also toured the whole country as well as France, and in Britain at least the reviews seem to have been uniformly rapturous.

One review complimented the performance of the *Bayadères* for its originality and diversity, offering 'much which astonishes and pleases and nothing that in any way offends'. Another sought to separate 'a superstitious and idolatrous creed' from dances which 'are capable of exciting the most exquisite sensibilities in the impassioned and sensual beholder; not only by every graceful variety of form and gesture, but by the symmetry of their revealed proportions, and the significant impression of the whole'. The same article extolled the moral virtues of the dancers and suggested that they and 'the young and handsome musicians' would have to be protected from the more lewd men and women around the theatre. In a remarkable encomium the review concluded:

> These dances are peculiar for the succession of graces they display, and must be seen more than once to be thoroughly understood and appreciated. Each of them is a theme or narration of dissimilar interest and details, but in which either passion or sentiment is conveyed in a form of originality that has never before been witnessed. There is nothing which seems to excite wonder, while the curiosity imperceptibly progresses to admiration. At length the beholder is lost in a reverie of delight, and he may fairly conclude that his soul has taken leave of his corporeal tenement to undergo a metempsychosis in the Elysian fields.[38]

It is a statement which seems free of irony and it appears to confirm the prime thesis of this book, that nineteenth-century commentators on the East, far from indulging in a monolithic discourse, were capable of separating out attitudes towards religion and politics from approaches to the arts. Even if the system that had produced the *Bayadères* was open to critical attack, the performance of the dancers and musicians was seen as offering unalloyed, even uplifting pleasure. The theme of the temple dancers was one that had already been explored by Goethe in his poem *Der Gott under die Bajadere*, turned into an opera in 1810 by the French composer Charles Catel, and later into a celebrated Russian ballet by Léon Minkus.

In this and in other productions, contemporary comment marvelled at the wonder of stage illusion, 'the whole of the adjuncts of an Indian city ... comfortably compressed into a small square place'.[39] There is no doubt that in the later nineteenth century the presentation of eastern characters, particularly Indian and Chinese, was unsympathetic, as I pointed out in *Propaganda and Empire*.[40] Nevertheless, the notion of a more sympathetic spectacle continued. Frequently in this period, the critics attacked the dramatic elements while extolling the stage settings. *The Grand Mogul* of 1884 attracted very critical reviews, one of which described the performance as 'depressing, even when it is not disgusting'. While the performance was 'dull' and the music 'very poor and stale' the costumes and scenery were 'brilliant', attracting vociferous applause each evening.[41] While the architecture, palms, trees and magnificence of the depiction of the Delhi fruit market, the sumptuous dresses, admirable scenery and beautiful broken light on the lake were much admired, the audience was 'indignant at the stupidity and bad taste exhibited'.

The same sorts of distinctions were made in respect of almost all the various operettas and plays set in India, Ceylon, China and Japan. Plots involving interracial relationships (always European male and Asian female), as in *A Chinese Honeymoon* of 1901, which ran for more than a thousand performances, and *The Cingalee* in 1904 were accepted without comment, but the reviews of these productions as well as of *The Mikado* were at pains to point out that the stage was offering a very unreal vision of South Asia, China or Japan.[42] Yet invariably the staging and above all the fans, costumes, jewels and artefacts were extolled for their beauty and their authenticity. Thus the arts and crafts of the East, at least those which had secured the admiration of the West and influenced the artistic movements of the late nineteenth century, were repeatedly separated from their political and social contexts.

Nobody viewed *The Mikado* of 1885, which Arthur Jacobs has described as perhaps the most successful of all the Savoy operas, as anything other than a satire upon English politics and society. Sullivan contributed music of great technical competence, some of it based on fragments of Japanese tunes supplied to him by Algernon Mitford (the future Lord Redesdale) who had worked in the British Embassy in Tokyo.[43] *The Mikado*'s opening run of 672 performances was a record for any Savoy opera up to that time, and it was also a huge success in the United States, Germany, Austria (with long runs in both Berlin and Vienna) and Denmark (though curiously it was never accepted in Belgium or France). Even the great critic Hanslick admired it. It was of course designed to satirise as well as draw upon the public fascination with Japan in the period, but it also set out to achieve 'authenticity' in its costuming.[44] The men's clothes were said to be from Japanese authorities. Valuable assistance was afforded by the directors and inhabitants of the Japanese village in Knightsbridge and Liberty's took large advertisements in the programmes.

One review declared that the Japan depicted was decidedly not the Japan of Sir Harry Parkes, 'but it is nonetheless a very interesting, not to say pleasant, Japan'.[45] Several commented on the artistic refinement of *The Mikado*. The *Pall Mall Gazette* reviewer remarked on the irresistible variety of rich and rare colours, always harmonious, some of the costumes having been brought specially from Japan and being a hundred to two hundred years old. The famous *Daily Telegraph* review, which announced that 'we are all being more or less Japanned', also extolled the perfection and beauty of the 'costumes, appointments, and scenery'.[46] When *The Mikado* was revived in 1901, there were similar ecstatic comments on the magnificence of the artistic spectacle.[47]

The only operetta to rival *The Mikado* was Sidney Jones's *The Geisha, the Story of a Tea House* which ran for over a thousand performances from 1896 and was also a great success in Europe. Again sets and costumes came in for most praise. The whole production was 'japanned' by Mr Arthur Diosy of the Japan Society (an associate of Christopher Dresser); the reviews extolled the superb costumes, the beauty of the 'wistaria' and 'chrysanthemum' scenes and the wonderful colour schemes (for example, the 'hotter tones of crimson, orange and amber, lit by white' in the second act). One remarked on the manner in which the costumes of the English girls jarred against the beautiful oriental background.[48] The equally long-running *A Chinese Honeymoon* was likewise acclaimed for its architecture, crafts, botanical display and costumes, while one reviewer noted its 'disregard of genuine Chinese manners and customs'.[49] The very popular and in many respects more grotesque *San Toy* received similar notices.[50] The chinoiserie of *The Chinese Lantern*, a play by Laurence Housman, was less admired, being dubbed 'puerile, and grotesque' by various reviews, a criticism clearly applied to the representation rather than the original culture.[51]

It might be thought that the stage presentation of Chinese and Japanese arts would be more likely to receive praise than those of territories that were long-standing possessions of the British Empire, but this is not the case. The intervals of *The Nautch Girl* were said to be particularly long so that the stage crew could handle the elaborate scenery.[52]

The Graphic described it as a great popular success because of its magnificent spectacle, its beautiful dresses and handsome scenery. The Savoy was crowded every night to see its 'truly gorgeous Indian raiment', although the prime theme of this costly show was to celebrate the throwing over of social and religious constraints. Similarly, the elaborate and complex staging of H. A. Jones's *Carnac Sahib* of 1899, set in the fictional Dilghaut and Fyzapore, was much admired, particularly the jewelled palace at Fyzapore. The production (though a failure) used music from Delibes's *Lakmé*, as well as a Hindu March by Raymond Roze and an Indian March by Sellenick. One review of *The Cingalee* considered the story to have 'just a sufficient thread of interest on which to hang a delightful embroidery of gay music, bright songs and lively dances'.[53] But most praise was, as always, reserved for the artistic impression: the setting was 'novel and superlatively beautiful'; 'the palace illuminations and wild revels were alone worthy of a visit to Daly's', with its 'deftly wrought crescendo of light and colour'; while much was made of the costumes and their influence on fashion. Similar comments were made about the Egyptian *Amasis* of 1906[54] and *Chu Chin Chow* of 1916, which was described as 'a pageant play', which attracted by reason of its 'gorgeous scenes of Eastern life'.[55] It was, as we have seen in Chapter 7, *Chu Chin Chow* which almost certainly convinced Puccini to set another eastern subject for what was to turn out to be his last opera.

One of the greatest climaxes to the spectacular approach to theatrical Orientalism was the grand Indian pageant *India* at Imre Kiralfy's 'Empire of India' Exhibition at Earl's Court in 1895.[56] This vast spectacle, performed in the 6,000-seat Empress Theatre, was ultimately a paean of praise to British rule in India, which presented a very selective and slanted account of Indian history and mythology to lead up to the consummation of Victoria's rule. Nevertheless, to achieve its effects it exulted in the spectacle of Indian arts and the grandeur of its past. As Kiralfy himself wrote:

> When, therefore, the subject of an Empire of India Exhibition came to my mind, it was associated with the idea of a beautiful re-production of leading events in the history of India; and as the object of an Exhibition is not alone to please but to instruct people, the combination of the two should more completely succeed. No better subject, to my mind, could be found for this combination than India, for its History is most interesting, its Mythology and its Poetry enchanting; its Architecture beyond comparison; its Arts and Manufactures delightful, and its Peoples interesting and picturesque.[57]

The spectacle should be seen in the context of the buildings which were erected at the exhibition, houses and carvings brought from Pune (formerly

Poona) by General Pitt-Rivers, the vast painted backdrops of Indian scenery around the exhibition grounds, and above all the eighty-five Indian craftsmen, including metalworkers, wood-carvers, silk- and carpet-weavers, who worked in the grounds, as they had done in the Colonial and Indian Exhibition of 1886.

The *Ballets Russes* and Orientalist stage design

In Chapter 3, we saw the manner in which Orientalism was taken up by each new movement in art, adopting a particularly radical form at the turn of the nineteenth and twentieth centuries. In the survey of music and opera in Chapter 7, it was again apparent that appeals to a European vision of the Orient enabled composers to strike out in fresh directions. The dramatic revolution in stage design and costumes which was roughly contemporaneous with – if slightly later than – these two movements also achieved its most forceful innovations through Orientalist forms, colours and motifs. Although these theatre designs have been seen as strikingly, almost shockingly new, they can be set into the longer tradition of Orientalist and spectacular theatre. As we have seen, the Orientalist productions of the nineteenth century were significant more for their designs and effects than for their plots. The new movement in the early twentieth century certainly heralded the arrival of high art in the theatre. Here was an undoubted revolution in quality, but it broke with what had gone before only in creating even greater sensation and more overwhelming spectacle.

Although these developments in stage design had a much wider incidence, they are inseparably associated with Diaghilev's *Ballets Russes*. Diaghilev drew on the work, among others, of Alexandre Benois, Nicholas Roerich, Sonia Delaunay and the greatest of them, Léon Bakst. Designers like Paul Poiret and Charles Ricketts were also associated with the movement. Almost all of these artists shared an interest in Japanese prints; most of them were influenced by Aubrey Beardsley; and they were all caught up in the artistic avant-garde represented by magazines like *The Yellow Book*, *Pan*, *The Studio* and Diaghilev's own *World of Art*. They all worked in other media, in book illustration, jewellery design, *haute couture*, and as artists in the widest sense, but much of their best work was created for the theatre. And the most sensational designs were produced for Diaghilev's Orientalist ballets.[58]

Orientalism, indeed, helped to foster two great revivals vital for the health of the musical theatre in the twentieth century. The first was in ballet itself. It was in a moribund state when it was revolutionised by Diaghilev and the new school of dancers he nurtured, as well as those like Pavlova who drifted off to create their own companies. Orientalist

subjects were the catalyst for wholly new body movements and lines in
dance, for fresh and exciting rhythms, for an erotic and sensual approach,
a raw and abandoned quality which filled the theatres and took the
artistic world by storm. Design, costume, fabric and colour contributed
to this outpouring of energies, enhancing the mood through an extraordinary unity of conception of music, dance and theatrical accessory.
Among the more notable productions were Roerich's designs for Borodin's
Polovtsian Dances (1909), Benois's *Petrouchka* of Igor Stravinsky (1911),
Bakst's *Schéhérazade* to the music of Rimsky-Korsakov (1910), Bakst's
Le Dieu Bleu with music by Reynaldo Hahn (1912) and Delaunay's
Cleopatra to music of Arensky and others (1918). Among Bakst's many
other designs were those for *Ballet Hindu* created for Pavlova's company
and set to the music of Serov, Mussorgsky and Rimsky-Korsakov.[59]

There were countless other Orientalist stage performances in the
same period, such as Ida Rubinstein's production of *Salome*, Ethel Levy's
musical reviews, and extravaganzas like *La Nuit Persane, Nabuchodnezar,
La Péri, Syrian Dances*, and many more. High society proceeded to
indulge in oriental soirées and fashions and jewellery adopted Orientalist
forms yet again. There were those who talked of Bakst and others as
the Delacroix and Ingres of costume, producing a Dionysian frenzy and
earthiness out of blinding colour harmonies, combining with music and
movement to create an orgiastic, ecstatic effect.

It is readily apparent that all of this can be analysed in the classic
Orientalist fashion. A mythical East, opulent, erotic and magical, was
being prefabricated yet again to appeal to jaded European taste. But this
is too facile. At another level of analysis, the perceived Orient was serving
to create a liberation in line and physical emphasis, a renaissance of
colour and a unity of concept that served to change the course of theatre
design. There were, indeed, direct oriental influences. A troupe of Siamese
dancers visited St Petersburg in 1900 and created a sensation; a group
of Cambodian dancers who appeared in Paris in 1906 were even more
influential. Bakst was enthralled by the detail of Mughal and Persian art.
Several designers travelled in the East and Roerich spent the last years of
his life in India. Roerich and Diaghilev purchased their fabrics for
Polovtsian Dances from merchandise brought from Central Asia to the St
Petersburg markets.[60] Bright greens and pinks, azure and orange, blues,
greens and yellows, mauve, black and gold not only produced the most
dramatic stage harmonies yet seen, but also interacted with the major
artistic movements of the period. Costumes and backcloths were designed with bold blocks of colour, intricate traceries of patterning, stripes,
chevrons or interlocking geometrical forms.

Clothed in such costumes, and set against flying drapes and exotic
backdrops, the dancers created new moods: religious reverie, majestic

display, unbridled sexuality or fabulous myth, conveyed by extremes of languor and muscular frenzy, slow unfolding patterns, twisting arabesques, sensual motions, themselves emblematic of the non-linear, curved and mobile character of eastern design. The key point, however, is that these Orientalist creations served to influence design, movement and production in the musical theatre generally. Those that ceased to have any connection at all to supposedly eastern themes still bore the mark of this revolution.

Both classical ballet and modern dance have scarcely escaped from it throughout the twentieth century. The Orientalist classics remain staple fare. Fokine's choreography is still used for the spectacular 'Polovtsian Dances' in modern productions of *Prince Igor*. More recent performances of *Schéhérazade* (those involving Rudolf Nureyev, for example) continued to reveal the opportunities afforded by Orientalist architecture, fabrics, design, props and furniture. Diaphanous costumes both covered and revealed. More uninhibited arm, leg and neck movements became possible, together with a great variety of female costume, bodices, pantaloons, long silken dresses, capes, turban-like headgear, costume jewellery, and so on. And interestingly, throughout all of these influences on ballet, music and design, there has never been any doubt that Russia was acting as the cultural bridgehead, the conveyor and interpreter of East to West. With this remarkable combination of art forms, it is impossible to find a single discourse, an inhibiting Othering which stereotypes in order to define the Self. Instead, perceptions of the East, however artificial and synthetic, produced a genuine revolution, major technical change, and above all an artistic world which was endlessly alluring and fascinating. Through it the audience sought to find a new Self, less grey and inhibited, a constructive merging of the West and the imagined East. Through fabric, colour, design and movement the artists were expressing excitement and admiration, never racial difference and disdain. With the *Ballets Russes* the Orientalist thesis of Edward Said seems at one level superficially confirmed and at another irretrievably disrupted.

The twentieth-century theatre and 'interculturalism'

In the twentieth-century, theatre directors and theoreticians in Europe and the United States have become increasingly interested in the many performance traditions of Asia and have sought to apply some of their basic principles to a reinvigoration of western drama. This movement reacted to the overwhelming realism of the Victorian theatre, attempting to find a new language of movement and a deeper psycho-physical acting presence against a wholly fresh and integral approach to stage design. The emphasis was on atmosphere rather than text, physical expression

rather than words, a subtle complexity in simplicity rather than the spectacular surface fussiness of the Victorian stage. While it was still possible
to subject the western classics to these techniques, producers also sought
refuge in both ends of the dramatic spectrum, the mythical and other-
worldly and both the ordinary and extraordinary events of daily life.

One of the most influential among the luminaries of this movement was Gordon Craig (1872–1966), the son of the great actress Ellen
Terry and the architect and designer, E. W. Godwin, whom we have
encountered in Chapter 5. While Craig was steeped in the Victorian
tradition and was a fervent admirer of Sir Henry Irving, who became
virtually his adoptive father, he also developed into one of the most
radical and innovative theorists of the twentieth-century theatre. In
artistic terms, he was influenced by Hubert von Herkommer and the
Symbolists. He was wildly eclectic and turned to various aspects of oriental theatre, particularly the Japanese Noh, Indian performance art, and
the shadow-plays of Indonesia and South-East Asia. He did not, however, visit the East, and he has been accused of an excessive deference
which merely mythologised and orientalised a rather indistinct and
undiscriminating eastern theatre. Nevertheless, in his journals, *The Mask*,
which appeared intermittently between 1908 and 1929 and *The Marionette*, which first appeared in 1918, he repeatedly turned to Asia for
inspiration.

Craig was searching for a non-naturalistic aesthetic, an abstract,
stylised and ritualistic theatre, characterised by light and rhythmic movement and moveable screens rather than scenery. In the pursuit of this
ideal theatre, he wrote articles in *The Mask* under many pseudonyms:
indeed most of the contents of the journal were written by him. One of
these *noms de plume*, John Semar, was derived from a favourite character,
Semar, of the Javanese shadow-plays. Indeed, it was his fascination with
the shadow theatre and with puppetry in general which led him to
collect marionettes, puppets, shadow figures and a great deal of material
associated with them. The Asian tradition of shadow theatre was becoming
better known in the West, partly through Dutch works, one major treatise being translated by one of Craig's friends, Mrs Carr, in 1907–08.[61]

The relationship between stylised movement and puppetry is obvious and one of Craig's debates with himself and others was the extent
to which the actor should lose his/her emotional autonomy in the pursuit
of a ritualised abstraction. Craig believed that something strikingly new
could only be created out of the perpetuation of an antique and deeply
embedded style. It was just such a visionary conformity, rooted in an
ancient and venerable tradition which Craig presumed to find in the
East, and in particular in India. Craig's deference was expressed in florid
and romantic prose: he referred to the 'exquisite fluting of the great and

lovely Krishna' and exclaimed that 'we are like fools beside wise men, we Europeans and Americans standing by Asiatics', those in the theatre being 'the most ignorant of all'.[62] Yet while he admired, he also distrusted the spirituality and 'noble artificiality', as he called it, of the Indian theatre. It may be that he found the shadow-play and the Noh tradition less intimidating, but ultimately he had inadequate first-hand knowledge of any of these theatrical forms.

There can be little doubt, however, that it was the discovery of the combination of dance, music and theatre in the Javanese and Balinese traditions which was to be influential over a wide range of arts. We have already seen the significance of these for classical composers and for the theatre designers active with the *Ballets Russes*, but they also influenced the radical stage. It was not only composers who encountered the Balinese gamelan and dancers featured at the Paris Colonial Exposition of 1931. The French poet, actor and theatre director, Antonin Artaud, was galvanised by their performance and as a result wrote a series of articles which were brought together as *The Theatre and its Double* in 1938. He had pioneered what he called the 'theatre of cruelty', a theatre which reflected the real world, featuring genuine action, violence and social taboos. For him the Indonesian performers reflected the underlying reality of the everyday world, expressed in a stylised manner which influenced his precise and balletic directorial manner.[63]

This combination of dance, music and theatrical arts suffuses Colin McPhee's account of his years on Bali in the 1930s. Although McPhee was a composer who dedicated himself to the study of the gamelan and the recording of its music in western notation (subsequently influencing Britten), it was the relationship of all the performing arts to everyday life, temple rituals, personal and political ceremonies, and the intense rivalry of the gamelan clubs which principally interested him.[64] His work was to have a considerable influence in the post-Second-World-War period. By the 1960s, however, Indian performing traditions were being plundered by radical and innovative western directors. The Polish director Grotowski visited southern India and drew on the Kathakali methods of exercising and training actors, including the use of yoga.

These methods were brought to bear on his production of the great Indian classic, the Shakuntala of Kalidasa, in 1960. The Shakuntala had indeed been produced in the West on several occasions, each one reflecting the particular emphasis of its period. Théophile Gautier produced it as a ballet–pantomime in Paris in 1858, replete with oriental textiles and architectural, botanical and zoological spectacle. In 1896 it had been produced in Paris again, this time with an aura of decadence thinly veiled by exotic spirituality. In 1914, the Russian director Tairov had rejected a theatre of social realism by presenting Kalidasa's classic in

Moscow as an example of what radical world theatre could do. Grotowski moved beyond all of these by emphasising movement, rhythm, stylised gesture and atmospheric yoga-induced reflectiveness rather than text. Grotowski was to influence the development of anthropological theatre, drawing on traditions derived not only from the East, but also from Africa and South America, as pursued by the Italian Eugenio Barba, the American Richard Schechner and the British director Peter Brook.

Each of these has come in for severe criticism from the Indian scholar Rustom Bharucha. He has seen these exponents of an eastern-influenced theatre as indulging in what he describes as the 'ambivalent ethics of cross-cultural borrowings', a 'naive and unexamined ethnocentricity' which enriches only one side, perpetuating the colonial relationship of appropriating, decontextualising and representing the 'Other'.[65] In particular, he has attacked Brook's critically acclaimed production of the *Mahabharata* as presenting nothing more than a 'flavour' of India, expropriating and reordering non-western material in an Orientalist framework. By excluding historical and cultural context, in Bharucha's view, Brook reduced and trivialised the great Sanskrit epic, cutting it off from its social setting and its crucial embedding in Hindu philosophy. He imposed upon it an inauthentic linearity and presented it with Shakespearian and pantomime conventions. In attempting to universalise the drama (using actors from all continents, for example), he shattered its central meaning. Thus, despite the close financial involvement of the Indian Government, it insulted Indian culture.[66]

In his challenging book, *Theatre and the World*, Bharucha is suspicious of most theatrical anthropology, mainly on the grounds of its basis in unequal exchange, its tendency to dehistoricise and to rip performance from its crucial social contexts. Only Grotowski is seen as 'pragmatic and non-reverential', ultimately abandoning the 'gesture clichés' of eastern theatrical traditions as inappropriate in a western setting. Thus, interculturalism is hopelessly compromised by its capacity to enrich only one side. Much of Bharucha's tenaciously presented argument is convincing, if his fundamental principle is accepted that trans-cultural influences can only be legitimated if they are mutually beneficial. (Incidentally, in castigating modern examples of intercultural theatre, he beautifully belies Said's Whiggish belief that with modern de-imperialised sensibilities, Orientalism can be replaced by more sympathetic responses.)

However, Bharucha's view seems to be a counsel of perfection: maybe exchanges of mutual respect and benefit do represent the hope for the future, but according to his paradigm the arts would have to steer clear of all exotic influences and the entire basis of this book would be undermined. The fact is that artistic traditions cannot be maintained in aspic. Purity of form and equality of transmission are themselves essentially dehistoricised concepts. Western theatrical traditions and Shakespearian performance did sweep India during British rule and were manipulated in ways that were as beneficial to Indian nationalist ideas as to the structures of imperial power. On the other hand, the western arts have been constantly dynamic, repeatedly seeking new sources of inspiration, often from perceptions (and misperceptions) of other cultures. That they manipulated, reinterpreted and misrepresented the originals in the process is beyond doubt, but in the theatre as in the other arts, radical movements seeking to free themselves of the conventions of a previous generation, invariably looked outwards, seeking inspiration from traditions other than their own. This process has to be understood and explained, not rejected as somehow illegitimate because it generally omitted to cherish the plundered culture and seek some form of equal exchange with it.

In conclusion, then, Orientalism in the theatre is a varied and highly complex phenomenon. There can be no doubt that texts and characterisation from the sixteenth century abound in stereotypes and unflattering satirical figures or that the legal and moral Other, as defined by Holder, is often given a strongly racial twist in the nineteenth century. But, as in the other arts, the verbal and visual discourse is never stable, never wholly clear in setting its supposedly binary programme. The exploration of the Other reveals much that attracted as well as repelled. Though satire was often clothed in Orientalist garb, few in the audience can have doubted that what they beheld was a version of Self. Asian and European characters merged merits and demerits, in some cases freely exchanged. As the *Times* review of 1813 indicated, the Orientalist theatre offered, both literally and metaphorically, brighter hues, starker absolutes, grander designs, all perceived to be highly desirable in the drabber world of northern Europe.

The spectacle of the East, so liberally displayed in the geographical expanses of scene painting and panoramas, the meteorological drama of lighting and effects, the architecture, botany, zoology, metal and other crafts, and above all the fabrics and colours of costume and drape in stage display, was repesented as eminently to be admired, even emulated. As the nineteenth century wore on and imperial rule became supposedly more strenuously underpinned, intellectually, technically and militarily, the complexity of the theatrical negotiation between East and West became, if anything, more profound. While the theatre displayed many burlesques, many ludicrous send-ups of Asian characters and situations, it was the highly visible Orientalist dramatic form which was being parodied as much as the East itself. And when the theatre is placed within its wider artistic context it is apparent that it too was reacting to the social, urban and aesthetic consequences of industrialisation. Exhibitions, displays and stage performances all held up another world through which a critique of the western could be developed.

When the new imperialism was at its height, the theatre, as with the other arts, sought new radical inspirations from the East. It was of course a perceived and often conflated East; influences represented another form of appropriation, operating on the basis of unequal exchange; but that cannot gainsay the fact that a dynamic inspiration was the result. Despite Bharucha's strictures, no tradition is hermetic, rigidly gripped in its own historicism. All are in a constant state of flux, developing and undergoing metamorphoses in line with, and often in reaction to political and social change. It is that complex interweaving of conformity and disruption, responding to dominant political, cultural and intellectual conventions, which renders the Orientalist theatre, in common with the other arts, so difficult to pin down in a monolithic discourse or a clear binarism.

Notes

1   John M. MacKenzie, *Propaganda and Empire* (Manchester, 1984), Chapter 2, 'The theatre of empire', pp. 39–66.

2   J. S. Bratton *et al.* (eds), *Acts of Supremacy: the British Empire and the Stage, 1790–1930* (Manchester, 1991), Paul Greenhalgh, *Ephemeral Vistas: the Expositions Universelles, Great Exhibitions and World Fairs, 1851–1939* (Manchester, 1988), the articles by Penny Summerfield and Ben Shephard in John M. MacKenzie (ed.), *Imperialism and Popular Culture* (Manchester, 1986) and by David Mayer and David Omissi in John M. MacKenzie (ed.), *Popular Imperialism and the Military, 1850–1950* (Manchester, 1992).

3   MacKenzie, *Propaganda*, Chapter 3; Jeffrey Richards charted the survival of late nineteenth-century ideas in the cinema of the 1930s in *Visions of Yesterday* (London, 1973).

4   Sari Jamil Nasir, *The Arabs and the English* (London, 1976) and 'The Image of the Arab in American Popular Culture', Ph.D. thesis (University of Illinois, 1962). Jeffrey Richards, *Swordsmen of the Screen*, Chapter 12, 'The sheikhs of Araby', pp. 271–83.

5   MacKenzie, *Propaganda*, p. 45.

6   J. S. Bratton, 'Theatre of war: the Crimea on the London stage, 1854–5' and Derek Forbes, 'Aquatic drama', both in David Bradby *et al.* (eds), *Performance and Politics in Popular Drama* (Cambridge, 1980).

7   Heidi Holder, 'Melodrama, realism and empire on the British stage' in Bratton *et al.*, *Acts of Supremacy*. See also the unrelentingly empirical Michael Booth, *English Melodrama* (London, 1965), particularly Chapter 3, 'Gothic and eastern melodrama'.

8   Penny Summerfield, 'Patriotism and empire: music-hall entertainment, 1870–1914' in MacKenzie (ed.), *Imperialism and Popular Culture*.

9   Michael Booth, *Victorian Spectacular Theatre, 1850–1910* (Cambridge, 1981).

10 For a stimulating examination of the 'Jack Tar' plays, see J. S. Bratton, 'British heroism and the structure of melodrama' in Bratton *et al.*, *Acts of Supremacy*.

11 John M. MacKenzie, 'Heroic myths of empire' in MacKenzie (ed.), *Popular Imperialism and the Military*; Holder, 'Melodrama, realism and empire'.

12   P. J. Marshall, 'Taming the exotic: the British and India in the seventeenth and eighteenth centuries' in G. S. Rousseau and Roy Porter (eds), *Exoticism in the Enlightenment* (Manchester, 1990), p. 56.

13   Brian Allen, 'From Plassey to Seringapatam: India and British history painting c. 1760– c. 1800' in C. A. Bayly (ed.), *The Raj: India and the British 1600–1947* (London, 1990), pp. 26–7; and John M. MacKenzie, 'Imperial art' in P. J. Marshall (ed.), *The Illustrated History of the British Empire* (Cambridge, forthcoming).

14   Bernard Smith, *European Vision and the South Pacific* (London, 1985), pp. 114–16. Philip de Loutherbourg was in charge of the costumes and décor and it was regarded as his most successful commission.

15   Marshall, 'Taming the exotic', p. 51.

16   David Mayer, *Harlequin in His Element: the English Pantomime, 1806–1836* (Cambridge, Mass., 1969).

17   Quoted in Mayer, *Harlequin*, p. 78.

18   I am grateful to David Mayer for information about the Orientalist theatre in 1811–12.

19   Quoted in Mayer, *Harlequin*, pp. 157–9.

20   John Ruskin, 'War' in *The Crown of Wild Olive* (London, 1909), p. 124.

21   Margaret J. Howell, *Byron Tonight: a Poet's Plays on the 19th Century Stage* (Windlesham, 1982), p. 53.

22   Seton Lloyd, *Foundations in the Dust: the Story of Mesopotamian Exploration* (London, 1980 – first published 1947), Chapters 7–9. It may well have been the publication of Layard's *Nineveh and its Remains* and *The Monuments of Nineveh* (both 1849), and subsequent publications in 1853 which prompted the revival of the play.

23   Howell, *Byron*, p. 75. Other critics were more sceptical, one describing it as 'a sort of Panorama of Assyria'.

24   Howell, *Byron*, p. 76.

25   Holder, 'Melodrama, realism and empire'.

26   The first parts of Murray's *Handbook for Travellers in India, Burma and Ceylon* were published between 1859 and 1882. They were brought together into a single volume in 1892 and by that time an account of the Mutiny was included, with a map and advice for tourists wishing to visit all the main Mutiny shrines. It was a sort of imperial pilgrimage.

27   Holder, 'Melodrama, realism and empire', p. 135.

28   On Ruskin's complex appeal, see John M. MacKenzie, 'Edward Said and the historians', *Nineteenth-Century Contexts*, 18 (1994), pp. 18–19. Interestingly, Holder has also pointed out (pp. 144–6) that those playwrights who sought a more radical dramatic renaissance in the late nineteenth century, figures like Henry Arthur Jones, G. B. Shaw, William Archer and Gilbert Murray, also turned to imperial (often eastern) themes to carve out new political and social conjunctures.

29   Bratton, 'British heroism'.

30   Bratton, 'British heroism', p. 59.

31   David Mayer (ed.), *Playing out the Empire: Ben-Hur and other Toga Plays and Films, a Critical Anthology* (Oxford, 1994).

32   Mayer, *Playing out the Empire*, p. 8.

33   Ralph Hyde, *Panoramania! The Art and Entertainment of the 'All-Embracing View'* (London, 1988).

34   Hyde, *Panoramania!* p. 28.

35   All the material in this section is derived from the individual play files in the Theatre Museum Archive at Covent Garden. The reviews cited are also to be found in these files.

36   Illusionists in the nineteenth century invariably presented themselves in Orient-
      alist garb. For a late example, see the article on the 'Great Lafayette' by A. C.
      McKerracher, 'The Last Illusion', *The Scots Magazine*, May 1985, pp. 166–71.
      The Prime Minister Benjamin Disraeli was often presented as an oriental illusion-
      ist in pulling off his dazzling political coups.
37   See reviews and pictures in *The Mirror*, 1 October 1838, *The Theatrical Register*,
      16 October 1838 and one which is unfortunately unidentified and from which
      the majority of the following quotations are derived.
38   Unidentified contemporary review in Covent Garden Museum file.
39   *ibid*.
40   *Propaganda and Empire*, p. 54.
41   See the reviews in the *Weekly Despatch*, 23 November 1884, the *Daily Telegraph*,
      19 November 1884, and *Entr'acte*, 22 November 1884.
42   See, for example, reviews of *The Mikado* of 1885, *A Chinese Honeymoon* of 1901
      and *The Chinese Lantern* of 1908.
43   Arthur Jacobs, *Arthur Sullivan* (Oxford, 1986), pp. 205, 210.
44   Gilbert and Sullivan had already lampooned the Japanese craze in *Patience*.
45   *Illustrated Sporting and Dramatic News*, 28 March 1885, where the reviewer
      suggested that W. S. Gilbert had created a new world from his inner conscious-
      ness that had nothing to do with the real Japan; *Pall Mall Gazette*, 16 March
      1885; *Daily News*, 16 March 1885. Interestingly, *Truth* subsequently suggested
      that Egypt would be the setting for the next Gilbert and Sullivan opera – 'a skit
      upon English commercial enterprise and humbug, as exemplified by the pre-
      tended British horror at annexing new territory'. Since there is no evidence that
      any such opera was being contemplated, it seems more than likely that the radical
      Truth was being ironical, using the success of *The Mikado* to propose a satirical
      opera on its own account. Jacobs in *Sullivan*, p. 226, seems to think that it was
      intended as a serious prediction.
46   *Daily Telegraph*, 16 March 1885.
47   In 1901, Liberty's was very closely involved in the provision of the costumes.
48   See unidentified reviews and that in *The Sketch*, 29 April 1896.
49   *The Sketch*, 16 October 1901 and other unidentified reviews.
50   *San Toy* and many other plays and light operas are considered in J. C. Trewin,
      The Edwardian Theatre (Oxford, 1976) and Mark Lubbock, *The Complete Book
      of Light Opera* (London, 1962).
51   *The Sketch*, 24 June 1908.
52   Programme for *The Nautch Girl*; reviews in the *Daily Graphic*, 1 July 1891; *Pall
      Mall Gazette*, 1 July 1891; *Illustrated London News*, 30 June 1891 and *Illus-
      trated Sporting and Dramatic News*, 18 July 1891.
53   *Illustrated London News*, 12 March 1904; *Daily Telegraph*, 7 March 1904.
54   *The Sketch*, 22 August 1906; *Illustrated London News*, 10 August 1906; *The
      Tatler*, 31 October 1906.
55   *The Tatler*, 6 September 1916. See also *The Stage* Year Book for 1917.
56   Breandan Gregory, 'Staging British India' in Bratton *et al.*, *Acts of Supremacy*.
57   Quoted in Gregory, 'Staging British India', p. 165.
58   The literature on these designers is vast, but useful material on Bakst, Ricketts
      and other artists can be found in the Fine Art Society, *Bakst* (centennial exhibi-
      tion, London 1976); Léon Bakst, *Esquisses de Décors et de Costumes, Arts,
      Graphiques, Peintures* (Leningrad, 1986); Joseph Derracott, *The World of Charles
      Ricketts* (London, 1980); Charles Ricketts, *Self Portrait, taken from the Letters
      and Journals*, compiled by T. Sturge Moore, ed. Cecil Lewis (London, 1939).
      Catherine Haill, *Theatre Posters* (London, 1983) offers an introduction to some
      Orientalist posters.

59   A remarkable collection of costumes from the *Ballets Russes* can be found in the Australian National Gallery in Canberra. See Robyn Healy and Michael Lloyd, *From Studio to Stage: Costumes and Designs from the Russian Ballet in the Australian National Gallery* (Canberra, 1990).

60   Healy and Lloyd, *Studio to Stage*, p. 16.

61   Edward Craig, *Gordon Craig: the Story of his Life* (London, 1968), pp. 306–7 and *passim*; Denis Bablet, *Edward Gordon Craig* (New York, 1966).

62   Rustom Bharucha, *Theatre and the World: Performance and the Politics of Culture* (London, 1993), pp. 17–22. Some of Craig's thoughts on oriental theatre can be found in 'Japanese Artists in the West', *The Mask*, 6 (1913) and 'Asia, America, Europe', *The Mask*, 8 (1918). Ananda Coomeraswamay conducted a lively debate with Craig, *The Mask*, 6 (1913).

63   Bharucha, *Theatre*, pp. 14–17.

64   Colin McPhee, *A House in Bali* (Singapore, 1979 – first published 1944 with many impressions thereafter).

65   Bharucha, *Theatre*, pp. 13–14.

66   Bharucha, *Theatre*, pp. 68–87.

Conclusion

IN HIS Wellek Library Lectures in Critical Theory, published as *Musical Elaborations*, Edward Said has produced his most unequivocal statement of a hermetic and stereotypical Western culture, mutually essentialising both West and East:

> For in the encounter between the West and its various 'Others' . . . there was often the tactic of drawing a defensive perimeter called 'the West' around anything done by individual nations or persons who constituted a self-appointed Western essence in themselves; this tactic protected against change and a supposed contamination brought forward threateningly by the very existence of the Other. In addition, such defensiveness permits a comforting retreat into an essentialised, basically unchanging Self. By the same token, there is a move to freeze the Other in a kind of basic objecthood.[1]

It is surprising that such a rigidly binary argument should have been made in a series of lectures about music, for the evidence of the arts suggests that the case is unsustainable. As the foregoing chapters have been relentlessly concerned to point out, the artistic record of imperial culture has in fact been one of constant change, instability, heterogeneity and sheer porousness. It is impossible to recognise either the 'essentialised, basically unchanging Self' or the freezing of 'the Other in a kind of basic objecthood'. The western arts in fact sought contamination at every turn, restlessly seeking renewal and reinvigoration through contacts with other traditions. And both Self and Other were locked into processes of mutual modification, sometimes slow but inexorable, sometimes running as fast as a recently unfrozen river.

Of course those other cultures were themselves highly heterogeneous. The approach to the eastern Other can only be fully understood through a recognition of the complexity of the range of Others which constituted at once both threat and potential liberation. Thus each of the European states, some only fully formed in the late nineteenth century, responded positively and negatively to each other, to the reinvocation of mythic pasts (Norse, Celtic, Germanic, for instance), to internal Others (including newly discovered and privileged folk traditions), to renewed cultural obsessions (medievalism and chivalry are good examples), as well as to other continents and their religious and artistic complexes. It is only when Orientalism is placed in this wider context that it begins to make sense as one of several cultural courts of appeal.

In art, it was used to recreate a feudal, chivalric, pre-industrial world of supposedly uncomplicated social relations, clear legal obligations and retributions, heroic connections with the environment, a supposedly appropriate separation of gender spheres, and enthusiasm for craft production. It also provided opportunities for the extension of techniques, the handling of bright light, powerful colours, abstract design, compositional rhythms and a sense of geographical space and meteorological extremes. In architecture, it offered fresh conjunctions, new syncretic approaches, the marriage of form to function, and a whole fresh language for the buildings designed for the rapidly growing leisure industry. In design, it produced new sensations over a whole range of artefacts, revolutionary approaches to ornament, different ways of handling space, colour, composition, texture, even a reversal of the 'scientific' developments of western art and design in perspective, optical adjustments and visual accuracy. In music, composers sought in the East an extension of instrumental language, different sonorities, new melodic possibilities and complex rhythmic patterns. In doing so, they attempted to establish both national and cosmopolitan styles. While in the theatre, character, spectacle, movement, design and fabric created a fresh visual and dramatic language, opportunities both for display and for satire, often a parodying of Self through the portrayal of the Other. In all these arts, the result was often the profound extension of mood and of psychological state, a dramatic liberation from existing conventions and constricting restraints; and in each of them the repeated appeal to a different cultural tradition infused radical movements more frequently than it propped up existing conservative ones.

Naturally, such appeals were frequently resisted and powerfully criticised. They were judged against other possible sources of inspiration, derived from the past, from previously obscured internal cultures, or from different intellectual movements. Orientalism was but one of a whole sequence of perceived or invented traditions invoked by the restless arts. As we saw particularly clearly in the music chapter, composers at different times turned to various eastern sources, as well as to many nearer home, such as Spain, Scotland, or the inspiration of the folk. In doing so, they were often seeking out a distinctive national style, pursuing a need to separate themselves from a dominant (usually German) tradition. But among these, the 'oriental obsession' was a continuing and constantly changing phenomenon, repeatedly adapted to the needs of the age and the yearning for innovation. Time and again, composers discovered their most distinctive voice through the handling of exotica. These were not passing fads, nor were they mere embellishments which ultimately left western forms unchanged. As we have seen, the capacity for assimilation often obscured the graft, but the resulting artistic organism was unquestionably new and different from that which had avoided all such contacts with the Other.

In music, as in the other arts, this process was rarely a matter of genuine representation; it seldom involved realistic facsimile. Sometimes it was concerned with stereotype and caricature, but in the majority of cases it was a matter of stimulation, extension, adaptation and absorption in the pursuit of a more or less syncretic form. Such a synthesis was indeed essential to the creative act. To be sure, it was invariably based upon perception rather than actuality, a constructed East rather than the real thing. As Oscar Wilde put it, long before Edward Said, 'the whole of Japan is a pure invention ... The Japanese people are ... simply a mode of style, an exquisite fancy of art.'[2] Yet this exquisite fancy was a mutually conceived invention. Ever since oriental carpets, ceramics and fabrics had begun to arrive in Europe (and indeed earlier in other parts of Asia) the needs of the market had produced their inevitable modifications. The interaction of European taste, demand, market forces and commodity production had operated through a process of natural selection to create an 'appropriate' East. Producer and consumer were wholly complicit in this process. This was equally true of those arts which did not involve moveable artefacts.

Yet even if the products and the visions or aural perceptions of eastern arts were thus devised and prefabricated rather than faithfully reproduced, none the less they represented characteristics, forms, techniques, moods, modes of thinking and feeling which were perceived to be radically divergent from – and therefore capable of transforming – those of Europe. However modified in production or refracted through a western prism, these traditions bore a shifting relationship to an under-lying reality. If they had not existed, been progressively unveiled and absorbed, there can be little doubt that the development of the western arts and associated taste would have been different. What's more, the artistic characteristics of the various Easts were not devised in order to facilitate rule, but to encourage an invigorating contamination. And, as we have seen, the influence of those oriental arts was at its most radical at precisely the supposed high point of European imperialism in the late nineteenth and early twentieth centuries. Indeed, they were often em-braced by artists, designers, musicians and other practitioners who were most out of sympathy with dominant political ideas. The coincidence of oriental interests and radical ideologies is striking in all the arts.

Thus, a fascination with Orientalism was as likely to be oppositional as consensual in relation to established power structures, a promoter of a ferment in ideas as in artistic innovation. This has continued to be so in the twentieth century in all those areas *not* covered in this book, radical religious movements, mysticism, philosophy, sexuality and the popular exploration of world music. Moreover, there has been a consid-erable degree of continuity in these processes. It is difficult to discover in any of the arts at whatever period sets of clearly delineated binary oppositions, sharp distinctions between the moral Self and the depraved Other. Rather has the whole experience been one of instabilities and fusions, attraction and repulsion, an awareness of characteristics to be peremptorily rejected as well as devoutly embraced. And of course the content and balance of this mixed bag of wished-for gems and undesir-able rejects changed over time.

Many modern scholars have begun to recognise these shifting ambivalences in the wide range of texts, literary, religious and philo-sophical, topographical and administrative, historical and anthropolo-gical, through which the East has been explored by the West. But the arts reflect these dualities both more obviously and in some ways more pro-foundly. Above all, the arts reflect the genuine refreshment repeatedly secured from drinking at eastern wells. Moreover, interesting parallels – as well as intriguing differences – can be found among them. The shift in interest (though these concerns are also heavily interleaved from the late eighteenth century) from the Ottoman Empire and the Middle East first to South Asia and then to the Far East is common to all. In each case, the appeal to changing Easts was used to reassess, redefine and reinvent significant aspects of the western arts. The increasing accessibil-ity of different areas of the East and of their respective arts led to a repeated dialectical restructuring of the trinity of language, form and mood.

In their introduction to *Exoticism in the Enlightenment* Rousseau

and Porter have argued that analysing the exotic was a particularly ex-
acting and invigorating challenge to eighteenth-century thinkers and
artists, that to a certain extent reactions to the East have been in a
downhill mode ever since, through the condescension of the Romantic
era, the racial exclusiveness of the period of high imperialism, to the
swings from overweening arrogance to the failure of confidence in the
twentieth century.[3] But the evidence of the arts fails to confirm such a
counter-progressive view. In the Enlightenment period, the arts of the
East were sampled, tasted and used as embellishments to create new
moods. As I have argued in each of my chapters, exotic ideas certainly
entered the bloodstream, but in a relatively weak solution.

Nevertheless, in the succeeding period concepts of the sublime
and the picturesque, of more potent emotional responses and heightened sensibilities, of revolutionary potential and individual heroic action
were all assumed to be readily discoverable in the East. In the Romantic
era, the vision of an oriental court of appeal becomes a profoundly
significant one. The Anglicists appeared to rubbish such an appeal to
exotica, even – as Macaulay did – to attack the taste for eastern ceramics
and other items of internal decoration. But none of the arts seems to
have responded to the suggestion that the western drawbridge should be
raised, or at least only lowered in order to facilitate the subduing of the
outer world to western technology and cultural modes. On the contrary,
before long the arts of eastern traditions were being used as a weapon
to attack the productive processes of industrialism, its resultant social
relations and its shoddy products. By the end of the century, perceptions
of eastern artistic canons were being used to mount a full-scale radical
assault on western conventions.

The radical inspiration of the late nineteenth and early twentieth
centuries is also an experience shared across all the arts, with little suggestion of time-lags in their responses. The remarkable sequence of
exhibitions through which the arts of other cultures were unveiled reflected not only the commodification and consumption of the world by
the West, the continuing organisation of knowledge and taxonomising
of cultures, but also the excitement of artists, designers, musicians and
performers at discovering fresh extensions of language, form and mood,
albeit complying with their own perceived needs for change. The climax
of this came in the twenty-five years preceding the First World War,
undoubtedly a period of great ferment, with Asia as a significant catalyst,
throughout all of the arts surveyed in this book. And invariably artists
developed a well-nigh reverential approach to those characteristics of
oriental arts from which they believed the West could benefit. It is true
that Japan figured prominently in this, but it was far from being a unique
source of eastern inspiration.

What's more, aspects of popular culture were not behindhand. There can be little doubt that stereotype and caricature, racially conscious attitudes, and notions of moral, technical and political superiority were highly prevalent here. But none the less, the same feeling of instability, of fascinating cross-race contact in both sexual and cultural fields, of the need to negotiate the dilemmas and contradictions of power emerges from the theatrical record. It is true that the responses of critics and of elements of the audience, particularly in the gallery, may well have been very different, but even so it is abundantly apparent that what was presented could seem endlessly attractive, another side of Self waiting to be released from repression or financial and social constraint. Just such a sense of desirable new moods, opportunities and attractive stereotypes of ease and leisure or of fantasy and illusion were promoted by the Orientalism of seaside architecture – in pier, tower, ballroom or bandstand – or of the theatre and the cinema. Aspects of art, design, music and drama undoubtedly percolated down, and when they did so in the form of satire and parody, they were fulfilling a long tradition of popular burlesque. Orientalism was but one vehicle, albeit a particularly visible and exciting one, in which such parodies could be conveyed. These burlesques are sometimes read in dismissive, even insulting ways, but they always imply affectionate knowledge; generally they creatively destabilise rather than destructively undermine.

In any case laughter is itself a highly unstable phenomenon. As the analysts of humour have always pointed out, it is never far from tears. Its sympathetic responses often emerge from a troubled sense of the nearness of the conditions portrayed. This is surely true of all great art (and the popular is not excluded from this category). Most art operates through opposites, laughter and tears, triumph and tragedy, the profane and the spiritual, violence and peace, the neurotic and the calm. It secures its elevating power through the exploration of such dualities, the fundamental realities of human existence.

This is equally true of the Orientalist arts. No true art can ever be founded upon a perpetual parade of cultural superiority, an outpouring of imperialist (sexist/racist) bile, an earnest expectation of decline and destruction, though the work of late twentieth-century scholars with particularly contemporary axes to grind attempts to project such single-minded negatives. Nor are the majority of consumers likely to purchase, look at or listen to that which they wholly denigrate, or seek to dominate and destroy. That notions of superiority and inferiority, racial feeling and pride can enter into the complex of sensations of those who imbibe such art cannot be denied, given the intellectual climate of the period, but the power of art comes from its capacity to disturb. Cultural cross-referencing, a sense of lost ideals, an appreciation of the beauty of a pre-industrial craftsmanship, a perception of a pure and vibrant land-scape, an awareness of more unbuttoned approaches to life and colour, unfettered responses to the human personality, emotional, sexual, lan-guorous, violent or ecstatic, can all coexist with value-laden and ethno-centric cultural and racial ideals.

The modern critique of Orientalism has generally committed that most fundamental of historical sins, the reading back of contemporary attitudes and prejudices into historical periods. The word 'barbaric' has been read in its modern one-dimensional meaning rather than in its nineteenth-century complexity, with its suggestions of the sublime, lack of restraint, an attractive colourful and dramatic approach, liberating new sensations on a grand scale. It was this kind of response which was expected of many Orientalist paintings, musical expression and dramatic performance. Appropriately contextualised readings substitute highly desirable crafts for technological backwardness, piety and learning for obscurantism, appealing languor for sloth, manly hunting and games-playing for childlike 'laziness', female elegance, repose and self-expression for male dominance and possession, release into exciting new emotional and physical sensations for primitive, animalistic responses.

Of course it is true that all of the cultural borrowings which con-stitute the widespread phenomenon of artistic Orientalism were secured in a political, social and economic atmosphere of unequal exchange. Few considered the ethics of trans- or interculturalism or sought to enhance and revive the donor culture. Most were egotistically involved in the single-minded pursuit of their own, often radical, artistic integrity. But the creative process is invariably a selfish one and this cannot nullify the value and power of the product. By the later nineteenth century, and with an increasingly sympathetic intensity in the twentieth, the first signs of collection and preservation, not just of cultural objects and the built environment, but also of the social, religious and philosophical contexts that engendered them, are on hand. Composers, for example, collected those elements of folk and exotic traditions that might be lost while still incorporating them into their own independent creative acts. This was as true of Béla Bartók in Europe and North Africa as it was of Colin McPhee in Bali. Other artists set about the same dual activity. They were still, it is true, responding to the needs of the West, often to destructive forces instituted by globalising cultures, but to suggest that they contri-buted to that destruction or failed to produce any preservation of lasting value is surely a counsel of despair.

Such attempts at conservation have not, however, been the subject of this book. I have not been concerned with Rustom Bharucha's anxi-eties about intercultural ethics, prescribing for mutually constructive cultural interaction in the future, however much I may feel sympathetic towards such an argument.[4] I have been concerned with what actually happened, with understanding Orientalism not only through the widest practical range of its manifestations, but also through the language and cultural contexts of its times and not ours. It has been, perhaps, an over-ambitious programme, but the whole point about responses to the East is that they have so often stimulated over-vaulting leaps of the imagination. Certainly the modern critics of Orientalism have been too procrustean. By creating a monolithic and binary vision of the past, they have too often damaged those intercultural relations which they seek to place on a more sympathetic basis for the future. In reality, Orientalism was endlessly protean, as often consumed by admiration and reverence as by denigration and depreciation. If these sensations were adopted solely to further the western arts, this does not invalidate the synthetic creative act which followed or the products which survive. Inevitably, some dross was produced in the process, but many masterpieces remain.

Notes

1   Edward W. Said, *Musical Elaborations* (London, 1991), p. 52.
2   Quoted in Tomoko Sato and Toshio Watanabe (eds), *Japan and Britain: an Aesthetic Dialogue, 1850–1930* (London, 1991), p. 40.
3   G. S. Rousseau and Roy Porter (eds), *Exoticism in the Enlightenment* (Manchester, 1990), introduction, particularly p. 7.
4   Rustom Bharucha, *Theatre and the World: Performance and the Politics of Culture* (London, 1993).

Select bibliography

Primary

In this work I have maintained my tradition of combining documentary and printed sources with visual and aural materials of all sorts. In 1984, when I published *Propaganda and Empire*, this was regarded as an unusual procedure for a 'conventional' historian. By 1994 it has become almost standard practice.

Many of the files on Orientalist productions were examined at the archive of the Theatre Museum in Covent Garden, London. Oriental and Orientalist artefacts and paintings were studied at the Victoria and Albert Museum, London, and many art galleries in the United Kingdom, too numerous to list. All the Orientalist exhibitions from 1982, cited in Chapter 3, were visited, and the purchasing policies and sales performance of the Mathaf Gallery were discussed with its director. In addition, I have visited many buildings with syncretic Orientalist influences, have listened to countless Orientalist pieces of music, both on record and in the concert-hall or studio, and attended performances of many operas set in the East. The riches of British broadcasting, in music magazine programmes, radio talks and television concerts and documentaries have also been plundered.

Secondary

Books

(The place of publication is London except where otherwise specified.)

Ackerman, Gerald M., *The Life and Work of Jean-Léon Gérôme* (Paris, 1986)

Ackroyd, Harold, *The Dream Palaces of Liverpool* (Birmingham, 1987)

Adamson, Susan M., *Seaside Piers* (1977)

Adburgham, Alison, *Liberty's: a Biography of a Shop* (1975)

Alcock, Sir Rutherford, *Art and Art Industry in Japan* (1878)

Alloula, Malek, *The Colonial Harem* (Manchester, 1986)

Allwood, John, *The Great Exhibitions* (1977)

Archer, Mildred, *Indian Architecture and the British, 1780–1830* (1968)

—— *Early Views of India: the Picturesque Journeys of Thomas and William Daniell* (1980)

—— *Company Paintings: Indian Paintings of the British Period* (1992)

Archer, Mildred and Falk, Toby, *India Revealed: the Art and Adventures of James and William Fraser, 1801–1935* (1989)

Archer, Mildred and Lightbown, Ronald, *India Observed: India as viewed by British Artists, 1760–1860* (1982)

Archer, Mildred, Rowell, Christopher and Skelton, Robert, *Treasures from India: the Clive Collection at Powis Castle* (1987)

Armstrong, Nancy J., *Fans* (1984)

—— *Fans from the Fitzwilliam* (Cambridge, 1985)

Aslet, Clive, *The Last Country Houses* (New Haven, 1982)

Atwell, David, *Cathedrals of the Movies* (1980)

August, Thomas G., *The Selling of the Empire: British and French Imperialist Propaganda, 1890–1914* (1985)

Ayers, John, Impey, Oliver and Mallet, J. V. G., *Porcelain for Palaces: the Fashion for Japan in Europe, 1650–1750* (1990)

Bakst, Léon, *Esquisses de Décors et de Costumes, Arts, Graphiques, Peintures* (Leningrad, 1986)

Bantock, Myrrha, *Granville Bantock: a Personal Portrait* (1972)

Barker, Francis *et al.* (eds), *The Politics of Theory* (Colchester, 1983)

—— *Literature, Politics and Theory* (1986)

Bauman, Thomas, *Die Entführung aus dem Serail* (Cambridge, 1987)

Bayly, C. A., *Imperial Meridian: the British Empire and the World, 1780–1830* (1989)

Bayly, C. A. (ed.), *The Raj: India and the British, 1600–1947* (1990)

Bearce, George D., *British Attitudes towards India, 1784–1858* (Oxford, 1961)

Beaumont, Antony, *Busoni, the Composer* (1985)

Bhabha, Homi K. *The Location of Culture* (1994)

Bhabha, Homi K. (ed.), *Nation and Narration* (1990)

Bharucha, Rustom, *Theatre and the World: Performance and the Politics of Culture* (1993)

Billcliffe, Roger, *Edward Atkinson Hornel* (Glasgow, 1982)

—— *The Glasgow Boys: the Glasgow School of Painting, 1875–1895* (1985)

Birdwood, George C. M., *The Industrial Arts of India* (1880)

Birks, Tony and Digby, Cornelia Wingfield, *Bernard Leach, Hamada and their Circle* (Oxford, 1990)

Black, Jeremy, *The British and the Grand Tour* (1985)

Bolt, Christine, *Victorian Attitudes to Race* (1971)

Booth, Michael, *English Melodrama* (1965)

—— *Victorian Spectacular Theatre, 1850–1910* (1981)

Bowers, Fabian, *Scriabin: a Biography of the Russian Composer, 1871–1914*, 2 vols. (Tokyo, 1969)

Bradby, David *et al.* (eds), *Performance and Politics in Popular Drama* (Cambridge, 1980)

Brantlinger, Patrick, *Rule of Darkness: British Literature and Imperialism, 1830–1914* (1988)

Bratton, J. S. *et al.* (eds), *Acts of Supremacy: the British Empire and the Stage, 1790–1930* (Manchester, 1991)

Breckenridge, Carol A. and van der Veer, Peter, *Orientalism and the Postcolonial Predicament* (Philadelphia, 1993)

Buchanan, William, *Mr Henry and Mr Hornel Visit Japan* (Glasgow, 1978)

Budden, Julian, *Verdi* (1985)

Cannon, Garland, *Oriental Jones: a Biography* (1964)

—— *The Life and Mind of Oriental Jones* (Cambridge, 1990)

Carner, Mosco, *Puccini: a Critical Biography* (1958)

Carner, Mosco (ed.), new edition of Guiseppe Adami (ed.), *Letters of Puccini* (1974)

Carrott, Richard, *The Egyptian Revival: its Sources, Monuments and Meaning, 1808–1858* (Berkeley, 1978)

Checkland, Olive, *Britain's Encounter with Meiji Japan, 1868–1912* (Edinburgh, 1989)

Chisaburo, F. Yamada, *Japanisme in Art: an International Symposium* (Tokyo, 1980)

Clayden, P. W., *England under Lord Beaconsfield* (1880)

Clayton, Peter A., *The Rediscovery of Ancient Egypt: Artists and Travellers in the Nineteenth Century* (1982)

—— *David Roberts' Egypt* (1985)

Clegg, Chris and Clegg, Rosemary, *The Dream Palaces of Birmingham* (Birmingham, 1983)

Clunas, Craig, *Chinese Export Watercolours* (1984)

Colley, Linda, *Britons: Forging the Nation, 1707–1837* (New Haven, 1992)

Conner, Patrick, *Oriental Architecture and the West* (1977)

—— *The China Trade, 1600–1860* (Brighton 1986)

Conner, Patrick (ed.), *The Inspiration of Egypt: its Influence on British Artists, Travellers and Designers, 1700–1900* (Brighton, 1983)

Craig, Edward, *Gordon Craig: the Story of his Life* (1968)

Cumming, Elizabeth, *Glasgow 1900: Art and Design* (Amsterdam, 1992)

Curl, James Stevens, *Egyptomania: the Egyptian Revival: a Recurring Theme in the History of Taste* (Manchester, 1994)

Daniell, Thomas and William, *Oriental Scenery, 1795–1807*, 4 series, each 2 vols. (1815)

Davies, Philip, *Splendours of the Raj: British Architecture in India, 1660–1947* (1985)

Dean, Winton, *Bizet* (1975)

Derracott, Joseph, *The World of Charles Ricketts* (1980)

de Schloezer, Boris, *Scriabin, Artist and Mystic*, trans. N. Slominsky (New York, 1990)

Dinkel, John, *The Royal Pavilion, Brighton* (1983)

Dresser, Christopher, *Principles of Decorative Design* (1973, first published 1873)

—— *Japan: its Architecture, Art and Art Manufactures* (1882)

Drew, John, *India and the Romantic Imagination* (Delhi, 1987)

Dutta, Krishna and Robinson, Andrew (eds), *Purabi* (1991)

Eastlake, Charles Locke, *Hints on Household Taste in Furniture, Upholstery and Other Details* (Dover, 1969, first published in book form in 1868)

Evans, Peter, *The Music of Benjamin Britten* (1979)

Fergusson, James, *On the Study of Indian Architecture* (1866, reprinted Varanasi, 1977)

—— *History of Indian and Eastern Architecture*, 2 vols. (New Delhi, 1972, first published 1876)

Findling, John F. and Pelle, Kimberly D. (eds), *Historical Dictionary of World's Fairs and Expositions, 1851–1988* (New York, 1990)

The Fine Art Society, *The Aesthetic Movement and the Cult of Japan* (1972)

—— *Bakst* (centennial exhibition, 1976)

—— *Eastern Encounters: Orientalist Painters in the Nineteenth Century* (1978)

—— *Travellers beyond the Grand Tour* (1980)

—— *The Travels of Edward Lear* (1983)

fine material for a dream . . . ? A Reappraisal of Orientalism: 19th and 20th Century Fine Art and Popular Culture Juxtaposed with Paintings, Video and Photography by Contemporary Artists (catalogue, Preston, Hull and Oldham, 1992)

Fisher, Michael H., *Indirect Rule in India: Residents and the Residency System, 1764–1857* (Delhi, 1991)

Fiske, Roger, *Scotland in Music* (Cambridge, 1983)

Fletcher, Banister, *A History of Architecture on the Comparative Method* (16th edn 1959)

Frayling, Christopher, *The Face of Tutankhamun* (1992)

Gilbert, Christopher, *The Life and Work of Thomas Chippendale* (Bristol, 1978)

Gilbert, James, *Perfect Cities, Chicago's Utopias of 1893* (Chicago, 1991)

Girouard, Mark, *The Victorian Country House* (New Haven, 1979)

—— *The Return to Camelot* (New Haven, 1981)

Glass, Philip, *Opera on the Beach: Philip Glass on his New World of Music Theatre* (1988)

Glasstone, Victor, *Victorian and Edwardian Theatres: an Architectural and Social Survey* (1975)

Gomme, Andor and Walker, David, *Architecture of Glasgow* (1968)

Greenacre, Francis and Stoddard, Sheena, *W. J. Müller 1812–1845* (Bristol, 1991)

Greenhalgh, Paul, *Ephemeral Vistas: the Expositions Universelles, Great Exhibitions and World Fairs, 1851–1939* (Manchester, 1988)

Guha, Ranajit and Spivak, Gayatri Chakravorty (eds), *Selected Subaltern Studies* (Oxford, 1988)

Guha-Thakurta, T., *The Making of a New 'Indian' Art: Artists, Aesthetics and Nationalism in Bengal, c.1850–1920* (Cambridge, 1992)

Guiterman, Helen and Llewellyn, Briony, *David Roberts* (1987)

Guy, John and Swallow, Deborah (eds), *Arts of India, 1550–1900* (1990)

Halén, Widar, *Christopher Dresser* (Oxford, 1990)

Harding, James, *Saint-Saëns and his Circle* (1965)

Head, Raymond, *The Indian Style* (1986)

Healy, Robyn and Lloyd, Michael, *From Studio to Stage: Costumes and Designs from the Russian Ballet in the Australian National Gallery* (Canberra, 1990)

Hillier, B., *Art Deco* (1985)

Hobsbawm, Eric and Ranger, Terence (eds), *The Invention of Tradition* (Cambridge, 1983)

Holden, Amanda (ed.), *Viking Opera Guide* (1993)

Holme, Charles, *The Influence of Japanese Art on English Design* (Warrington, 1890)

Holst, Imogen, *Gustav Holst* (1938)

Hornel, E. A., *Japan* (Castle Douglas, 1895)

Howard, David, *Chinese Armorial Porcelain* (1974)

Howard, David and Ayers, John, *China for the West* (1978)

Howell, Margaret J., *Byron Tonight: a Poet's Plays on the Nineteenth-Century Stage* (Windlesham, 1982)

Hunterian Art Gallery, *James McNeill Whistler at the Hunterian Art Gallery: an Illustrated Guide* (Glasgow, 1990)

Hutchins, Francis G., *The Illusion of Permanence: British Imperialism in India* (Princeton, 1967)

Hyam, Ronald, *Empire and Sexuality: the British Experience* (Manchester, 1990)

Hyde, Ralph, *Panoramania! The Art and Entertainment of the 'All-Embracing View'* (1988)

Impey, Oliver, *Chinoiserie: the Impact of Oriental Styles in Western Art and Decoration* (1977)

Inden, Ronald, *Imagining India* (Oxford, 1990)

Irving, Robert Grant, *Indian Summer: Lutyens, Baker and Imperial Delhi* (New Haven, 1981)

Irwin, John, *Shawls, a Study in Indo-European Taste* (1955)

—— *The Kashmir Shawl* (1973)

Irwin, John and Brett, Katharine, *The Origins of Chintz, with a Catalogue of Indo-European Cotton-Paintings in the Victoria and Albert Museum, London and the Royal Ontario Museum, Toronto* (1970)

Jacobs, Arthur, *Arthur Sullivan* (Oxford, 1986)

James, C. F., *An Artist on the March: Paintings of India, Abyssinia and Kashmir by Colonel Cornelius Francis James, 1938–1889* (St Peter Port, 1989)

Jarry, Madeleine, *Chinoiserie: Chinese Influences on European Decorative Art, Seventeenth and Eighteenth Centuries* (London, 1981)

Jefferson, Alan, *The Operas of Richard Strauss in Britain, 1910–63* (1963)

John, Nicholas (series editor), *The Magic Flute*, Opera Guide Series (1980)

—— *Aida*, Opera Guide Series (1980)

—— *Madam Butterfly*, Opera Guide Series (1980)

—— *Così fan Tutte*, Opera Guide Series (1983)

—— *Turandot*, Opera Guide Series (1984)

—— *Salome/Elektra*, Opera Guide Series (1988)

Jones, Owen, *The Grammar of Ornament* (1986, first published 1856)

Kabbani, Rana, *Europe's Myths of Orient: Devise and Rule* (1986)

Kenna, Rudolph, *Glasgow Art Deco* (Glasgow, 1985)

Kennedy, Michael, *Britten* (1981)

Kinchin, Perilla and Kinchin, Juliet, *Glasgow's Great Exhibitions, 1888, 1901, 1911, 1938, 1988* (Glasgow, 1988)

King, Anthony D., *The Bungalow: the Production of a Global Culture* (1984)

King, Donald and Sylvester, David, *The Eastern Carpet in the Western World from the Fifteenth to the Seventeenth Century* (1983)

Kopf, David, *British Orientalism and the Bengal Renaissance: the Dynamics of Indian Modernisation, 1773–1835* (Berkeley, 1969)

Lambert, Susan, *Pattern and Design: Designs for the Decorative Arts 1480–1980* (1983)

Larner, Gerald and Larner, Celia, *The Glasgow Style* (1980)

Leask, Nigel, *British Romantic Writers and the East: Anxieties of Empire* (Cambridge, 1992)

Levy, Mervyn, *Liberty Style: the Classic Years, 1898–1910* (1986)

Lewis, Wyndham, *Journey into Barbary*, ed. C. J. Fox (Harmondsworth, 1987)

Llewellyn, Briony, *The Orient Observed: Images of the Middle East from the Searight Collection* (1989)

Llewellyn, Briony and Newton, Charles, *The People and Places of Constantinople: Watercolours by Amadeo, Count Preziosi* (1985)

Lloyd, Seton, *Foundations in the Dust: the Story of Mesopotamian Exploration* (1980, first published 1947)

Lockett, Terence A., *Oriental Expressions: the Influence of the Orient on British Ceramics* (Stoke-on-Trent, 1989)

Lockspeiser, Edward, *Debussy* (1963)

Longford, Elizabeth, *A Pilgrimage of Passion: the Life of Wilfrid Scawen Blunt* (1979)

Lorimer, Douglas A, *Colour, Class and the Victorians* (Leicester, 1978)

Louden, T., *The Cinemas of Cinema City* (Glasgow, 1983)

Lovelace, Antonia, *Art for Industry: the Glasgow–Japan Exchange of 1878* (Glasgow, 1991)

Lowe, Lisa, *Critical Terrains: French and British Orientalisms* (Ithaca, 1991)

Lubbock, Mark, *The Complete Book of Light Opera* (1962)

McCully, Bruce, *English Education and the Origins of Indian Nationalism* (New York, 1942)

MacDonald, Malcolm, *John Foulds* (Rickmansworth, 1975)

McFadzean, Ronald, *The Life and Work of Alexander Thomson* (1979)

MacKenzie, John M., *Propaganda and Empire* (Manchester, 1984)
—— *The Empire of Nature* (Manchester, 1988)
Macleod, Robert, *Style and Society: Architectural Ideology in Britain, 1815–1914* (1971)
—— *Charles Rennie Mackintosh: Architect and Artist* (1983)
McPhee, Colin, *A House in Bali* (Singapore, 1979, first published 1944)
—— *Music in Bali* (New York, 1966)
McWilliam, Colin (ed.), *The Buildings of Glasgow* (1990)
Mahler, Alma, *Gustav Mahler: Memories and Letters*, trans. Donald Mitchell (1973)
Majeed, Javed, *Ungoverned Imaginings: James Mill's The History of British India and Orientalism* (Oxford, 1992)
Mathaf Gallery, *Lands Without Shade: the Orient through Western Eyes, an Exhibition at the Zamana Gallery* (1985)
Mayer, David, *Harlequin in His Element: the English Pantomime, 1806–1836* (Cambridge, Mass., 1969)
Mayer, David (ed.), *Playing out the Empire: Ben-Hur and other Toga Plays and Films, a Critical Anthology* (Oxford, 1994)
Mayor, Susan, *Collecting Fans* (1980)
Melman, Billie, *Women's Orients: English Women in the Middle East, 1718–1918* (1992)
Mendus, Susan and Rendall, Jane (eds), *Sexuality and Subordination: Interdisciplinary Studies of Gender in the Nineteenth Century* (1989)
Menpes, Mortimer, *The Durbar* (1903)
—— *Japan: a Record in Colour* (1903)
Metcalf, Thomas R., *The Aftermath of Revolt* (Princeton, 1965)
—— *An Imperial Vision: Indian Architecture and Britain's Raj* (1989)
Miller, Christopher L., *Blank Darkness: Africanist Discourse in French* (Chicago, 1985)
Mills, Sara, *Discourses of Difference: Women's Travel Writing and Colonialism* (1991)
Mitter, Partha, *Much Maligned Monsters: a History of European Reactions to Indian Art* (Oxford, 1977)
Moon, Karen, *George Walton: Designer and Architect* (Oxford, 1993)
Moore-Gilbert, B. J., *Kipling and Orientalism* (1986)
Morris, Barbara, *Liberty Design, 1874–1914* (1989)
Mukherjee, S. N., *Sir William Jones: a Study in Eighteenth-Century British Attitudes to India* (Cambridge, 1968)
Nasir, Sari Jamil, *The Arabs and the English* (1976)
Orledge, Robert, *Debussy and the Theatre* (Cambridge, 1982)
Ormond, Richard, *Sir Edwin Landseer* (1982)
Parry, Benita, *Delusions and Discoveries* (1972)
Pemble, John, *The Mediterranean Passion: Victorians and Edwardians in the South* (Oxford, 1987)
Pointon, Marcia, *Bonnington, Francia and Wyld: an exhibition at the Victoria and Albert Museum* (1985)
Porter, Dennis, *Haunted Journeys: Desire and Transgression in European Travel Writings* (Princeton, l991)
Pratt, Mary Louise, *Imperial Eyes: Travel Writing and Transculturation* (1992)
Reade, Brian, *Aubrey Beardsley* (1987)
Régamey, Félix, *Japan in Art and Industry* (1893)
Richards, Jeffrey, *Swordsmen of the Screen* (1977)
Richards, Jeffrey and MacKenzie, John M., *The Railway Station: a Social History* (Oxford, l986)
Ricketts, Charles, *Self Portrait, taken from the Letters and Journals*, compiled by T. Sturge Moore, ed. Cecil Lewis (1939)
Riley, Valerie, *Paisley Pattern* (Glasgow, 1985)
Robertson, Pamela, *Charles Rennie Mackintosh: the Architectural Papers* (Glasgow, 1990)

Rosenthal, Donald A., *Orientalism: the Near East in French Painting, 1800–1880* (Rochester, NY, 1982)

Rousseau, G. S. and Porter, Roy (eds), *Exoticism in the Enlightenment* (Manchester, 1990)

Said, Edward W., *Orientalism* (1978)

—— *The World, the Text and the Critic* (Cambridge, Mass., 1983)

—— *Musical Elaborations* (1991)

—— *Culture and Imperialism* (1993)

Saint-Saëns, Camille, *Outspoken Essays on Music* (Westport, Conn., 1970, first published 1922)

Salusinszky, Imre, *Criticism in Society* (New York, 1987)

Sato, Tomoko and Watanabe, Toshio (eds), *Japan and Britain: an Aesthetic Dialogue, 1850–1930* (1991)

Schneider, William H., *An Empire for the Masses: the French Popular Image of Africa, 1870–1900* (1982)

Schwab, Raymond, *La Renaissance Orientale* (Paris, 1950)

Seal, Anil, *The Emergence of Indian Nationalism* (Cambridge, 1971)

Searight, Sarah, Llewellyn, Briony *et al.*, *Romantic Lebanon: the European View, 1700–1900* (1986)

Scottish National Portrait Gallery, *Visions of the Ottoman Empire*, exhibition catalogue (1994)

Sharafuddin, Mohammed, *Islam and Romantic Orientalism* (1993)

Sharp, Dennis, *The Picture Palace* (1969)

Shearer, David R., *Why Paisley?* (Paisley, 1985)

—— *Paisley Shawls* (Paisley, n.d.)

Shepherd, Naomi, *The Zealous Intruders: the Western Rediscovery of Palestine* (1987)

Short, Michael, *Gustav Holst: the Man and His Music* (Oxford, 1990)

Short, Michael (ed.), *Gustav Holst: Letters to W. G. Whittaker* (Glasgow 1974)

Sim, Katharine, *David Roberts RA, 1796–1864: a Biography* (1984)

Smith, Bernard, *European Vision and the South Pacific* (1985, first published 1959)

—— *Australian Painting 1788–1960* (Melbourne, 1971)

—— *Imagining the Pacific* (New Haven, 1992)

Sotheby's, *Important Orientalist Paintings from the Collection of Coral Petroleum Inc.* (New York, 1985)

Spalding, Frances, *Whistler* (Oxford, 1979)

Spivak, Gayatri Chakravorty, *In Other Worlds: Essays in Cultural Politics* (1987)

Sprinker, Michael, *Edward Said: a Critical Reader* (Oxford, 1992)

Stafford, Robert, *Scientist of Empire: Sir Roderick Murchison, Scientific Exploration and Victorian Imperialism* (Cambridge, 1989)

Stevens, Mary Anne, *The Orientalists: Delacroix to Matisse, European Painters in North Africa and the Near East* (1984)

Stokes, Eric, *The English Utilitarians and India* (Oxford, 1959)

Stradling, Robert and Hughes, Meirion, *The English Musical Renaissance, 1860–1940* (1993)

Suleri, Sara, *The Rhetoric of English India* (1992)

Sullivan, Michael, *The Meeting of Eastern and Western Art* (1973)

Sutton, Denys, *The Art of James McNeill Whistler* (1963)

Sweetman, John, *The Oriental Obsession: Islamic Inspiration in British and American Art and Architecture, 1500–1920* (Cambridge, 1988)

Sylvester, David, *Islamic Carpets from the Collection of Joseph V. McMullan* (1972)

Symonds, Julian, *Oxford and Empire: the Last Lost Cause* (1986)

Taylor, Hilary, *James McNeill Whistler* (1978)

Taylor, Philip M., *The Projection of Britain: British Overseas Publicity and Propaganda, 1919–1939* (Cambridge, 1981)

Thacker, Christopher, *The Wildness Pleases* (1983)

Thompson, E. P., *William Morris* (1977)

Thompson, James, *The East: Imagined, Experienced, Remembered, Orientalist Nineteenth-Century Painting* (Dublin and Liverpool, 1988)

Thornton, A. P., *Doctrines of Imperialism* (New York, 1963)

—— *For the File on Empire* (1968)

Thornton, Lynne, *The Orientalists: Painter–Travellers, 1828–1908* (Paris, 1983)

Tidrick, Kathryn, *Empire and the English Character* (1990)

Toplis, Ian, *The Foreign Office: an Architectural History* (1987)

Trewin, J. C., *The Edwardian Theatre* (Oxford, 1986)

Truman, Charles, *The Sèvres Egyptian Service, 1810–12* (1982)

Vergo, Peter, *Vienna 1900: Vienna, Scotland and the European Avant-Garde* (Edinburgh, 1983)

Verrier, Michelle, *The Orientalists* (1979)

Victoria and Albert Museum, *Art and the East India Trade* (1970)

—— *Liberty's 1875–1975* (1975)

—— *Rococo: Art and Design in Hogarth's England* (1984)

Viswanathan, Gauri, *Masks of Conquest* (1989)

Walker, Brian M., *Frank Matcham: Theatre Architect* (Belfast, 1980)

Walton, John and Fischer, Richard, *British Piers* (1987)

Warrack, John, *Carl Maria von Weber* (Cambridge, 1976)

Warrack, John (ed.), *Carl Maria von Weber: Writings on Music*, trans. Martin Cooper (Cambridge, 1981)

Watney, B., *Eighteenth-Century English Blue and White Porcelain* (1979)

Wiener, Martin, *English Culture and the Decline of the Industrial Spirit, 1850–1980* (Cambridge, 1981)

Worsdall, Frank, *The City that Disappeared: Glasgow's Demolished Architecture* (Glasgow, 1981)

Young, Andrew McLaren (ed.), *Charles Rennie Mackintosh: Architecture, Design, Painting* (Edinburgh, 1968)

Zatlin, Linda Gertler, *Aubrey Beardsley and Victorian Sexual Politics* (Oxford, 1990)

Articles, pamphlets and theses

Arberry, Arthur J., 'British Contributions to Persian Studies' (1942)

Bhabha, Homi K., 'The other question: difference, discrimination and the discourse of colonialism' in Francis Barker *et al.* (eds), *The Politics of Theory* (Colchester, 1983), 148–72

—— 'Of mimicry and man: the ambivalence of colonial discourse', *October*, 28 (spring 1984), 125–33

—— 'Signs taken for wonders: questions of ambivalence and authority under a tree outside Delhi, May 1817', *Critical Inquiry*, 12 (1985), 144–65

—— 'DissemiNation: time, narrative and the margins of the modern nation' in Bhabha, Homi (ed.), *Nation and Narration* (1990), 291–321

Bowen, Harold, 'British Contributions to Turkish Studies' (1945)

Bratton, J. S., 'British heroism and the structure of melodrama' in Bratton *et al.*, *Acts of Supremacy* (1991), 18–61

Brockington, J. L., 'Warren Hastings and Orientalism' in Geoffrey Carnall and Colin Nicholson (eds), *The Impeachment of Warren Hastings* (Edinburgh, 1989), 91–108

Chatterjee, Sir Attul and Burn, Sir Richard, 'British Contributions to Indian Studies' (1943)

Chatterjee, Partha, 'Their own words? An essay for Edward Said' in Michael Sprinker, *Edward Said: a Critical Reader* (Oxford, 1992), 194–220

Chrisman, Laura, 'The imperial unconscious? Representations of imperial discourse', *Critical Inquiry*, 32, 3 (1990), 38–58

Cohn, Bernard S., 'Representing authority in Victorian India' in Eric Hobsbawm and Terence Ranger (eds), *The Invention of Tradition* (Cambridge, 1983), 165–209

Cox, Ian, 'The ornamental ironwork of Walter Macfarlane and Co.', *Scottish Art Review*, XVII (1991), 3–7

de Groot, Joanna, '"Sex" and "Race": the construction of language and image in the nineteenth century' in Susan Mendus and Jane Rendall (eds), *Sexuality and Subordination: Interdisciplinary Studies of Gender in the Nineteenth Century* (1989), 89–128

Driver, Felix, 'Geography's empire: histories of geographical knowledge', *Society and Space*, 10 (1992), 23–40

Farmer, Henry George, 'Oriental influences on occidental military music', *Islamic Culture*, 15 (April 1941), 239–40

Ferriday, Peter, 'The peacock room', *Architectural Review*, CXXV (1959), 407–14

Fox, Richard G., 'East of Said' in Michael Sprinker, *Edward Said: a Critical Reader* (Oxford, 1992), 144–56

Gellner, Ernest, 'The mightier pen', *Times Literary Supplement*, 19 February 1993, 3–4

Gregory, Breandan, 'Staging British India' in J. S. Bratton *et al.*, *Acts of Supremacy: the British Empire and the Stage, 1790–1930* (Manchester, 1991), 150–78

Holder, Heidi, 'Melodrama, realism and empire on the British Stage' in J. S. Bratton *et al.*, *Acts of Supremacy: the British Empire and the Stage, 1790–1930* (Manchester, 1991), 129–49

Howe, Stephen, 'When the sun did set', *The Times Higher Education Supplement*, 13 November 1992, 17

Jameson, Fredric, 'Modernism and imperialism' in Terry Eagleton, Fredric Jameson and Edward W. Said, *Nationalism, Colonialism and Literature* (Minneapolis, 1990), 43–66

Kopf, David, 'Hermeneutics versus history', *Journal of Asian Studies*, XXXIX (1980), 494–506

Lewis, Bernard, 'British Contributions to Arabic Studies' (1941)

MacKenzie, John M., 'Propaganda and the BBC Empire Service' in Jeremy Hawthorn (ed.), *Propaganda, Persuasion and Polemic* (1987), 37–53

—— 'Occidentalism: counterpoint and counter-polemic', *Journal of Historical Geography* 19 (1993), 339–44

—— 'Scotland and the Empire', *International History Review*, XV (1993), 714–39

—— 'Edward Said and the historians' *Nineteenth-Century Contexts*, 18 (1994), 9–25

McKerracher, A. C., 'The last illusion', *The Scots Magazine*, May 1985, 166–71

McLaren, Martha, 'Writing and Making History, Thomas Munro, John Malcolm and Mountstuart Elphinstone: Three Scotsmen in the History and Historiography of British India', Ph.D. thesis, Simon Fraser University (1992)

Marshall, P. J., 'Warren Hastings as scholar and patron' in Anne Whiteman, J. S. Bromley and P. G. M. Dickson (eds), *Statesmen, Scholars and Merchants: Essays in Eighteenth-Century History Presented to Dame Lucy Sutherland* (Oxford, 1973), 242–62

—— 'Oriental studies' in L. S. Sutherland and L. G. Mitchell (eds), *The History of the University of Oxford, Vol. V, the Eighteenth Century* (Oxford, 1986), 551–63

—— 'Taming the exotic: the British and India in the seventeenth and eighteenth centuries' in G. S. Rousseau and Roy Porter (eds), *Exoticism in the Enlightenment* (Manchester, 1990), 46–67

—— 'No fatal impact? The elusive history of imperial Britain', *The Times Literary Supplement*, 12 March 1993, 8–10

Meyer, Eve R., '*Turquerie* and eighteenth–century music', *Eighteenth-Century Studies*, 7 (1973–74), 474–88

Nasir, Sari Jamil, 'The Image of the Arab in American Popular Culture', Ph.D. thesis, University of Illinois (1962)

Netton, George Henry, 'The mysteries of Islam' in G. S. Rousseau and Roy Porter (eds), *Exoticism in the Enlightenment* (Manchester, 1990), 23–45

Nochlin, Linda, 'The Imaginary Orient', *Art in America*, (May 1983), 118–31, 187–91

O'Hanlon, Rosalind, 'Recovering the subject: subaltern studies and histories of resistance in colonial South Asia', *Modern Asian Studies*, 22 (1988), 189–224

Parry, Benita, 'Problems in current theories of colonial discourse,' *Oxford Literary Review*, 9 (1987), 27–58

—— 'Overlapping territories and intertwined histories: Edward Said's postcolonial cosmopolitanism' in Michael Sprinker, *Edward Said: a Critical Reader* (Oxford 1992), 19–47

Porter, Dennis, 'Orientalism and its problems' in Francis Barker *et al.* (eds), *The Politics of Theory* (Colchester, 1983), 179–83

Prakash, Gyan, 'Writing post-Orientalist histories of the Third World: Perspectives from Indian historiography', *Comparative Studies in Society and History*, 32 (1990), 383–408

Rendall, Jane, 'Scottish Orientalism: from Robertson to James Mill', *The Historical Journal*, 25 (1982), 43–69

Rockwell, John, 'The Orient, the visual arts and the evolution of minimalism: Philip Glass' in *All-American Music: Composition in the Late Twentieth Century* (New York, 1983), 109–22

Said, Edward W., 'Opponents, audiences, constituencies and community' in H. Foster (eds), *Postmodern Culture* (1985), 135–59

—— 'Orientalism reconsidered' in Francis Barker *et al.* (eds), *Literature, Politics and Theory* (1986), 210–29

—— 'Representing the colonized: anthropology's interlocutors', *Critical Inquiry*, 15 (1989), 210–29

Saxbee, Helen, 'An Orient Exhibited: the Exhibition of the Chinese Collection in England in the 1840s', Ph.D. thesis, Royal College of Art, London, 1990

Spivak, Gayatri Chakravorty, 'Can the subaltern speak?' in Cary Nelson and Lawrence Gossberg (eds), *Marxism and the Interpretation of Culture* (1988), 271–313

Spivak, Gayatri Chakravorty, 'Poststructuralism, marginality, postcoloniality and value' in Peter Collier and Helga Geyer-Ryan (eds), *Literary Theory Today* (Cambridge, 1990), 219–44

Trotter, David, 'Colonial subjects', *Critical Quarterly*, 32 (1990), 3–20

Wilson, Amrit, 'Reappraising Orientalism' in *fine material for a dream. . . . ?*, unpaginated

Wilson, W. Daniel, 'Turks on the eighteenth-century operatic stage and European political, military, and cultural history', *Eighteenth-Century Life*, 2 (1985), 79–92

Index

Page numbers in **bold** indicate illustrations